PENGUIN BOOKS

ALL GODS CHILDREN

Carroll Stoner is associate features editor of the
Chicago *Sun-Times*. She is the former editor of the
Philadelphia *Inquirer*'s *Today* magazine and "Living" section, which she changed from a traditional
women's page to a prize-winning general-news
feature section. Ms. Stoner was chosen one of the
Outstanding Young Women of America in 1974.
She lives with her husband in Chicago and is the
mother of a young son and two teenage stepchil-
dren. She is an alumna of the University of Minnesota and studied at the University of Mexico,
Mexico City.

Jo Anne Parke began her journalism career as a
member of the Washington, D.C., press corps.
After graduation from Pennsylvania State University and study at the University of Strasbourg,
France, she joined the Washington *Star* as a reporter. She has been a writer and editor for several
American newspapers and most recently was
modern-living editor of the *Floridian* magazine of
the St. Petersburg *Times*. Ms. Parke presently
writes on social issues, families, and the arts for the
Philadelphia *Inquirer* and national magazines. She
resides in suburban Philadelphia with her husband,
a broadcasting executive, and their two young
children.

ALL GODS CHILDREN

The Cult Experience–
Salvation or Slavery?

by Carroll Stoner and Jo Anne Parke

PENGUIN BOOKS

Penguin Books Ltd, Harmondsworth,
Middlesex, England
Penguin Books, 625 Madison Avenue,
New York, New York 10022, U.S.A.
Penguin Books Australia Ltd, Ringwood,
Victoria, Australia
Penguin Books Canada Limited, 2801 John Street,
Markham, Ontario, Canada L3R 1B4
Penguin Books (N.Z.) Ltd, 182–190 Wairau Road,
Auckland 10, New Zealand

First published in the United States of America by
Chilton Book Company 1977
First published in Canada by Thomas Nelson & Sons, Limited, 1977
Published in Penguin Books 1979

LIBRARY OF CONGRESS CATALOGING IN PUBLICATION DATA
Stoner, Carroll.
All gods children.
Reprint of the 1977 ed. published by Chilton
Book Co., Radnor, Pa.
Bibliography: p. 459.
Includes index.
1. Cults. 2. Youth—Religious life.
I. Parke, Jo Anne, joint author. II. Title.
[BP603.S8 1978]   200'.9   78–15001
ISBN 0 14 00.5055 8

Printed in the United States of America by
Offset Paperback Mfrs., Inc., Dallas, Pennsylvania
Set in Times Roman

To my husband and children
J.P.

In Memoriam: W.W.G. and E.M.G.
And to Bob
C.S.

Contents

COPING WITH THE CRISIS

Acknowledgments

We want to express appreciation to all those families who opened their homes to us, shared their stories and experiences, and helped us put together the pieces of the religious cult puzzle. Since many of them are unaccustomed to public scrutiny they prefer to remain anonymous. For this reason, throughout the book we have changed the names of some individuals to protect their privacy.

To Elizabeth Coleman Albertson whose friendship, clear-headed originality, patient encouragement, and sound advice bolstered us through the entire writing of this book, our special thanks.

To Nini and Terry Coleman; George and Betty Slaughter; the Coles; Elaine Leiberman; Mimi and Sidney Jaffe; Dr. George Swope; Morris, Judy, and Jerry Yanoff, who helped us understand why this story needed to be told, our thanks.

To the journalists who made a similar journey, especially Barbara Ross, Vera Glaser, and Nadine Walker, our gratitude.

To Elizabeth Darling, whose private investigation of religious cults gave us assurance that the republic is in no danger with citizens as alert as she, appreciation.

To those whose professional study closely paralleled our own and who graciously shared their experiences with us—Richard Delgado, Stanley Bernstein, and the Reverend Dr. William Hendricks—we are indebted. For sharing his thoughts with us we owe special thanks to Martin Orne, M.D.

' Father Kent Burtner's and Rabbi Maurice Davis's concern for the temporal and spiritual lives of young Americans heartened us.

To all the young people who shared their thoughts, feelings, and experiences with us, particularly those at the Unification Church Theological Seminary and at the Divine Light Mission ashram in Philadelphia, our gratitude.

A special thank you goes to Susan Reinbold, who started as our guide and became our friend. Toni and Butch Clarkson, Joe Anctil, and Vishna Laksha and his family all helped us to understand their commitment.

We thank Curt and Henrietta Crampton and Alan and Giovanna Wood, who relived painful experiences in the hope that others may learn from them, and the Robert Wilcox family and Dot Heller and her son Rick for sharing their knowledge.

Our very special thank you goes to James Gordon, M.D., whose own reasoning left a permanent mark on our point of view, and to Cynthia Slaughter, who charted the journey before us—and to friends Paula Dranov, Carole Hainsfurther, Ellen Berman, M.D., and Perry Berman, M.D., whose advice and good counsel never failed to brighten our perspective. To our friend and teacher Charles Puffenbarger of the Washington *Post* and to Larry Swindell of the Philadelphia *Inquirer* who were more helpful than they know, and to the *Inquirer*'s Eugene Roberts for the gift of time, our thanks.

To our editors Glen Ruh and Joan Bingham whose patience and skill proved invaluable, our deepest appreciation.

Introduction

This is a book about young people and their families. It is, only peripherally, a book about religion. The seed of this book began to grow while we were working together on a magazine story about the effects of raising children outside organized religion.

While we were involved in that research, we began to see signs of another far more disturbing religious phenomenon that was affecting thousands of mostly middle class families. Friends and colleagues told us about young people they knew, frequently from nominally religious families, who believed they had found salvation in religions that were in no way part of the mainstream of American Christianity or Judaism, but unorthodox groups with gnostic beliefs led by resident messiahs or gurus. These groups were called "cults" by everyone but their own members and were earmarked by their members' willingness to give up personal freedom and live under unusual and often severely limiting restrictions.

Some parents of these young people had reacted by banding together in loosely organized groups to fight the cults and they were anxious to tell us their own stories. As parents we could vividly identify with their despair.

Still, while some parents claimed to want "only what is best" for their children, their definition of "best" often seemed to us to be a narrow one that fit only their own concepts of success or failure. We found ourselves countering with questions about their children's personal freedoms and civil liberties, arguing that young people have the right to decide what to do with their own lives even if such decisions include membership in offbeat and restrictive religious groups.

Several mothers confessed that they decided to rescue and deprogram their sons and daughters from religious cults only when their appearance or behavior became socially unacceptable.

"He got so bad, we couldn't take him anywhere," one mother told us about her son.

It seemed as if presentability somehow overrode the parents' acceptance of the normal adolescent search.

In several instances, new messiahs began to figure in headlines, as their political, financial, and religious goals were questioned by increasingly vocal anticult parents' groups. The parents of the new believers and the cults became involved in legal suits and counter suits, charging abduction, psychological kidnapping, and involuntary imprisonment.

We discovered that an entirely new profession, one that has yet to be clearly defined, grew out of the efforts of parents to reunite families separated and hurt by a son's or daughter's commitment to the new faiths. The new professionals call themselves "deprogrammers." It was on these deprogrammers that many parents began to pin their hopes for their children's salvation. And both parents and deprogrammers felt justified in breaking laws to rectify the wrongs they felt had been done. Some found themselves at the center of a legal storm that is still raging.

Soon, it seemed everyone we met had a story to tell about someone they knew or had heard of—a cousin, neighbor, or a friend—whose life had been touched by some new and "bizarre" form of godliness. Most of the stories were related with a sense of fear, derision, and anger which seemed to reflect a value that our middle class society generally holds: Fanaticism of any kind is to be scorned. Will these young people be forever alienated from the mass of society? Are the new religious leaders misleading American young people? Are they usurping the talent and productivity of youth for destructive ends? To the sophisticated and nonreligious, it is wrong that young Americans can get so wrapped up in God and religion at a time in their lives when they should be studying, working, playing, and laying the groundwork for productive, mature lives.

By the early 1970s, the American middle class had either left the churches of its childhood or so secularized them that for many God had taken a back seat to social action. But the year 1975 was a turning point for the orthodox, mainstream religions in the United States. Inner-city religious schools and churches were still closing their doors as the last faithful worshipers abandoned the cities for the more affluent suburbs. But the continuing decline in attendance at neighborhood churches and temples finally abated. The big movement was back to God.

Interestingly enough, the new growth within the religions of this almost totally Judeo–Christian country was not within the stodgy, static forms of the faith the people had fled, or within the socially progressive form orthodoxy had adopted. Instead the new growth was reflected in the radically dogmatic, fundamentalist forces within Protestantism, Catholicism, and Judaism.

Charismatic prayer meetings drew thousands of once complacent Catholics into their midst. Pentecostal revivalist experience became commonplace as the numbers of "born again" Christians increased and as they discovered proselytizing and witnessing. Hasidic Jews took to prayer vans and street corner preaching to exhort fellow Jews back to a more intense religious experience. In many instances the revitalized believers were viewed with suspicion by the more traditional members of the faiths they represented.

And in a nearly parallel reaction, new religious movements surfaced outside the umbrella of religious establishment. These too were questioned, not only by members of mainstream faiths, but also by the skeptics, who put little store in any brand of religion.

In our investigation we began to suspect that we wouldn't find the truth near the surface of the story. We became fascinated by the story behind these new religions, a story that we felt needed to be told. It was not in the headlines of the stories we'd read. The whole truth would be heard not only from outraged cult-members' parents, but also in the words of these members themselves. We decided to examine the despondency of the parents, the dreams of their children, and the motives of the new religious leaders. We wanted to understand what it is about our contemporary culture that makes it ripe for a resurgence of old religions and a birth of new faiths and new messiahs. If our research showed these new religions to be as pernicious as their critics claimed, we wanted to show people how to avoid cult membership. We also would explore ways of dealing with pressure on members' families when cult involvement was a fact.

We tended during the first months of our research to be almost totally on the side of the counter-cult parents, as though parenthood itself is a demarcation separating the young—cult members in this case —from the adults. As we studied newspaper and magazine clippings from around the country we found that we were not alone in wanting to disapprove of these new religions with their deviant theologies, their confounding ways, and the sometimes arrogant conviction that they alone can save the world. Reporters wrote of religious cults entirely from the point of view of parents, former cult members, and deprogrammers—angry victims of these groups. Rarely were any of the "true believers" allowed to have their say, to tell how they felt, why they left homes, campuses, and careers to practice full-time faith. They seldom had the chance even to explain why they chose lives of self-denial over the lives of material success their parents had planned for them.

A barrage of charges and counter charges of "brainwashing" came from both the cults and the deprogrammers. Former cult members charged that the cults had subjected them to techniques of mind control and ego destruction. Spokesmen for the new religions labeled the charges "ridiculous." We had to wonder if these young people were really subjected to mind control or if they were merely looking for an excuse or rationale for joining the group in the first place.

Cult members who returned to their new religions after being subjected to failed deprogramming sessions told stories of deprogrammings where they had been handcuffed, deprived of sleep, involuntarily imprisoned, and "brainwashed." Parents and deprogrammers claimed that they were justified in their tactics, for the cults had first deprived their children of their rights. They were, after all, "only trying to rectify a wrong."

Our search was not without trepidation. Parents, former cult members, and deprogrammers warned us, "They'll get you. They can hypnotize you right on the street corner. Don't listen to them for long or expose yourself to their recruiting techniques, or you may end up joining."

There were more implications that we might be in danger. One American reporter, Claudia Ross, was found stabbed to death and her typewriter symbolically smashed after she wrote an article damaging to the Children of God in the Bangkok *Post Daily,* an English-language newspaper in Thailand. And there were persistent rumors about the unexplained deaths of two reporters who attempted to write about the Scientology movement. They were only rumors, and although we heard the stories again and again, we could not document them or find their source. Other threat and harassment stories were common. Many former cult members live with unlisted telephone numbers in fear of the cloud of possible harm hanging over their lives.

The images of fear became very real when we were alone in strange cities, asking what some people thought were too many questions. On a country road in the heat of a Texas summer night, we were followed and our car forced into a ditch. We will never be sure if it was a religious cult fanatic or a "good old boy" with too much moonshine in him who forced our car off the road. At the time we thought it was the former but in retrospect, the drunk theory seems more likely. Finally our fear, which diminished slowly, disappeared.

We gathered academic studies, dissertations by those interested in the cults from the point of view of religion and sociology, and papers written by psychologists and psychiatrists. We interviewed dozens of clergymen and psychiatrists and read so much about brainwashing and thought control our own heads were aswim.

Then we went to religious rallies and festivals, to services, gab sessions, and introductory lectures and seminars about the new religions. We intruded as little as possible, sometimes identifying ourselves as interested journalists working on a long-term project, but more often quietly observing and absorbing.

We visited Unification Church seminary and recruiting centers and stood on street corners with their fund-raising teams. We read their literature and studied their materials. We interviewed hundreds of current and former cult members and their families. We listened to their stories with interest and compassion. We learned to love the young people of this generation—the generation of our younger brothers and sisters.

During the months of our observation we saw things we would not, at the outset of our investigation, have believed. We saw the young cult members with glassy eyes and plastic smiles that make them look like the "zombies" their parents claim they have become. We saw also bright-eyed, intelligent young converts who expressed rage and anger at a society they feel has rejected them or badly needs improving. We saw others who only wanted to be left alone to live lives they consider good and wholesome.

We heard sermons that blasted the United States and its values. We heard half-truths, distortions, exaggerations, and outright lies. But we heard these from both the cults and their critics. Early in our work, we decided that the real issue of the religious cult question lies not in their theologies, but in their practices. We feel the basic questions are whether or not these groups are exploiting their young members for unstated or surreptitious purposes, whether or not life within the groups is physically or mentally healthy, and whether or not these groups will have any long-range detrimental effects on our society or our nation.

As citizens, we were horrified by the story of a twelve-year-old boy who was taken by his mother, who did not have legal custody of her son, into the Hare Krishnas, where he was hidden, possibly in a French Krishna commune. His father's pain and fear is real but unspoken—he is afraid he will never see his son again.

And as young men and women quit college, left jobs and prospects behind them, and chose totalitarian lives, we wondered with their parents how this happened to some of our best and brightest.

"There but for the grace of God . . ." is written on the soul of every parent who sees another in distress. For what, in the end, is more vulnerable than parenthood? Yet our children too are vulnerable. And the reason behind their needs is a troublesome part of the story. While parental guilt can be overwhelming, we are all part of a society that has spawned these exploitative groups. While the family's pain is genuine, parental concern must not be confused with possessiveness. There must be a time when parents relinquish the tenuous hold on their children.

We have attempted to understand why today's youth is particularly vulnerable to the pleas and promises of new messiahs. We understand that their lot, growing up in a confusing and ever-changing world, in a society that has promised them everything, has not been an easy one. We've come to see that some institutions and some families have failed our young people.

Religious freedom demands that any religion, no matter how bizarre its theology, be allowed to flourish. We've listened to civil libertarians argue that these cults should be protected as religions. On the other side of the issue we've heard parents argue persuasively that the first amendment to our Constitution should be modified for Americans' own protection.

Society must ask itself if it has a responsibility to

regulate totalitarian groups that require absolute
obedience to a living godhead and which inspire contempt for our laws and values. Can it allow the conventional family to be undermined, as these groups
systematically attempt to do? Should the people tol-
erate religious recruiting methods that are not only
intimidating, but are as deliberately deceitful as any
fraudulent sales scheme consumer agencies seek to
protect us against? Does any group that chooses to
call itself a religion have the right to control or dom-
inate all of a person's time during the years when he
could be building a foundation for a productive and
satisfying life?

We question whether spending twelve-hour days
soliciting money for a church is a realistic way to
serve either God or mankind. We question whether
any of the deceptive recruiting means used by these
religions ever justify their ends, however altruistic.
We believe young adults, who are members of religious cults, have the obligation to examine both sides
of the cult issue. We have tried to present ideas for
parents to use to help their sons and daughters understand the gravity of making a permanent life
choice while in a state of highly charged emotion-
alism.

But when a consenting adult, with full information before him, decides to follow a messiah, however controversial, ought he to be allowed to serve
his god in peace? And if these religions intend to
continue to grow and become part of an expanded
religious establishment, must they not conform to
our system of laws, both moral and judicial?

The first amendment to the United States Con-

stitution was designed to protect religious freedom
for all Americans and for all time. We do not believe
the Bill of Rights should be tampered with, no matter how justifiable or expedient such an action may
seem to the critics of religious cults. We agree with
U.S. Supreme Court Justice Lewis F. Powell, who
observed in 1974 that there is no such thing as a
false idea: "However pernicious an opinion may
seem, we depend for its correction not on the con-
sciences of judges and juries, but on the competition
of other ideas."

It is in this spirit that we present this book. We
hope that with knowledge and understanding of the
cult experience young Americans and their families
can obviate the pain that comes from ignorance.

THE NEW RELIGIONS...
WHY NOW?

Recruiting

This is an age of messiahs, a time when new religions are proliferating. Each campus has its share of gurus, and young people are flocking to join religious movements that are often cults. Depending on how a cult is defined, estimates of their numbers range from the hundreds to the thousands. Some seem to be gaining momentum and becoming forces to be reckoned with by the rest of society. Others are small, look harmless, and appear to be nothing more than havens for aimless young people. Many do not deserve the denigration that has been leveled at them by critics who lump all new religious groups together in one derogatory category—cults. Time may prove that some of the movements are, in fact, legitimate endeavors at new forms of religious expression.

And yet there are enough messiahs around, commandeering the time and energy of thousands of disciples, to make a definition of the most pernicious type of cult a necessary part of the education of young people.

What then is a religious cult? One dictionary defines it as "a minority religious group regarded as spurious or unorthodox." The definition elaborates, saying "great or excessive devotion or dedication to some person, idea, or thing."

For thousands of disapproving parents of cult members those two phrases alone are enough to define a cult. But when a person encounters a new religious movement, such a simplistic definition may not be enough to help him evaluate it. Here are some additional criteria a person may use to determine the legitimacy of a new religion.

—A cult has a living leader. Cult doctrine is based on his revelations which either supplant or supplement traditional religious doctrine and scripture.

—The cult leader is the sole judge of the quality of a member's faith and he enjoys absolute authority over the members. He often lives in kingly splendor while his subjects live in poverty.

—A cult promises a system in which a convert may work to save the world and humanity, but actually sponsors no community-improvement programs.

—The daily work of nearly all cult members is demeaning and utilizes little of their potential in terms of intelligence, training, or education.

—Religious cults are exclusive social systems, claiming that their members will achieve salvation (or happiness). Members are taught to believe that they are "superior" to those outside of the group.

—To be a member of a cult a person must remove himself from society and cut himself off from job, education, friends, and family.

—Methods of ego-destruction and thought control are part of a religious cult's recruiting and indoctrination practices.

—Cults discourage critical analysis by dictating the suppression of negative thoughts, therefore fostering a dependency on the cult's authority that arrests the maturation process.

—The cult rituals and practices are psychologically unwholesome, and in some cases physically dangerous when they involve the use of drugs or perverse sexual rites.

Here then is an explanation of the recruiting methods used by some religious cults to help amass the numbers of followers that each hopes will help it toward respectability.

BY THE LIGHT OF SUN MOON

During a television interview Neil Salonen, president of Sun Moon's Unification Church in the United States, warned his archrival, Rabbi Maurice Davis, not to confuse Moon's Divine Principle with the methods used by the Korean evangelist to swell the ranks of his followers. Salonen said the Moonies use the most effective techniques they know of to recruit and teach members and that if they found a better way, they'd start using it tomorrow.

On busy city street corners, in student unions, and on grassy campus malls across the United States, Sun's Moonies are constantly looking for new recruits. The group admits it is in a growth stage, devoting nearly all its energy to fund-raising and working to get new members. In the fall of 1975 it was reported that Moon's church had communal living centers set up in 120 American cities and recruiting teams covering 150 college campuses.

If a young person gives a minute to a Moonie pitchman, he'll get a lecture. Between that first lecture and a conversion to the Moon faith, days filled with "love bombing," lectures, and hours of nonstop activity may be his experience. And once a recruit becomes a full-blown follower of the new messiah he will stop short of little, even the exploitation (though he'll call it salvation) of his friends, brothers, and sisters to reap new followers for Moon. Almost without exception, members of the Unification Church claim that finding the Reverend Moon was the single most important event in their lives. Also without exception, former members say they were deceived and duped into contributing to one of the "biggest con jobs in history." Therein lies the mystery of the Unification Church.

In the past few years the Unification Church has spent millions of dollars to polish its tarnished image. But much of the advertising, like the classified ads placed in college newspapers and the flyers distributed on campuses, is designed to get recruits.

At Queen's College in New York, members of the Collegiate Association for Research of Principle (CARP), one of the names used by Unification Church groups at some colleges, handed out flyers which asked, "Are you ready to accept the challenge of a new age? If so we are really anxious to meet you. . . . Let's join hands together to build a better world."

This ad was placed in the campus newspaper at Southern Methodist University in Dallas, Texas:

PIONEERS
Seeking creative conscientious young men & women to pioneer new paths toward the betterment of mankind.
Call Dana   10:30 a.m.–1:30 p.m.
Monday–Friday   526-3415

Many others like it were paid for by the Unification Church under the auspices of one of the cover groups the church hides behind. It is through this kind of evasive advertising and personal evangelism that the Moonies plan to mobilize an ideological army of young people determined to unite the world in a new age of faith. Recruiters are told to watch on the streets and campuses for the lonely. Several former members say they knew the backpack and guitar case were symbols of rootlessness and therefore those carrying them were special targets for recruitment.

The Unification Church's emphasis on evangelism is not the rhetorical expression alone that it has become in so many Christian sects. Bringing in spiritual children is tied directly to the Moonies' hope for salvation. To become eligible for the Reverend Moon's marriage blessing, a symbolic and sacramental rite within Unification theology, a follower must not only put in years of devoted labor on his messiah's behalf, he must also bring in at least three new followers to the messiah's flock. The marriage blessing is not only an outward sign that a devotee has been acknowledged "saved" by the Reverend Moon, but it is the sole legitimate outlet for sexual expression recognized by the Unification Church. Members are admonished and expected to remain celibate until married.

Here is a typical story of how a person can become a Moon follower.

"She had a haunting expression. It was as though her bright smile and sad eyes didn't match. But I didn't pay much attention then because she was so nice. She was interested in me and I was so lonely. She asked my name. 'That's such a nice name,' she said. 'Let me tell you about this place where I live. We have a beautiful life together and everyone is full of joy. Why don't you come over for dinner and meet the rest of my family?' "

That's how it begins, becoming a Moonie. This story, with slight variations, has been repeated to us by every Moonie and former Moonie we've interviewed. The young recruit will probably take his new acquaintance (who will almost always be of the opposite sex) up on the dinner invitation because she will be persistent, and he will go along with her solicitations because it's easier than making a decision not to. He will begin the process of conversion to the Unification Church. Recruits rarely decide to become Moonies. They just evolve into Moonies by putting off the decision.

When the young recruit arrives at the Moonie house, he often won't know that it's a part of the Unification Church and his new friend may not tell him. He'll be greeted at the door by his recruiter and her "brothers and sisters." They will shower him with affection and attention and share dinner with him, followed by music, singing, and a lecture. The lecture is an attempt to paint a picture of a better world, using clichés and platitudes. Though there will be little in the lecture that he can disagree with, it will hardly inspire the hope intended in the young recruit's heart. The mammoth dose of friendship he has received from the "brothers and sisters" will do that. At the end of the evening he'll be invited to a weekend workshop where they tell him he will be able to learn more about the movement and spend more time with his new friends.

He doesn't know and he isn't told that the object of the weekend seminar is to get him to give up his studies, his friends, his family, and the rest of his life, to serve the purpose of a religious leader he's never met, and possibly never heard about. He still may not even know that the commune is a religious organization. During introductory lectures we've attended, the name of the Reverend Moon is never uttered. The recruit only knows that he's met a bunch of very nice kids, he likes them, they seem to like him, they want to change the world, and he has been lonely lately. If he had access to more complete information, he'd probably turn down the weekend invitation.

On the weekend retreat the young recruit will have little time to contemplate what he is experiencing. He will be surrounded by attentive recruiters at all times, in some cases even when he goes to the bathroom. He will be kept busy from dawn to the early hours of the morning with lectures that em-

phasize positive goals, calisthenics, sharing and confessional sessions, and lots of singing. The weekend
retreat will end in a hard-sell pitch to attend a week-
long workshop. By this time the young man has an
idea that this is a religious movement and may have
some inkling of Sun Moon's direction of it. But he is
alone. He has been discouraged, almost forbidden,
from talking to any other recruit. If he's had too
much togetherness or if his commitments on the outside world are calling to him, he'll probably say no
to the next step. Present and former Unification
Church members estimate that more than half the
prospects who attend the weekend seminars never go
on to the workshops. Yet, if he's among those who
do attend the next workshop, the odds are he'll become a Moonie, if he hasn't become one already.

WHAT MAKES THE LIGHT DIVINE?

The Divine Light Mission is attempting to take a
more respectable approach in its efforts to attract
new premies (as the devotees are called), and it will
be no coincidence if the new methods are also more
financially advantageous for the Mission. Once Divine Light proselytized among druggies and drop-
outs, promising a constant high without drugs, much
as the Krishnas did. But a contemporary premie
recruit is more likely to be a student, musician,
artist, lawyer, or teacher—a well-educated man or
woman who is, or is destined to become, a solid
member of the community.

Some of the communal houses where premies live
have been closed, but five of the largest and most

successful remain open. Many of today's young premies are scattered about cities in communal apartments, rather than together in one large communal house. However, their physical dispersion seems in no way to have altered their communal dedication to the Mission. But a whirlpool of controversy swirls around the system of ashrams (the communal houses where devotees live together).

In the beginning the group looked for followers who wanted to devote all of their time to Mission work and their newfound meditative techniques. Complaints began, charging that the group was a religious cult out to capture the minds and spirits of unaware young men and women who had wanted only to expand their minds and improve their psyches, but instead fell into a full-time premie trap.

Enthralled by the guru's meditative techniques, young people by the score succumbed to the entreaties of newfound Mission friends to move into an ashram and devote their lives to Mission work. Once inside an ashram, they often became as fanatical and as single-minded as members of the most extreme religious cults. It wasn't long before the Guru Maharaj Ji's Divine Light Mission was being called a pernicious religious cult on the order of the Unification Church, Love Israel's Church of Armageddon, the Krishna Consciousness Movement, and others around the country that persuade converts to give up everything for lives of sacrifice and concentration on new group goals.

In order to evaluate charges that Divine Light is a destructive religious cult, it is important to compare the Mission to both the most deceitful religious cults and to the self-help programs which neither offer communal life structures nor encourage practitioners to give up all outside interests. Some compare Divine Light's meditative "knowledge" techniques to the meditation practices of Transcendental Meditation, explaining that both are do-it-yourself systems that can be used to enrich one's life.

But the comparison does not work. The Mission's three-pronged program does not depend solely on the techniques of meditation, but also on satsang, or reinforcement of a belief in the benefits of meditation through discussion with others who do it, and on service work performed for the Mission without pay.

To get the most out of being a premie, a follower is encouraged to practice vegetarianism and celibacy as well as abstention from the use of alcohol, tobacco, and drugs. Premies will say that nothing is forbidden in Divine Light, but they will also emphasize that each follower ought to give his first allegiance to the Mission. Consequently fervent believers form new friendships with fellow believers, eventually cutting ties with disapproving friends outside of Divine Light and ultimately breaking with their families who do not condone or endorse their new lifestyles. A college student who sets up an altar to Guru Maharaj Ji in his dormitory room and sits quietly meditating may be the subject of derision and scorn. He can be no more comfortable with his practices while living at home with parents who are obviously antagonistic toward his new beliefs. The final step in disassociation with the outside world often comes when a premie leaves his home and friends to move into the communal living structure provided by the Mission. Here, with other like-minded premies, he can practice "knowledge" full-time and devote his life to the service of his guru and the Mission.

While the ashrams have often been self-supporting they have not been a good source of income for the Mission. Unlike the Moonies, the Children of God, or the Hare Krishnas, Divine Light Mission members do not sell anything. They do not solicit on street corners, selling candy, flowers, peanuts, or literature. And unlike the Church of Scientology, Guru Maharaj Ji's group does not charge for the courses or the teaching of the techniques of "knowledge." The group gets its money through gifts and the tithing of its members. The more gainfully employed a premie is, the higher the tithe the Mission receives.

The Divine Light Mission knows that to close all the ashrams, which are not only communal residences but also serve communities as a central meeting place where premies can come for nightly satsang, would seriously disrupt the group's cohesion. Instead, today's premies, whether they live in ashrams, communal apartments, or in their own homes, are encouraged to come regularly to the ashram for satsang or reinforcement of their beliefs. They are encouraged to remember what Mission spokesman Joe Anctil told us, "The ashram is a state of mind, not a place to live."

Premies recruit to their ranks by personal witnessing to friends and to strangers. A young woman premie who works as a full-time secretary at a Catholic college says she feels confident that some of her associates at work will become interested in Divine

Light once they are impressed with her gentle ways and peaceful demeanor, qualities she is sure are fruits of her Divine Light practice.

The group also appeals through newspaper and Yellow Page advertising in cities where it has centers. Theirs is a soft-sell approach, and it seems to work.

There is a heightened interest in mind-expansion techniques in the United States, so it isn't surprising that continuing numbers of young people are finding their way to Divine Light centers to hear about the knowledge. We have attended the introductory lectures that come before the techniques of meditation are taught to recruits and we were amazed by two things. There were, each night, more than twenty new people at the lectures, all of whom were there because a friend had marveled to them about the fruits of the experience of meditation. And the lectures were so vague, filled with so much profundity and so little concrete information that we wondered how the lecturers were able to keep the attention of the recruits, let alone convert them.

But meditation is intriguing and mysterious and the Divine Light premies are, individually, compelling witnesses for their faith. True premies say they are happier than before. They believe that the liquid they taste when they put their tongues to the back of their throats in one technique of the knowledge is indeed nectar, not the mucus of a post-nasal drip. They believe the light they experience when they press on their eyes is sight through a "third eye," the pineal gland, which the guru contends is the vestige of an extra eye humans had at some point in their evolution. Premies don't allow that the sensation of light might simply be a physiological reaction to pressure on the cornea. They also believe that the vibrations they feel and hear when they cup their hands over their ears put them in touch with the source of all life.

What the premies really have may not be the truth of all truths, but just another effective method for meditating, for altering one's consciousness. What they may not understand is that they could learn to meditate for free and with no continuing obligations from a book at the library. Meditation, when practiced as a calming, leveling device, is a method of attaining a degree of inner peace and tranquility that should not be discounted. However, it does stand scientifically as a consciousness-altering technique and under its influence a mind is susceptible to suggestion. It is a medically accepted means of alleviating the ravages of stress. But when practiced to excess, meditation can "bliss out" a person to the point of inactivity and inertia, stifling creativity much the same way overindulgence with alcohol or marijuana can. These excesses are the major fears of Divine Light's opponents.

IN THE CLEARING OF THE MIND

The Church of Scientology holds a special attraction for those who are, or think they are, in trouble. Young adults who are trying to sort out life goals and options are good candidates for Scientology's message as set down by Scientology's creator, Ron Hubbard.

And yet Scientology differs markedly from the religious cults included in this book. This group that calls itself a religion does not recruit its membership exclusively from the ranks of college students and young adults. Scientologists rarely live in communal systems. Most Scientologists continue to live in the outside world, working at jobs and functioning as productive members of society.

But some of the recruiting practices Scientologists use are the same kind of techniques used by religious cult members, especially those used on college campuses and with young adults.

The case of Charlie Wilson is a typical story of how a young person meets up with Scientologists and ends up deeply in their debt, alienated from family and friends, and dropped out of college and everything he had planned. Charlie was a popular student at a large Midwestern university when he met a Scientologist recruiter. He had lots of friends and his relationship with his family was a warm and loving one. His frequent letters and telephone calls to his grandparents were not out of duty, but because he counted these two active septuagenarians among his friends. Within a few months of the time this young man became a Scientologist, he had dropped out of college and cut himself off from friends and family.

Charlie can count himself among the hundreds of thousands of individuals who have had either a passing or a permanent relationship with the nondenominational Church of Scientology in the quarter of a century since the movement was conceived. In spite of Charlie's limited membership in the church—he was involved for less than a year—he says he is certain that his brief infatuation with Scientology will have lasting effects on his life, few of them good ones.

Critics of Scientology include former Scientologists who claim they were hypnotized during "processing" (a system in which Scientologists are helped to confront what they call engrams or psychic scars). Parents, spouses, and friends of those who have embraced this search for enlightenment with the fervor of religious fanatics charge that the movement uses processing to control the thoughts of followers, and to introduce negative information that then becomes a part of the psyche. Some charge that the Church of Scientology reduces followers to the status of "working slaves," with jobs in the movement to pay the high price the group charges as tuition for the courses and sessions needed to become a "clear" or totally improved human being.

Scientology's critics draw a comparison between the system and psychoanalysis and psychotherapy, saying, "If a psychologist or a psychiatrist offered to employ a patient who could no longer afford to pay for his treatment, the mental health professional would be doing the same thing Scientology does when it allows and encourages those who can't pay for courses to work for little pay in exchange for their processing."

Psychiatrists and psychologists do not recruit patients on college campuses and in front of their offices. They do not have to convince potential patients of their weaknesses and problems. Nor do they claim that they alone can effect cures. Scientologists do, however, stand in front of churches, luring outsiders in so they can benefit from "this wonderful system of self-improvement."

Stories of young people spending their college funds within a matter of weeks on Scientology courses, of careers that were abandoned and jobs lost abound as those opposed to Scientology describe how converts single-mindedly pursue the goal of "clear-thinking freedom."

And yet, as with the Divine Light Mission, thousands of practitioners of this belief system profess to gain inner peace from Scientology. One such Scientologist says she spent between $10,000 and $15,000 within a few months of the time she joined the church and claims that Scientology alone, among all the philosophies she has studied, has helped her to live a better life. "I can't speak for the organization, but I know it works for me. It has improved my life and helped me do a better job."

This young professional woman has a high-level job that she professes to enjoy. Her employers are happy with her and say she is one of their most valuable employees. One friend says it seems to have made her very calm, almost a little too tranquil, but then counters quickly that these are qualities the woman always wanted, and that Scientology has made her seem more content.

Because the young woman drew on savings, the courses did not represent financial hardship, and her family claims she has "never looked or felt better." Who is to say that Scientology has, in fact, harmed her?

Former Scientologists and their parents who are now angry and disillusioned with the system say this calm may be the symptom of some deeper problem and caution us to look carefully for the negative aspects of the "Scientology addiction."

Scientologists say the competent professional member is the rule, the young member who wants to give up everything for the sake of his new belief, the exception. They admit that it does happen, but they also contend that Scientology dismisses from active membership those members who are caught up in family problems. "We tell them to go home and to work out the conflicts before they come back," spokesmen say.

Former members deny that they were ever shut out from full membership when their parents complained. They say they were told to "handle" their families, to do anything in their power to get their families to approve of Scientology. The young people also say that they were counseled by a Scientologist on just how to "handle" the situation. Never, they say, were they encouraged to get a job outside of Scientology, to go back to school, or to get on with the lives they had left behind.

Charlie Wilson is back in college now, working hard and professing gratitude for the deprogramming that freed him from what he calls the "grips of Scientology." He claims to have been coerced into total commitment because his life problems were made to seem insurmountable outside the group.

Charlie tells the story of his recruitment. It is similar to those told by many others. "I met a girl in front of a bank in the town where I was going to school. She asked me, 'What are the three most important subjects in your life?'

"I answered, 'Health, environment, and philosophy.'

"She said, 'You should buy the book *Dianetics* and read it if you really mean that.'

"She was pretty, and I like pretty girls. I enjoyed talking with her, so I bought the book from her for two dollars and I gave her my phone number.

That was a mistake because she and her Scientology friends began calling me twice a week. I always avoided talking with them when they called. But one day I was in my room, feeling sick with a cold, and all my friends were in classes when she called. I was very down, so when she called I talked to her. She invited me to come to the church to see a film.

"My roommate said that I was crazy to go, but I went anyway. The film turned out to be an old BBC interview with Ron Hubbard. After the film they had a discussion of the riddle of why people have problems with mental or physical health when it is the soul that is really in trouble.

"They told me how pleased they were to have someone of 'my caliber' in Scientology and took me to see some of the organization's higher-ups when they were in town. I was flattered," Charlie says.

"I took their first course in communication techniques. Then I really jumped in and tried to spend all my spare time in Scientology. My grades began to suffer. Eventually, I left school and went home to live so I could continue working with the group. The only important thing in my life was getting 'clear,' which I figured would take a few years. My relationship with my family deteriorated, and I stopped seeing all my old friends. I was about to marry a woman in the movement, someone much older than I, someone I didn't even love," he says as though he still cannot believe it, "and then my parents arranged for my deprogramming."

Charlie Wilson was deprogrammed in less than two days with Ted Patrick. He is now back in college, with funds provided by affluent parents. Whether he would have worked at Scientology for a while and then returned to college, none the worse for the experience and just a few years older than the rest of his classmates, will never be known.

But he says he will never forgive Scientology for deceiving him.

AROUSING THE CONSCIOUSNESS FOR KRISHNA

Many of the young people who gravitate to Swami Prabhupada's Krishna group fancy themselves the "wretched refuse" of an uncaring, unfathomable society. They are young people who couldn't, or wouldn't, find a place for themselves. They seek, as convert Peter Boyle sought, a place where they can escape from the tribulations of a world that has bogged them down. They find a religious movement that condones and encourages introspection and singular spiritual growth, within a community of like souls.

Peter had been knocked around by life and had reached a point when he could no longer deal with it and its tribulations alone. He knew that the followers of Prabhupada's brand of Hinduism had set themselves apart from the mainstream of American life. But Peter, in his mind, was already apart from the mainstream and he didn't want to be there anymore.

Others who are drawn to the Krishnas fancy themselves the cream of society. Their backgrounds as honor students and class leaders bear out their flattering self-images. Why then do they join a group where self-denial and everything about their lives removes them from a society where they function so well? Former Krishna John McCabe was a success when he joined the movement after an early graduation from high school. John's academic future was bright but he says that almost everything had always been too easy for him. His sister, Pat, reminds us that everything wasn't as rosy as John remembers. Their mother died while they were teen-agers, after an arduous battle with cancer, and their father quickly remarried his much younger secretary.

Still John insists he found his first real challenge in Krishna. Almost six years after he joined, John had once again risen to the top of the class, only this time he had become one of the first American swamis in the Krishna movement. And again he became bored. "I began to see that chanting and meditating were not really the best ways to change the world," he says. "But I still hope to make some changes in things." And so he left the movement.

There is no mistaking the Hare Krishnas with their saffron robes, rosarylike beads, shaven heads, and "holy" ghostlike pallor. Still, most of these young devotees of this strange amalgam of religion and enterprise are not as easily lured from the maelstrom of society as are the Moonies and some of their young cultist counterparts. And when it is all over, they will not be so easily reassimilated into it.

More than members of other cults, the Krishnas must decide to become members. They must make conscious decisions, for the differences between Krishna and the rest of society are too well-defined for a convert to miss. Many Krishnas look upon their adopted, highly structured, and deeply spiritual way of life as freedom. But freedom is not an easy subject to discuss with a Krishna devotee. His concept of freedom is not at all like that which the framers of the U.S. Constitution had in mind, a freedom concomitant with individual responsibility.

Yet with all its rules and repression of the individual's personality, Krishna does offer freedom from the rigors, challenges, and laws of contemporary society, a society in which these young people could not, or did not want to, find a place.

Many of the devotees of the Indian "holy man" who heads this cult were counterculture casualties of the sixties, who had been part of the drug culture and its exploration of philosophy and mystical religious thought. Krishna Consciousness was a convenient manifestation of Eastern religion. Since it was already stirring on the street corners of Berkeley, Boulder, and Antioch, the seekers didn't have to make a trek to India to find a guru. The young druggies of the sixties sought Eastern religion's meditative techniques as a mind-expanding complement or substitute for drug experimentation.

But older adolescents and young adults who experiment with consciousness-expanding hallucino-

genic drugs are not the only ones attracted to
Krishna. Their younger, marijuana-smoking counterparts are also subject to a soft-sell Krishna pitch. It
can't be a secret to an astute parent that much of the
incense burned by teen-agers is used to create an
atmosphere that will separate the young person's
room from the rest of the house and mask the smell
of cigarette or marijuana smoke. The Krishnas know
this and manufacture and market incense, a brand
called "Spiritual Sky." On the back of packages of
Spiritual Sky incense are directions on how to send
for information about "mind expansion." The mind
expansion information is about the wonders of the
Krishna movement.

Swami Prabhupada offers his young followers a
chance to practice the techniques of Eastern meditation and a chance to leave behind a world that
made them uneasy. "Don't worry about school or
your job. It doesn't matter. Krishna will take care of
everything!" he tells them.

This swami gives service to "Lord Krishna," an
ancient godhead whose presence is richly documented in Vedic scripture and Indian mythology.
But Prabhupada's movement has grown rich through
street corner and airport solicitation by his bands of
"blissed out" followers. And, say Krishna critics, he
has done little to feed or care for the poor in his
native India or elsewhere.

Krishna's hard sell is reserved, not for recruiting
new members, but for marketing the volumes of
magazines and books produced in Krishna-operated
printing plants. Members are taught that this literature will raise the consciousness and increase the

chances for salvation of those who buy it. And so, determined to save souls for Krishna, the devotees accost the prospective clients, sometimes violently, in airports and shopping malls. The gentle Krishna demeanor belies the hard sell tactics, as many who have failed to purchase their tracts can attest. A young military man and his family, still groggy from a transatlantic flight, arrived at Denver's Stapleton International Airport to be assaulted by the sales pitch of yellow-robed Krishnas who followed them persistently through the expanse of this mammoth airport demanding that they buy a book. The young man's wife, with two infants in her arms, was about to throw the unwanted book in a trash can when we met her. In Chicago's O'Hare Airport alone, over fifty Krishna-associated assault and battery cases have been reported to airport police within a few months.

Although their primary goal in streets, airports, and malls is to sell literature, the Krishnas rarely miss a chance to convert a potential member. They advertise "free Indian banquets with music and dance" on college campuses and in most of the major U.S. cities. At these Sunday evening dinners the Krishna speakers invoke their prospects to leave behind a life of "lust and intoxicants" to follow the "true, happier" way of life they offer. "Just look around you, who do you know who is really happy?" they ask. "We are truly happy in our love for Krishna and our devotion," they tell their recruits.

Peter Boyle was a lonely young man when he first met the Krishnas on the Boston Common. They tried to sell him a magazine, but he didn't have any money. They gently, and promptly, invited Peter to come to their commune to share a "free feast."

Peter Boyle's mother was near death in a Boston hospital. He had no friends in that city and was lonely. Peter had been unhappy with his job as a merchant seaman and had not been able to find more satisfying work.

"I went to their dinner and brought some of their literature back with me to the YMCA where I was living." Peter recalls. "A week later I saw them in the park and again they invited me to dinner.

"They were very nice and paid a lot of attention to me. I began to increase my visits to twice a week and ultimately one guy told me they wanted me to stay." Peter told them he couldn't stay because of his mother's illness and his financial obligations to her. "They told me, and they believed it, that Krishna would take care of everything. I guess I believed it too.

"I went in for the security and friendship they offered me," Peter remembers. "But, I was misled. Before I joined Krishna, I was the object of all of their attentions when I went to visit. The day after I moved into the group I found myself cleaning their toilet. I didn't even mind. I had hypnotized myself with their mantra . . . Hare Krishna, Hare Krishna, Krishna Krishna, Hare Hare Hare Rama, Hare Rama, Rama Rama, Hare Hare."

HURRY, THE END IS NEAR

The power of fear is obvious in the evangelism of David (Moses) Berg's Children of God. In their street corner witnessing these young disciples invoke their fellow man to give up worldly ways and follow them toward God before it is too late. In the past they have been a "little off" in their predictions of a coming apocalypse. The end of the world they predicted would come with Kohoutek fizzled along with the highly publicized fizzle of the comet. So far Mother Nature has failed to comply with Berg's prophesies about death by earthquake in the state of California. Still the Children of God predict that doom is just around the corner.

In the beginning the Children of God were more freaky in appearance than they were in doctrine. That was back when "Moses" was still preaching the gospel according to Matthew, Mark, Luke, and John and the Children looked like any of the garden-variety flower children in the early Jesus movement. They were hundreds strong. Young people who looked like hippies, preaching the "word of God" in city streets.

In those days they were even able to get support from the parents of some members. In Dallas, Texas, the heart of the Bible Belt, true-believing Baptist mothers joined an organization to support the Children of God and praised the group for leading their offspring to the Bible. Mrs. Mary Gottwalls, who had a son and a daughter in COG, is no longer so favorably inclined toward the group as she once was. But she is still grateful to the Children of God for exciting her daughter's interest in the Bible. "I just bought her a new Bible, because she wore out the one we had given her for her eighteenth birthday," Mrs. Gottwalls told us.

Mrs. Gottwalls' daughter joined the Children of God when she was eighteen, bore two children in the cult, and was pregnant with a third when she left in early 1976, at the age of twenty-four. The young mother had to leave her oldest child with his father and the Children of God in Italy, in order to get out. Still, Mrs. Gottwalls bears no acrimony toward the cult, though she says, "I can understand how some parents can become frustrated."

The Baptist Bible Belt rapture with the Children of God was short-lived, for in 1970 the prophetic side of "Moses" Berg's nature came into full flower and he began preaching a gospel according to David. Berg began to see himself as God's chosen messenger for those "last days on earth." It is at this point in his ministry that lurid sexual descriptions enter his preaching and his "Mo" (for Moses) letters. Herbert J. Wallenstein, who headed the investigation for the attorney general's office in New York, told *Newsweek* magazine, "His letters are blatantly pornographic, complete with sketches and diagrams. We didn't even want to reproduce them in our report."

COG tactics are designed first to unnerve and then witnessing tips for recruiting and fund raising. The group tells its members: "Eye contact is very important. Give 'em a look of love and watch their hearts turn out. Watch your breath! Be sure to brush your teeth and use mints. You can blow away a lot of potential 'givers.' Try hopping on a school bus and asking the kids if they want to go to heaven. Tell them they can if they ask Jesus into their hearts. Pray with them and don't forget to leave some literature with them before you hop off. One day about three of us were able to do this with about forty busloads of school kids.

"When at a concert or a high school when kids are moving fast it often helps to shorten your speech to 'Can you help with change for kids?' or 'Any change for kids?' When you mention children it really touches people's hearts to give better donations. You should enjoy 'litnessing' (what the COG's call their witnessing-fund-raising-evangelism and dispensing of literature) as much as lovemaking."

COG tactics are designed first to unnerve and then to go for recruitment when the subject is off his guard, when his defenses are down. They time their sieges of college campuses to coincide with exam time. They ridicule those who "don't know the Bible" and threaten them that "the government is going to take away all the Bibles so you'd better hurry up and learn it." They constantly warn prospects that the "end of the earth is near." Each new Child of God is expected to study the Bible twelve hours a day, and when he isn't reading the Bible, he will be listening to biblical tapes or loudspeakers which blare Bible verses all day long.

Former Children of God members tell how they had to earn meals and rest by memorizing Bible verses. One story is told and retold. It seems a young retarded man fell in with a COG commune and had such difficulty memorizing the required number of verses that he was simply not fed for days. His parents finally found him in a dehydrated, debilitated condition. He had lost more than 20 pounds in a few days and was thoroughly confused by all the "nice people who wouldn't give him anything to eat." A psychologist who saw him after his "rescue" tells how it did not take very long to bring him back to reality, since his reality was so limited. But other former members of the Children of God have not found readjustment to the world outside their cult so easy.

In one of his Mo letters on recruiting called "The Look of Love," Berg tells his followers how to look at a prospective recruit, "If there's real spiritual contact in a look, it's just like getting naked into bed with someone. . . ."

The group makes no effort to hide its free sexual attitudes when recruiting if such an appeal is considered effective with the prospective member. These attitudes are for many converts one of the appealing features of the Children of God. In other cases, former members say they were not told of the free and easy sexual mores because recruiters knew it would "turn them off." But once they are devoted, full-time Children of God, young women members are encouraged to use their sexual charms to secure followers for Berg.

In his letter "Flirty, Flirty, Little Fishy," Berg employs vivid sexual imagery and symbolism to show his young women COG's how to use eroticism to secure new followers. "You're such a cute little fishy! So Pretty! You roll those big eyes at them and peck them with that pretty little mouth and you flirt all around them! You wrap your pretty fins around them and you wiggle your little tail between their legs."

And again, "These two, the bait and the fish become one flesh, both on the hook of my spirit. See?

You see? You see? His mouth comes to devour you! You both become one, first in the flesh, then by my spirit. If you're afraid to give it to them just because of a little pride and regard for convention, you could even lose them because of your God-damned pride and concern about what they THINK about you! To hell with what they think about you! . . . That's not your business to be concerned about that."

Current-day Children of God give these letters equal status with the Bible and are powerful witnesses since their tales of the end of the earth are potent and fear-evoking stories. For their street corner witnessing and evangelism the COG's are able, even trained, to assault the privacy of those they encounter. They will invade the last remnant of private space a person reserves for himself—the distance one keeps between himself and a person with whom he may be conversing. A COG encounter is much more than eye contact and witnessing, it is eyeball-to-eyeball confrontation, breathing in the very air the assailant has just breathed out, being touched as you listen. The Children of God approach, assault, and demand, "Do you believe in God? What are you doing about it?" They succeed in effectively unnerving even some of the steadiest of psyches.

The Lefkowitz report contains the testimony of a fourteen-year-old girl who said she had been raped repeatedly at a COG commune. When she complained, a leader told her that such forced sex would "increase the tribe."

Some of the controversial Mo letters are destined only for the leaders of the Children of God, some for all the disciples, and some for the general public as

well. The COG communes often reprint certain of
the Mo letters and sell them to the public to raise
funds. "Flirty, Flirty, Little Fishy" was not meant
for public consumption. Only the "fishies" were
meant to read that. But when these "classified" Mo
letters fall into the public domain, it is easy to see
why parents of Children of God members weep and
worry for their children.

Sandy Cole, a young woman in her mid-twenties
and a long-time member of the Children of God,
fled the Children in Puerto Rico for the safety of her
parents' home in Moorestown, New Jersey, because
the group had planned to "marry her off" to a Puerto
Rican man twice her age in order, she said, "to secure his devotion for the Children of God." In spite
of her distaste for the arranged marriage and a subsequent deprogramming arranged by her parents
and Ted Patrick, the magnetism of the Children of
God prevailed, and Sandy Cole went back.

All new religions vigorously seek new members.
Many recruit heavily from the ranks of college students and young adults whose combination of idealism and disillusionment may make them willing and
eager converts. Members of all religions, and especially those called cults, justify their evangelism and
their recruiting techniques with the same reasoning
that proselytizing religions always use, "We have
found the truth and are compelled to share it."

And the leaders of the new religions know that to
command respect they must command a substantial
following. Cult leaders without a large and prosper-
ous following are dismissed as "religious nuts."

Unification Church leader Mark Lee says it well: "If the Reverend Moon were standing in rags on a corner of Harlem, who would pay attention to him?" The Reverend Moon, with his thousands of clean-cut followers, cannot be ignored. The dozens of pictures of him with United States senators and congressmen attest to power that until recently went unquestioned.

The Unification Church openly admits to being in a growth stage, and says that is why it concentrates on recruiting members and fund raising. With its claim to a worldwide mission to unify all faiths under the umbrella leadership of the Reverend Sun Myung Moon, followers say they are willingly giving up their lives in service to the cause. It is not until after they have left this group that most Moonies are willing to admit that the Church should not have taken such a huge amount of their time and energy.

It is not that the new religions want more followers that distinguishes them from recognized mainstream faiths. It is the unconventional ways they go about getting their new members that makes them different and suspect.

Christian sects too are zealous in the pursuit of converts. They have a compulsion to "share the good news"—the word of Christ and the promise of redemption that is contained in the gospels of the New Testament. Yet, with all its zeal, Christianity is cautious as it advises potential members to convert from sincere inner conviction and desire and not because of conflict and temporary life problems.

A few of the evangelical, fundamentalist, or charismatic sects within organized Christianity encourage sudden, emotional conversions similar to the Wesleyan conversions in eighteenth-century England. But most sects, including the largest one of all, Roman Catholicism, insist on a program of study, contemplation, and soul-searching before they will consider a convert for membership.

In their own defense, religious cults often try to liken their communal living systems to the monasteries and convents of Catholic religious orders. Dr. Martin Orne, University of Pennsylvania psychiatrist and expert on brainwashing, who testified for the defense at the Patricia Hearst bank robbery trial, contends that while "there are many similarities between a Catholic nun's training and that of a Moonie," the two systems are not really comparable. He reminds us that when a young woman becomes a nun, she is not alienated from her family. "Her family usually shares in the belief system," he says. "And nuns are also not living in a system where the head of the order lives in a manner befitting kings."

Still, family disapproval is not enough cause for condemnation of new religions. Another important difference between cults and mainline religions is the way the sects within Christendom show strong concern for improving a person's life as it is. If a potential convert to most mainstream religions has problems in his daily life, he is not encouraged to run away from those problems and seek refuge in a new life system. Roman Catholic orders of nuns, priests, and brothers do not recruit on street corners. Most religious sects will tell a potential convert that through belief in God and with God's help he can improve his life. We know of no accepted religious group that deceives its recruits or witholds information from them in the conversion process.

Each segment of society recognizes the power of cult leaders for its own reason. Parents, whose family units have been fractured by a religious cult, eye the leader with fear and anger. Realtors, businessmen, and politicians often pay him court, hoping he may transfer some of his influence or funds over to them. Million-dollar property sales to the Reverend Moon's Church have made some real estate salesmen wealthy themselves. Bona fide clergymen, on the other hand, regard the cult leaders with a mixture of the curiosity and contempt they reserve for heretics. But all the attention a cult leader gets comes because of the size and influence of his flock. And so, not incidentally, does the real essence of his power: wealth. When a cult disciple, working the streets selling peanuts, candy, flowers, or literature can earn $200 a day tax-free, every devotee is worth at least this much to the cult leader. More members mean more money and more money means an increase in power.

Not all the new religions actually sell goods. Some get their money directly from the membership, as the Divine Light Mission does. The Mission and its guru are supported mainly through the gifts and "tithes" of premies, or followers of the Guru Maharaj Ji. Premies who live within the ashrams either turn over all their income from outside jobs to the Mission in exchange for food, clothing, and shelter, or work for the Mission itself and get, in exchange, the necessities of life and the privilege of living in the commune.

Many of those living outside the communal living

system of Divine Light do not appear to be giving everything up in order to practice the techniques of "knowledge" as the Guru teaches them. And when viewed as a supportive system, and not as a total commitment, Divine Light may not be a religious cult at all. But in the Divine Light Mission, and to some degree in Scientology, a total life-system is there for a young person to run into, leaving what is generally considered normal life behind him. Many adults and many young people do not seem to need to devote their entire lives to such a system, but rather take from it what they need. Without going into an analysis of the addictive-type personality —the person who becomes totally or habitually involved in everything he does—it is important to recognize that there do seem to be some young people who are more likely to become caught up in the religious cult or self-improvement system than others. The groups, it seems, exploit their weakness.

If the young people who are the prime targets of cult recruiters don't understand themselves, the cult seems to understand them and their vulnerabilities very well. Hope springs eternal, especially in the hearts of the disillusioned and disoriented young. It is by building on the natural hopes of the young —for a better world, for a better life sometime in the future—that the disciples of contemporary gurus and messiahs hope to recruit others to their way of life.

Although the rhetoric, dogma, and devotions of each of these exclusive religious societies differ markedly, the recruiting practices of all have common elements in theory and in practice. Each one has put together a marketing program for its peculiar brand of faith that appeals to that unique combination of optimism, idealism, and narcissism that is present in every personality. Some of the marketing strategies are so inherently dishonest that if they were being used to sell material goods or secular services they would astound even Ralph Nader's consumer watchdog raiders.

In spite of the old saw to the contrary, "flattery will get you somewhere," and the cults know it. The young who join these movements are willing subjects for flattery. During the postadolescent stage young people are possessors of huge but fragile egos that need constant reinforcement. They often find it easier to see themselves through the eyes of others than to go through a sometimes painful process of self-recognition.

When his interest is heightened by flattery, a prospective cult member will listen eagerly as a recruiter describes in vague platitudes a wonderful microcosm of a new order that the group has already established. "After all," he reasons, "if these people think I am great, they can't be all wrong."

When describing the new way of life, the cult recruiters may carefully avoid or even deny that the group is a religion. Visitors at the Creative Community Project in California are told specifically that the group is not a religion. Recruiters avoid speaking of a lifetime commitment or describing the concessions that may have to be made in order to belong. "You owe it to yourself, to come, to see, to hear," the prospect is told. He is invited to the cult's commune, house, or meeting place to share in a picture of nirvana the recruiter paints in broad strokes. And, if a prospect accepts the recruiters' invitation, it is the beginning of a conversion that may end all of his contact with the outside world, except when it serves the cult's purpose.

It is ironic that individuality and self-centeredness, the qualities of an individual's personality the cults first appeal to, are also the first qualities the cult seeks to take away from a person once he joins. The new religions recruit on the basis of individuality but operate on the premise of "group think" and group action. There is certainly less individual expression in the cults than there is in the world at large. In some of the groups the members dress and even look alike. Hare Krishnas adopt a uniform, though unconventional, mode of dress. Moonies, with their short hair, conservative clothes, old-fashioned eyeglasses, and constant smiles, begin to resemble one another.

After a study of the recruits and recruiting practices of the Divine Light Mission, Hare Krishna, the Unification Church, the Children of God, and the Church of Scientology, it is obvious that it is not so much religiosity that the young cultists are seeking, as it is a better and more fulfilling way to live their lives. Cult leaders know this well.

Dr. Saul Levine, a psychiatrist on the faculty of the University of Toronto, determined in his study of religious cult members, as we did in our own, that those who joined these groups were almost universally nonreligious before they met the cults. They were seeking, not religion, but fruits of religious experience—peace, happiness, and self-fulfillment in the highest purpose anyone can choose for his life, the creation of a better world. And they were open for suggestions on how to go about working toward this elusive goal.

The sixties were marked by secular group action to save or change the world. Young and old marched with Martin Luther King from Selma to Montgomery. The young joined Eugene McCarthy in vigorous political efforts to end the war in Vietnam. In the sixties youth had purpose and direction. But "Dr. King was assassinated, Bobby Kennedy was assassinated, McCarthy lied to them, Johnson lied to them," Rabbi Davis points out. "American youth entered the seventies disillusioned and deceived."

In the seventies cult leaders have come along with a different appeal, "save the world, but save yourself first." The appeal to egocentricity inspires trust, even in the untrusting.

The religious conversion of young adults is what Harvard-educated theologian Herbert W. Richardson calls an "ideological or vocational conversion." Dr. Richardson (a part-time faculty member at the Unification Church's Barrytown, New York, seminary and a professor at the theological seminary of the University of Toronto) says that between the ages of eighteen and twenty-five adults are ripe for conversion to an ideology. He contends that a religious conversion at this time of life is often confused with getting hold of one's own will or independence. "A child has neither a culture nor values when he is born, he assumes those of his parents. Conversions in young adults are stabs at rebellion and independence."

Gail Sheehy outlined the phases of adulthood the

way the Gesell Institute outlined the phases of child-hood. In her book, *Passages,* she calls the syndrome "piggy-backing."

Dr. Richardson doesn't note, as Ms. Sheehy did, that the lifestyle or ideology one adopts as a form of rebellion or a stab at independence may be even less help to him in his struggle for identity than than that of his parents which he rejects.

In a permissive society where behavior knows few boundaries, relative answers are given to the direct questions of our young. They find it difficult to rebel when all the rules are flexible.

In a time when no one has a handle on all truth, it is conceivable that anyone who can claim, with a straight face, to have all the answers will be able to gather a following. He doesn't have to recite his answers. He must only claim to be privy to them, and promise eager adherents that all will be revealed to them too, in time.

When this kind of absolutism is conveyed along with a purpose—such as the betterment of mankind—a cult leader is bound to become something of a pied piper. It even happens when it is apparent to any who question that the stated goals of a movement and its activities are often opposed to each other. However, the contradictory practices of a movement don't seem to spark the curiosity of its followers. Once they have become ardent cultists, they cling to the vague, higher purpose they espouse.

A cult holds out nirvana as an attainable goal. It promises the revelation of truth and the fruits of experience, in increasing degrees, as a novice grows toward maturity in his faith.

Guru Maharaj Ji claims to understand the key to the essence and spirit of knowledge and truth. He says he is in touch with the force of life that lurks in the inner recesses of all living things. He promises the same to those who will follow him. "He who seeks truth, finds it," the young guru tells his disciples. If by chance a new devotee doesn't find what the guru promises when he practices the guru's meditative techniques, the fault of course is not the guru's but the premies. A disappointed premie will be told that he "hasn't grown enough" to experience the "knowledge." Consequently, he will keep coming back to the oracle for a taste of the truth he has been promised, and so desperately seeks. It is mystifying to see young people become so dependent on the praise and promises of a cult or its leader that they will do nearly anything they are told to do.

Some cult critics, including the controversial deprogrammer and hero of most anticult parents, Ted Patrick, charge religious cults with using hypnotism to recruit young men and women into their ranks. Patrick told the California State Senate Subcommittee on Children and Youth that these groups use "on-the-spot hypnosis," when recruiting. ". . . A person can come up to a person on the street and talk about anything. They can be singing or playing a guitar and the only thing they want you to do is look them straight in the eyes for five or ten minutes and you believe everything and go with these people."

We have yet to meet a cult member, or former cultist, who has convinced us that he was hypnotized into a new religion. But it does seem apparent that some religious cults use recruiting practices that in the world of business would be labeled "deceptive marketing practices." An honest contract between religion and convert cannot be made if information about the group, its identity, and the degree of commitment necessary for members to belong is withheld. It is not coincidental that the Creative Community Project, an adjunct of the Unification Church in California, denies its affiliation with the Moon cult. It is the cult's most successful recruiting wing.

A prospective member is showered with affection and attention. He is made to feel important as friendship, love, peer support, and approval are heaped on him. In fact, all of these conditions will exist within the group if he joins, but no one is told of the attendant price of each of the "gifts." Moonies and other cultists call this "love bombing," and "loving them up," and they know how effective it is. They themselves joined the same way.

The Moonies try to justify these practices by calling them "heavenly deceptions." Other religious cults admit that they feel the end justifies any means. Justice Louis Brandeis wrote, "One can never be sure of the ends, political, social, economic. . . . Lying and sneaking are always bad, no matter what the ends. We must, and we can, be sure of the ethics of the means, if not the ends." Justice Brandeis could have been writing about a million instances of short-sighted ethics. He could have been writing about religious cults.

Theology

Man is a religious creature. In his journey through time he has embraced and discarded thousands of gods and as many religions. Some gods caught man's fancy, inspired his imagination, and prevailed as expressions of ultimate truths. Religious belief has always been supposed on a leap of faith—a leap from despair to promise. To explain the inexplicable and to give meaning to the human condition the notion of a supernatural force has always been with man. A creator God, by many names, is the bedrock upon which all the great religions of the world are built.

If one respects religious freedom, the right of a religious cult to exist should not be gauged by how its theology compares to any other belief system. The question must not be whether or not a religion is unorthodox, but whether or not its theology is so perverse that its practice becomes unwholesome either for its disciples or the mass of society. Many respected people in this overwhelmingly Judeo–Christian nation are members of religions which conflict with the basic tenets of Christianity or Judaism, or are agnostics or atheists.

Still, if young Christians and Jews become involved with one of the new faiths they ought to understand how religious cults differ from orthodoxy. Cults are not always, as they often claim, methods of expression for Christian or Jewish beliefs, or nondenominational churches compatible with all belief. In their initial conversion approaches, cult recruiters often discredit the differences and assert that their doctrines are universal and acceptable to members of any religion.

Out of the pool of stagnant enthusiasm where organized religion found itself in the 1960s has come a rebirth of interest in religious expression. Religious awakenings and reformations have occurred at intervals throughout history. The resurgence of old faiths is part of this cyclical phenomenon, for any institution can stagnate for only so long before it either disappears or adapts to the needs of the society it is meant to serve.

During the sixties in America many forces converged to question or to overthrow traditional establishment values. The birth-control pill, the atomic bomb, and other results of modern technology were making themselves felt as they influenced and altered the course of history. Man had to wonder if the old formulas and time-tested values were still relevant. As society began to question its own ways and goals a practical methodology for successful existence became obscured. Left with little to hold onto, some survivors of the upheaval turned inward to drugs. Others moved to rural communes where values were based on the simple life, back to nature, and down with technology. Many more, trying to interpret the transcendental implication of what was happening in their society, turned to God.

Here is a brief explanation of five of the new belief systems.

Unification Church theology, as set down by Sun Myung Moon in the church's codes of faith, Divine Principle, has become Korea's most controversial, if not its most profitable, export. Emissaries for Moon's theology carry to the homelands of the missionaries, who once brought Christianity to Asia, a new and revised version of the credo those missionaries once so eagerly sought to share. The Western world often confuses Moon's theology with the Christianity it mimics. Unification theology is not Christianity. Rather it is a peculiar alloy of Christianity, Taoism, and Buddhism, which has its roots in the Reverend Moon's interpretation of Judeo–Christian scripture.

At times the Moon faith resembles a political movement, since the ultimate goal of Divine Principle is the worldwide unification of all religions into a theocracy, not incidentally, headed by the Korean evangelist. Church doctrine teaches that Korea, Moon's birthplace, is hallowed ground—the New Israel—and it has political overtones as well, for Unification Church members have been active in enlisting continued American military and financial support for the war-torn land.

The Divine Principle is based on the premise that man needs to be restored to God's divine grace, a condition he lost because of original sin, and that grace can be restored by the payment of indemnity (penance) and the advent of a new messiah (the Reverend Moon).

The Principle begins with the creation of man—God created the race of man to be his children, not his servants—and starts to differ from orthodox Christianity with the Reverend Moon's interpretation of the fall of man from the Book of Genesis. (Moon's interpretation of original sin is even more explicit than the literal biblical version. He tells his believers that Eve had physical sexual relations with the archangel Lucifer.) Lucifer (created by God to be a servant, as were all the angels) was jealous of God's children, Adam and Eve, according to Moon's teachings. Therefore, Lucifer decided to take Eve away from Adam. Physical union between Lucifer and Eve was possible, Moon's apologist Young Oon Kim explained in a letter to Dr. William Hendricks of Southwest Baptist Theological Seminary in Fort Worth, Texas, because "contact between a spirit and an earthly man is not very different from contact between two earthly beings. Therefore sexual union between a human being and an angel is actually possible."

According to Unification Church theology, soon after her sexual union with the devil, Eve recognized that Adam had been meant, by God, to be her rightful husband. So Eve promptly seduced Adam, instead of waiting to be joined with him in marriage by God. Eve's blood was tainted by her sexual intercourse with Lucifer and her subsequent seduction of Adam caused the fall of man. Moon's followers believe that this fall from grace made Adam and Eve, and all of their descendants, children of Satan, rather than children of God.

Ms. Kim, in her book *Divine Principle and Its Application,* explains that man's subsequent resurrection (or restoration) is taking place in three stages.

In the first stage—the formation stage or the Old Testament stage—man had to get close enough to God before he could even begin working with him again. Ms. Kim writes, "To start the dispensation of resurrection, a foundation first had to be laid. Toward this end God began working in Adam's family. During the 2,000 years after Adam, God continued to work through men to lay the foundation. But until Abraham and his family were chosen, the foundation was not laid because those who were called failed the task."

The family of Abraham, the Jews, were justified before God by their observance of Mosaic Law. Yet because of their low spiritual status, God didn't speak directly to them. He sent them messages through his angels. The family of Abraham never became children of God, only God's servants, according to Ms. Kim.

The second stage is the growth stage or the New Testament stage. On the basis of the foundation laid by the children of Israel, God sent Jesus Christ. His mission was to raise mankind again to the stage of perfection—one with God. But, according to Divine Principle, because he was crucified, Christ was not able to marry and begin a perfect family of man and therefore failed in his mission. Those faithful to the teachings of Christ in the New Testament are justified before God, achieving the growth stage, and moving one step closer to perfection.

During the third stage, the perfection or com-

pleted Testament stage, God again sent an advo-
cate to earth, the Lord of the Second Advent. Man
can be resurrected to the perfection stage—spiritually and physically—by accepting this Lord and
serving him. Ms. Kim writes, "Through the ministry
of the Second Advent, mankind will be brought into
the position of God's children not merely in idea
but in reality. Mankind will enter into a complete
union with God." In the completed Testament stage
man will be justified before God by following and
attending the teachings of the Lord of the Second
Advent rather than Mosaic Law or the teachings of
Jesus.

The Divine Principle is rich in dualistic concepts.
It considers man and woman to be manifestations
of God's male and female nature and sexual union
to be the completion of the God nature. Divine
Principle polarizes good and evil into Satanic and
Godly forces and deals heavily in the separation of
man's nature into spiritual and physical qualities.
With the ultimate reunion of God and man, in the
completion of the perfection stage, man's physical
and spiritual natures will be reunited and mankind
itself will be united under one religion—Unification.

In order to achieve the ultimate union with God,
Moon says, man has to redeem himself. God will
not intervene on his behalf. According to Moon,
God will only do 95 percent of the work. Man must
comply by supplying 5 percent of the effort. God
assists by sending anointed ones to help man with
his redemption. Jesus Christ was such an anointed
one, the Principle says. The Reverend Moon, who is
the implied Lord of the Second Advent, is another.

Christ would have succeeded in his mission if man had not interfered with God's plan. Men (the Jews who crucified Christ) caused the failure of the mission. Man's spiritual salvation was achieved by the crucifixion, but his physical salvation is still forthcoming. "Jesus was chosen to be Lord of Lord, but because he could not complete his work he was unable to attain that position," Ms. Kim writes. According to Unification theology Christ's position is that of a second God, on the order of a Hindu avatar, but by no means God himself.

Man's restoration to God can be achieved by a process of paying indemnity for sin. Certain historical figures, such as Christ, have helped to pay the penance through sacrifices but none has made, as the Anglican *Book of Common Prayer* claims Christ did, "a full, perfect, and sufficient sacrifice." The interest on the wages of sin is compounded; each subsequent savior must pay for the failure of those who came before. Only the Lord of the Second Advent will be powerful enough to complete the restoration of man to God.

The eschatological dogma of the Unification Church is appealing and hopeful for it includes no gory stories about the end of the earth and eternal suffering. It suggests the strife the world is experiencing right now is the turmoil predicted in the Book of Revelations.

Instead of doctrine of spiritual life after physical death, the Divine Principle refers to a time when there will be no death. The spiritual and physical world will be one, united with God, in the Restoration.

There is a worrisome prophecy in Divine Princi-

ple, that of an inevitable confrontation between the
forces of good and the forces of evil. It is this twist
to the principle that especially concerns parents of
young American Moonies who fear their children
might go off to fight for their "messiah" in a war.
The confrontation, according to Unification theology,
will be a war between the forces of democracy and
the forces of communism and it will take place in
Korea, the birthplace of the Lord of the Second
Advent.

The Unification Church's official line to those outside the faith is that the Reverend Moon is not wor-
shipped as a god. However, even a casual study of
church publications reveals that this is not the case.
A booklet biography, published by the Unification
Church, describes Sun Myung Moon's birth: "Few
were aware of the universal significance of the quiet
Bethlehem scene 2,000 years ago when Jesus Christ,
Son of God, was born. The saying, 'history is made
at night,' was again proven in 1920. On January 6
of that year an event of similar significance took
place in the province of Pyung-buk, North Korea.
On this day, unnoticed by all, a child was born who
was destined to be appointed the most difficult
task in history—remaking the world. History will
mark this day as the beginning of a cosmic transition."

The Unification Church biography of Moon goes
on to explain how he became aware of his mission
at sixteen when, ". . . deep in prayer . . . Jesus appeared to him and told him he was chosen to complete the mission Jesus had begun 2,000 years ago."
The booklet states that throughout the Reverend

Moon's life those who know him have often had visions or dreams that showed him to be the son of God.

In 1960 Sun Moon was married to a teen-age Korean girl, Hak Ja Han. The Unification Church says this was Moon's second marriage—and it was allowed by God because Moon's first wife did not understand his mission. South Korean public records reveal only two marriages for the evangelist, but there are reports that he was married to a third woman during the late 1940s in North Korea. The reports cannot be documented since North Korean records are not available. Moon's current wife, a strikingly beautiful woman, has borne him nine "perfect sinless children." The Moon family lives in Irvington, New York, on a large estate. The school-age children of the "Perfect Parents" attend exclusive private schools in Westchester County.

It seems that it was Moon's marriage to Hak Ja Han that Ms. Kim was referring to when she wrote, explaining that the Lord of the Second Advent was able to discover Satan's hidden crime and subjugate him. "It is he who, through his prosecution and subjugation of Satan, established the crossing point between good and evil in 1960. At that time, the marriage of the lamb prophesied in the nineteenth chapter of Revelations took place. Thus the Lord of the Second Advent and his bride became the true parents of mankind."

The marriage blessing of the Reverend Moon is the only rite in the Unification Church which resembles a sacrament in the traditional sense. The hundreds of young people who have received this blessing in the mass marriage ceremonies where Moon has officiated are considered to be among the first to be restored to the status of children of God. They are considered to be among the 144,000 who were predicted to be saved first in the Book of Revelation. Ms. Kim writes, "The number . . . is symbolic. . . . It represents a limited number of people who will share in the first resurrection and form the foundation for the restoration of mankind."

Church members believe they are absolved of original sin through Moon's marriage blessing. According to Korean religious scholars, several sects hold the same literal interpretation of original sin as the Moon church, and these groups practice a sexual rite called "pikarume," or blood-cleansing, to purify souls of Eve's misdeed. Supposedly a woman could have the taint of Satan's blood, which had been passed on to the human race by Eve, removed by copulating with the sect leader or another man who had already been "purified." Those who describe this practice say men were ostensibly "purified" by engaging in the sex act with a "pure" woman. Blood-cleansing among members of the Moon church was reported in "A Brief Outline of Sun Myung Moon's Doctrine and the Movement of His Group," published in the journal of the Royal Asiatic Society.

Dr. Sa-hun Sin, a religious authority who has written a book on heretical movements, says that a woman who was once affiliated with the Moon church related stories of the ritual and her own involvement in it to him.

Moon and his followers vehemently deny these charges, and avow the ritual was never practiced.

There is no reason to suspect that today's Unification Church condones blood-cleansing. If anything, a contemporary Moonie is more, not less, chaste than the average young adult.

The Divine Light Mission (from its Denver offices in a Victorian building resembling a turn-of-the-century department store that has been remodeled, but never renovated) is trying to tell the world that it is not a religion. While the philosophy of the young Guru Maharaj Ji, leader of the movement, has no elaborate theology, what theology is has reflects Hinduism, not Christianity and Judaism, from whose ranks come the masses of its membership.

The Divine Light Mission gives equal billing to all well-known religions and their scriptures, the Torah and all the Old Testament, the New Testament, the Koran, and the Bhagavadgita. Perhaps because the movement originated in India it emphasizes the teachings of the Hindu scriptures, the Bhagavadgita. The God of Divine Light resembles the impersonal concept of infinite power and energy of the Hindu omnipresence more than it does Western man's image of a rational and willful God who created the Universe and has a plan for it.

Premies learn that their guru is a messiah in a direct line of Perfect Masters that includes Jesus Christ, Buddha, Mohammed, Lord Krishna, Shri Hans (the young guru's late father), and the guru himself. The issue of conflict between Divine Light teachings and Christianity or Judaism is seen in the answer to a premie's question: "Just who is the Guru Maharaj Ji?"

The answer often given by other premies is, "The Guru Maharaj Ji is God." Sometimes he is told that the Hindu faith, the springboard of Divine Light, holds that God can have many manifestations, many incarnations.

A rabbi reminds us, "For Jews there can be no other God but God." Christians, who have accepted the divinity of Jesus Christ as the son of God and savior of man, do not accept the idea of many incarnations.

Leaders of the Divine Light Mission contend the movement is not a religion. They now say their work has been impeded by the Hindu trappings that many followers have invoked to "enrich the experience of meditation." But whether premies have promoted "Hindu trappings and their guru's divinity," in much the same way many Americans and Europeans have sought the life explanations in Eastern religion and writing, or whether the Guru Maharaj Ji himself claims that he is God is a question of some importance.

The methods of self-discipline practiced by premies are (other) aspects of Hinduism which have found their way into Divine Light philosophy. Celibacy, abstention from the use of tobacco, alcohol, and drugs, and the mission's highly touted vegetarian diet are stepping stones on the divinely lit path to enlightenment. And in true Hindu fashion, the Mission acts, not as a lawgiver but as a dispenser of advice. The disciplines are recommended, not commanded.

Maharaj Ji teaches that God is the source of all life. "God is an omniscient power that is hidden in the secret recesses of all living things. . . ." The guru claims that he alone has the key to the knowledge of the source of God. He has promised his premies that with this key (his meditative techniques), they can get in touch with this source. His God is, then, an energy that is always present and cannot be removed by temporal circumstances. Maharaj Ji does not claim to give God to his devotees, but to put them in touch with the God that has been present in them all along.

Armed with the knowledge of his own private God, a premie should be able, according to the guru, to handle any situation with maturity and strength. "The mind and the thoughts are obstacles to the experience of God," the guru says. His interpretation of the knowledge is an experience rather than an intellectualization of the deity.

The young "Perfect Master" of the Divine Light premies, whose full name is Prem Pal Singh Rawat, was a tiny boy when his father, Shri Hans Ji, traveled about India spreading the word of the knowledge. Although he was the son of a wealthy family, Shri Hans took his ministry to the poor. When little Prem's father died, his mother, ignoring the Western tradition of primogeniture, named the youngest of her four sons as the inheritor of his father's mission.

Together the family continued to minister to the poor for several years and the widow and her four sons became known in their region of India as the "holy family." Divine Light came to the United States after a drug-dealer, in India to close a deal, stumbled upon the ministry and persuaded the teen-

age guru to visit him in the United States. The dis-
coverer of Guru Maharaj Ji (Great King) put a
strong arm on his cohorts, back in Boulder, Colorado, to finance the trip, and they obliged. Maharaj
Ji's benefactors had no apparent intention to capital-
ize on the crusade they designed for him, but they
did provide the boy guru with all the public relations acumen known to the world of pop culture.
One of the members of the group had worked for
the rock group "The Grateful Dead" and was
well-versed in the promotional tactics of the record-
ing industry.

And so the chubby holy boy and his religion
were "sold" to the American people using the same
gimmickry Procter & Gamble employs to sell soap.
More than 80,000 "souls" have, during the past few
years, received the guru's knowledge. He has become
wealthy. The Divine Light Mission grew from a tiny
band of missionaries to a massive business empire.
The guru began leading a life that was not in keeping with his image as a holy man, and his mother
fumed. He countered by saying that the "souls" in
the United States were "poor in spirit but not in
body," which by implication says one must live
frugally only when trying to evangelize among the
poor, and not the affluent.

Today the Mission of Maharaj Ji stands mired in
controversy. Joe Anctil, spokesman and public relations director for the group, seems determined to
lift the Mission from the muck, even if it means
changing its doctrine, as well as its image. At one
time the premies called their guru "Lord of the Universe." Now the Mission tells them to call him a
teacher.

Anctil and his staff are using the same high-powered public relations techniques to change the Mission's image that the guru's original benefactors used to promote the movement in the first place. Divine Light leaders seem to think their Mission has more of a future if it concentrates on becoming a business which trains people in the techniques of meditation and discipline than it does if it continues as a religion, worshiping the contemporary incarnation of God.

"This is not India," say Divine Light leaders today. "The Hindu trip is all right there, but for Americans it's phony." And yet the Guru Maharaj Ji says, as Vedantic Hinduism also purports, that the creator-god (Brahman) has incarnated Himself many times in human forms, and will do so again and again. Vedantic Hindus call these incarnations, "avatars," or super-saviors.

"The truth is one, sages call it by various names," Ramakrishna, a leader of the Vedantic Hindus once told his followers. Maharaj Ji and the Divine Light Mission seem to agree.

And so the Mission denies no God, but asserts that its guru is on an equal plane with all Gods. The group says it is compatible with other religions. But for those who recognize the God of the Israelites or the Divinity of Christ, Divine Light is surely a compromise.

The International Society for Krishna Consciousness is a religion. Not only do Krishna devotees say so, but 200 American religious scholars signed a petition to that effect at a conference held in 1976 in St. Louis. Members of the American Academy of

Religion, Society of Biblical Literature, and the American School of Oriental Research signed such a petition to show their support of the Krishna movement and to attest to its right to religious liberty.

The Krishna society, founded in New York in 1965 by its leader A. C. Bhaktivedanta, Swami Prabhupada, is the American version of a branch of Hinduism in the same way that the Baptists and the Lutherans are sects of Christianity. Their relationship with the Krishnas in India has been termed "quarrelsome," but the Hare Krishnas have won some legal battles in Indian courts, having to do with guru succession, or Prabhupada's right to lead his flock toward God.

Brahman, the creator God, is the central godhead figure to all Hindus. However, Hinduism is a polytheistic faith with many secondary and demi-gods. It is on the hierarchy of these secondary Gods that sects of Hinduism differ. One of the two major divisions of Hindu faith is Sivaism, which holds that the God Siva is the supreme manifestation of Brahman.

The other Hindu division, Vishnuism, contends that the God Vishnu is its supreme lord. Within Vishnuism, the dominant form of Hinduism, there are two separations, Vedantic Hinduism and Krishna. Vedantic Hinduism caught the imagination of Aldous Huxley and other Western intellectuals early in this century, for it embodies the spiritual disciplines of Christianity, Judaism, and Islam and is thought by many to be compatible with all religions. Ramakrishna, onetime leader of the Vedantic Hindus, reflected on Hindu philosophy when he said, "Many faiths are only different paths to one reality,

God." Vishnu fundamentalists believe that all other Gods, except for Vishnu, are lesser deities or super-savior avatars. Vedantics justify their apparent ecumenism by allowing that Christ, Mohammed, Buddha, and Moses were all avatars. (The many incarnations of God in Vedantic belief is the basic premise of the Divine Light Mission as well.)

The Krishnas believe it is the other way around. Lord Krishna was the ultimate manifestation of the creator god, Brahman, and therefore Vishnu was merely an avatar. Krishna Chaitanya (his name means Krishna consciousness), a charismatic holy man in sixteenth-century India, is the founder of contemporary Krishna doctrine. Chaitanya's form of Hinduism was a faith of the people. He told followers that they could "earn" their way to salvation and didn't have to be born into the right caste or social strata to be eligible for it. The sixteenth-century spiritual master is considered by today's Krishnas to be an avatar, who preached that direct love for the Lord Krishna, in the form of chanting, singing, and dancing, was the best way to rid the soul of ignorance and bad karma (predestined failure) to gain salvation.

Although the vigorous, physical worship-rituals of the sect were condemned by the more restrained Hindus, Chaitanya possessed a powerful personality and was able to secure many conversions to his brand of faith, even from among the intelligentsia of his time. For several centuries the sect endured, changing little and ministering to its followers in India.

In the 1960s Swami Prabhupada, who was heading

the Indian movement at the time, brought Krishna
Consciousness to the United States. If he had a hunch
the Krishna brand of Hinduism would be successful in the United States, he was right. Those were ripe
times for Eastern gurus. The Beatles and Mia
Farrow, along with many other stars and affluent
Americans, had traveled to India to sit at the feet of
a wise guru. Interest in Eastern religion was running
high. When the media became intrigued with the
aged holy man, he was on his way. From a Greenwich Village storefront in New York City, the Swami
began preaching his ascetic philosophy. Swami Prabhupada conducted open-air evangelical events in
the Village's Washington Square that drew Allen
Ginsberg and other counter-culture heroes. Television, and the press, always on the lookout for the
unusual, covered the gatherings with the same
enthusiasm they spent on Baby Jane Holzer, Andy
Warhol, and other media-wrought characters of the
era.

The Swami preaches that the world is in an age
of decline, headed for a downfall, which, although it
won't come for nearly half a million years, is un-
avoidable. The Krishnas' chanting and dancing, they
believe, may stave off the inevitable, but the real
reason for the group's existence is for them to save
as many souls as possible before the end comes.
After the predicted apocalypse, Lord Krishna will
come to earth again and save his devotees. The
demonic world, made up of everyone but the Krishnas, will be demolished.

Krishna Consciousness devotees in the United
States engage in a practice which theologians call

antinomianism. It comes from the term "antinomy," which means the opposition of two apparent truths. The Krishnas believe that they, the true believers, have been freed from moral law by the grace of their god. Their scorn for the laws of this nation (their alleged harboring of runaway minors, assaults during fund raising, and their dogged sales persistence in the face of consumer protection laws) comes from the assumption that they are above the law. It is difficult to say whether this practice is part of the belief structure of Krishna, or an accommodation to the persecution and scorn the "strange young men and women in Indian garb" have had to suffer in order to practice their faith.

But even if their lawlessness is an American-bred addition to the creed, the Swami himself couldn't have known that the American culture would influence his religion far more than his faith has influenced American culture. In India, the segments of a man's corporal and spiritual life are clearly delineated. A man is first a student, then a husband and father and a member of the community. Later, after his wordly duties have been discharged, a man can, as the Swami has done, discard his worldly life for spiritual pursuits.

In the United States, however, the Hare Krishnas recruit the young and the very young, sometimes teen-age girls and boys, to follow a strict spiritual life. The movement here tries to amalgamate the spiritual and the worldly facets of a man's life, making him a servant of God and a servant of man at the same time. There are no holy women in Indian Krishna temples, and the Krishna feminism, limited as it may seem to Westerners, is foreign to Indians, who call these American additions to Hinduism ridiculous.

The idea of children within a temple is also outrageous to the Indian believers. The Hare Krishnas began a school (called "gurukula") in Dallas, where they sent the offspring of devotees—once they were out of the toddler stage—to segregate them from their parents and to educate them in the ways of Krishna, away from worldly temptations.

The children at the gurukula led severe lives with no toys, storybooks, or even the great American "pacifier," television. Their classes taught them no science or geography or mathematics, and the only books they used were religious books.

Public sentiment and subsequent legislation forced the closing of the Krishna school in Dallas, but the strange life of the American Krishna devotee continues. He believes:

1. By cultivating a bona fide spiritual science, we can be free from anxiety and come to a state of pure, unending, blissful consciousness.

2. We are not bodies but eternal spirit souls, parts and parcels of God (Krishna). As such we are all brothers, and Krishna is ultimately our common father.

3. Krishna is the eternal, all-knowing, omnipresent, all-powerful, and all-attractive personality of the godhead.

4. The absolute truth is contained in all the great scriptures of the world; however, the Bhagavadgita is the literal record of God's actual words.

5. We should learn Vedic knowledge from a genuine spiritual master (Prabhupada).

6. Before we eat, we should offer to the Lord the food that sustains us. Then the food becomes Krishna and purifies us.

7. We should perform all our actions as offerings to Krishna and do nothing for our own sense gratification.

8. The easiest method for most people to achieve the mature stage of love of God is to chant the holy name of the Lord in the mantra, Hare Krishna, Hare Krishna, Krishna Krishna, Hare Hare, Hare Rama, Hare Rama, Rama Rama, Hare Hare.

The Krishna life is strange by almost any definition, since it is neither in keeping with the traditional practices of the Krishna faith, nor in step with the American society where it intrudes.

The Scientology movement is considered a church in the United States, where it is relatively simple for any group that chooses to call itself a religion to do so under the law.

Scientology has been called "the branch of psychology that treats of human ability." It has been described as the "largest mental health organization in the world, the science of knowing how to know." In the United States, where this brainchild of science fiction writer and philosopher Lafayette Ronald Hubbard operates as a religion, it promises potential converts clear-thinking happiness in this lifetime and eventual freedom from death of the "thetan" or soul. This nirvana can all be obtained, Scien-

tology's creator claims, through the study and process of erasing "engrams" or scars of bad experience
from the soul and psyche. These engrams are, Hubbard claims, the cause of all aberration in human
behavior.

Hubbard founded Scientology in 1951, following the publication of his book, *Dianetics: The Modern Science of Mental Health*. The book describes
a system called "processing," where converts work
to erase these bad memories of scars (the engrams) that may have formed in their lifetime, while
the subject was in the fetal stage, or in previous lifetimes. The Scientology processor, or "auditor" as
he's called, helps the subject to locate and confront
these engrams by means of conditioning and discussion techniques. The subject's reponses are measured
by means of an E-Meter, a psycho-galvanometer,
which is a crude form of emotion or lie detector that
measures galvanic skin response during a one-to-one
confrontation between auditor and processor.

Theoretically, as a person relives the traumatic
events in current and past lives, he will be able to
free himself from the effects of the bad information
and experience that have been fed into his mind
and psyche and then become "clear" and opti-
mize his potential. Reams of material have been
written on the subject of dianetics and Scientology.
This is only a brief explanation of how the system
works.

Scientologists, along with hundreds of lesser-
known groups, have found that the guarantee of religious freedom of the American Bill of Rights, and
a religion's resulting exemption from both taxes and

government scrutiny, can benefit both the movement and its adherents. The statutory definition of religion, in the United States, is a broad one. The government, particularly the courts of its judicial branch, has allowed wide scope in the interpretation of laws pertaining to religious institutions. One early court opinion, according to the Internal Revenue Service, states that "religion is not confined to sect or ritual. The symbols of one religion are anathema to another."

The government regulates religions through other laws which define how they should act in order to achieve tax exempt status. A religion, according to the Internal Revenue Service code, may not have a substantial portion of its net income inure to a private individual. A religion may not devote a substantial part of its efforts to propagandizing for political causes, and it may not participate in political campaigns.

Other laws, such as zoning regulations and ordinances which govern soliciting, also apply to religious institutions. No laws deal with what a religion's beliefs are, or ought to be.

In his early writings, Scientology's founder, L. Ron Hubbard, referred to his philosophy as a science. In 1952 he organized Scientology for the practice of that science. But in 1955 the group incorporated as a religion. In the certificate of incorporation for the Founding Church of Scientology in the District of Columbia, the group said the Founding Church was to "act as a parent church for the religious faith known as 'Scientology' and to act as a church for the religious worship of that faith."

A tax case opinion, handed down by the U.S. Court of Claims in 1969, defines the beliefs of the Church of Scientology: "The beliefs center around the spirit or thetan which is said to reside within the physical body of every human being. Scientologists believe that the spirit is immortal and that it receives a new body upon the death of the body in which it resides."

This interpretation of reincarnation that is part of Scientology beliefs continues in the doctrine. The thetan is impeded in its many lives by aberrations or engrams which result from wrongdoing and bad experiences. Allowing some latitude of religious definition and expression, engrams can be explained as "sins" by and against the individual the soul inhabits. Scientologists say memories of the scars on the soul are stored in a deep subconscious mind, and only through the practice of Scientology can they be remembered, confronted, and finally erased, thus freeing the soul from bondage.

L. Ron Hubbard is both the head of the church and the faith's only prophet. A hierarchy of clergy has grown up around the practice of Scientology, since many of the auditors and processors of the movement, those who help members "confront" engrams and free themselves, are also its ministers. The meeting places and classrooms of Scientology are called missions or churches. The group conducts some rituals of a religious nature, often services which are said to be compatible with other faiths. It is, say Scientologists, possible to be a Presbyterian, Catholic, or Jew, and still practice Scientology. Clergy of other faiths don't always agree. Ministers of the Church of Scientology perform legal marriages and baptisms which mention neither eternal salvation nor God.

David (Moses) Berg's Children of God movement is not a church and it has no churches. It is a religion, though, a faith apart and unto itself. Spouting Bible verses and wearing crosses, the Children of God bear all the outward signs of Christian missionaries. Yet they are not what they seem to be. The Children of God movement is a perverse extension, some say a mockery, of Christianity.

Members of COG are often confused with the young fundamentalist Christian "Jesus people," who, like them, stand on street corners witnessing for Christ. However alien the Jesus people may seem to middle-class straights, with their crosses and cassocks, long hair and jeans, they are generally honest representatives of orthodox Christianity. On the other hand, while the Children of God are disciples of Christ, they are also, and primarily, disciples of David Berg. They give precedence to the prophecies and revelations of their leader over lessons from the Bible. A Child of God believes that his leader receives regular divine revelations from God. Berg puts these revelations and prophecies into writing for his disciples. They are called Mo letters. To a member of COG, a Mo letter is as important as the Bible. Possibly more important.

Berg tells his disciples that he is the fulfillment of many prophesies that concerned Christ himself. A pamphlet, *The True Story of Moses and the Children of God,* quotes Berg as saying he was blessed in his mother's womb so he would be like Moses, Jeremiah, Ezekiel, Daniel, even David. David Berg claims powers for himself saying, "You could even rebuke the devil in the name of David and he will flee. No power in the world can stand against the power of David."

Children of God are nomads, wandering from commune to commune on the directives of their contemporary Moses. They believe they have been given divine license to disregard moral and legislated law. A letter from Berg to COG communes tells leaders how members can avoid being arrested if they have broken the law. "You can ask to see the warrant. Make sure who it is for, and while you are stalling, someone else can inform the disciple, who then has a perfect right to run out the door if he wants to."

Most members of the Children of God, like those in other religious cults, believe the world is rotten. They compare it to the Egypt of the Pharaohs and say that they alone are the "true servants of God." At war with the rest of the world, they are exempt from its rules. When the COGs resort to lying and stealing to "procure" supplies for their colonies, they call it "spoiling Egypt."

The issue of their Christianity becomes even more confusing for those who know the Children of God. The group condones what many would describe as foul or pornographic language and sexual behavior that is shocking to anyone who believes in the privacy of sex, the admonition against adultery in the sixth commandment, or the sanctity of marriage. Berg has taken, according to New York Attorney General Louis Lefkowitz's report into the practices of the Children of God, "a positive position on incestuous behavior, youthful intercourse, and the nonsanctity of marriage and the family."

—On incest: "There are also many biblical exceptions to so-called incest. . . . In fact, there would be no human race if Adam and Even's two sons, Cain and Abel had not married their sisters because there was no one else to marry."

—On youthful intercourse: "I found little girls as fascinated by my own erections and quite as willing to feel them as I was to attempt to explore their more hidden inner recesses."

—On God and sex: "We have a very sexy God and a very sexy religion and a very sexy leader with an extremely sexy young following. . . . I frequently examine the bodies of women, because I am a man, and a woman's physical and sexual attributes are appealing to me."

—On marriage: "God had broken up the marriages of almost all our entire leadership at some time or other, with one or two exceptions who are apart from their partners most of the time anyway. I have certainly seen a lot of good fruit in these since this has happened and it has born good amongst the kids. Is breaking up families anything new with God? God is in the business of breaking up families, little private families. If you have not forsaken your husband or wife for the Lord at some time or other, you have not forsaken at all. . . . Are you willing to lay down your life—even your wife—for a starving brother or sister?"

Berg has, according to witnesses at the New York hearings, conducted marriage ceremonies uniting

couples who were already legally married to others.
He has condoned polygamy for certain members
of his flock. Berg's own proclivity for polygamy is
documented in the Lefkowitz report: "Proof that
Berg practices what he preaches was obtained
through testimony of a witness who had attended a
'mass bethrothal' (marriage ceremony) directed by
Berg. He announced that he was 'taking another wife'
and thereupon, in the presence of his wife (Jane
Berg), other members and their infant children con-
summated the 'marriage' to a young girl who had
taken his fancy."

Mainstream clergymen say that practices like
these are "proof positive" that the Children of God
"mock the faith they pretend to mimic."

The questionable practices of the Children of
God are not readily apparent to one who visits a
COG commune for the first time, either as an observer or as a prospective member. It is easy to assume that the group is a legitimate Christian group
when one sees the Children, away from Berg's
physical presence, where days are spent in prayer
and Bible study, and where Bible verses blare from
loudspeakers. Many former COGs say that the
sexual practices and sexual license of the group was
kept from them for a long, long time, until they
could be "trusted with the secret."

Messiahs and Gurus

We are living in a messianic age when every campus has a guru and each new religious movement claims a leader with divine powers. Who are these men who claim godly sanction for their actions and why do young Americans flock to their sides? Each messiah's and guru's background and philosophy marks his group as surely as parents, unwittingly or intentionally, stamp their sons' and daughters' characters with their own images. Here is biographical information on a few of the best-known leaders of the new religious cults.

SUN MYUNG MOON

Sun Myung Moon is an object of adoration and of scorn. His church is running aground in a mucky bog of controversy and allegations of political and financial intrigue. Yet his loyal followers, the sons and daughters of middle class America—the children of businessmen, teachers, doctors, and lawyers —still stand by his side, smiling and praying and working, telling all who will listen that he is not a scoundrel, but the one and only hope of the world.

The evangelist, who later brought his own strange brand of religion to the North American continent, was born on January 6, 1920, in a small village in what is now North Korea. His parents called him Yong Myung Moon—Shining Dragon—a name he would later change. His parents were Presbyterians, members of Korea's largest Christian denomination. The Presbyterian missionaries had been active prose-lytizers among the Koreans for some time before Moon was born.

The Moon legend tells us that even as a small child he was different—more spiritual than the other children at the school he attended in his home vil-lage of Kwangju Sangsa Ri. When young Moon had learned as much as he could at the small village school, his parents sent him south to Seoul to high school. He attended Tong Yang Sang Kong, a com-mercial and industrial engineering school in Seoul, and became increasingly involved in religion. While he was in high school Moon was a member of two churches, one a traditional Protestant church and the other a sect of pentecostals, according to Dr. Sa-hun Sin, a Korean scholar who has written on the heretical sects. Near his home in the north, Moon and Young Oon Kim (who would later become one of Moon's most loyal disciples) were both, as teen-agers, members of a pentecostal church in Pyong-yang. In the 1930s Korean pentecostals had already begun to predict that a new messiah would be born in that nation.

It is probable that Moon already knew of this prophecy when, at sixteen, he had the vision while deep in prayer in which he claims Christ came to him and told him that he (Moon) was the messiah. According to Unification Church beliefs, Jesus himself appeared to Moon and said, "You will be the completer of man's salvation by being the second coming of Christ."

After high school, Moon went to Japan where he says he studied for a degree in engineering at Waseda University. There appears to be no record of Moon's enrollment at the school. Dr. Sin explains, "It seems he was dismissed from the school because of his complaints to the school, his conflicts with the Japanese, and especially because of his scandalous affairs." However, the Korean clergyman does not elaborate on any of Moon's alleged activities at the Japanese university. A number of mainline Korean religious authorities say they think "he [Moon] misrepresents the truth when he says he is a college graduate."

Alan Tate Wood, a former American follower of Moon, whose duties included presidency of the Freedom Leadership Foundation, a right-wing, anticommunist organization for American youth which is sponsored by the Unification Church, was also head of Moon's One World Crusade for the state of Maryland where he built a factory to manufacture candles the Moonies sell on the streets to raise money.

Wood was often in the evangelist's company and says that Moon's command of English is fragmentary. "He learned just enough to converse with the American troops who occupied his native land. He would ask, 'Wood happy? Wood feel good? Wood okay?'"

But the former top-level Moonie also said,

"Moon's charisma is highly underrated. In one meeting he has the ability to convince even dissidents that he is their greatest friend. I was told that Moon's Korean dialect is that of a peasant, not an educated man. He speaks Korean the way a hillbilly would speak English."

In 1944, while the war in the Pacific was still raging, Moon left Japan and returned to his native Korea, which was still one country. With the mandate of his vision in mind, Moon set out to establish a following of his own among the pentecostals there. Orthodox Korean churchmen, who are among Moon's most vocal detractors, claim that most of his early followers were people "known to be religious fanatics."

About the same time, these same sources report, Moon married Choe Son-gil. After six months the couple was divorced, but Moon's first wife bore her husband a son. Now in her early fifties, Choe Son-gil is said to live in a rented room in Seoul. She gave Moon custody of the boy when he was thirteen years old, the Korean churchmen say.

In the late 1940s Moon, his biographers tell us, spent six months studying the Bible with Kim Paeng-mun, also known as Paik Moon Kim, another man who had designated himself as a reincarnation of the Messiah. The Korean Christian critics of the Unification Church (for whom the Divine Principle holds no fascination, no matter whose it is) accuse Moon of further deception, claiming that he stole the theology from his mentor, Kim.

In 1946 Moon changed his name from Shining Dragon to Shining Sun and Moon, a convenient change, especially for the English-speaking world where Sun and Moon have the connotation of the beginning and the end, the alpha and the omega.

Records of the Presbyterian Church in Korea show that by 1948 the sect had had enough of Moon's "heresy" and excommunicated him. The Presbyterian denomination was the prominent Christian sect in Korea. Still, many Koreans were simultaneously members of the mainstream church and smaller pentecostal groups. These multiple memberships were tolerated due to the nation's tradition of many and diverse faiths. So it isn't surprising that the Presbyterians didn't disassociate themselves from Moon until after he had started to build his own following.

The most damaging allegations in Dr. Sin's book, *Heresy and Criticism on Modern Times and Our Way of Life,* written in 1957, stem from his interview with Tug-on Chong, who had been a Moon follower in the 1940s. Dr. Sin says the woman told him of pikarume ceremonies in the Moon group, saying she had taken part in them. Moonies say her stories are merely an attempt to discredit their leader.

The Reverend Moon has reportedly been married to three women. Church spokesmen acknowledge two of the unions, saying that Moon was ultimately destined to find the right mate to be the "perfect mother" for mankind. (Today, of course, serial marriages are not uncommon.) Reports of Moon's second marriage come from a group of Korean religious scholars, including Dr. S. H. Shin, a professor at Seoul National University; Dr. Y. H. Jyoo, a teacher at Kon-Kuk University; and Dr.

M. H. Tank, a lecturer at several Korean Christian
seminaries. The scholars conducted careful research
and say Moon also married Myung Hee Kim, who
bore him a second son. Alan Tate Wood says he
learned of the boy while he was a member of the
Unification Church. Wood understands "the boy was
killed, as a teen-ager, in a train accident in Korea."

It is known that Moon was imprisoned in North
Korea's Hungnam Prison during the war that divided the nation in the late 1940s and early 1950s.
There are varying accounts of the charges leading
to his arrest. The official Unification line is that its
messiah went to jail for his anticommunist activities.
The Korean scholars, who conducted extensive research into Moon's past (checking marriage and
birth records as well as other government records)
say that he didn't adopt his anticommunist stance
until 1962, after Park Chung Hee had come to
power in South Korea.

Dr. Sin implies, in a lecture he delivered in May
1975 at the Houston Girls School in Taejon City,
Korea, that if Moon had been pursued or persecuted
by the North Korean Communists, he could have
escaped, rather than be imprisoned. Dr. Sin said that
a Protestant minister, Reverend Tokkosam, who
had been acquainted with Moon in North Korea,
told him of going to Moon for assistance when he
(Tokkosam) had been trying to escape to the south
in the late 1940s.

There are also stories relating Moon's rescue from
the Hungnam Prison. Both renditions agree that
United Nations troops liberated the prison; however,
Dr. Sin's version says that Moon and two of his fol-

lowers were taken to Pusan, South Korea, aboard a navy vessel. The official Unification Church story, very much part of the Moon lore that young converts study, contends that Moon escaped to South Korea under his own power.

The official Moon pamphlet reads:

> As the UN forces swept through North Korea, many refugees fled to freedom in the south. Sun Myung Moon refused to flee however, until he had first returned to Pyung-yang, more than 100 miles away [from the prison] to gather his followers. He knocked at the door of each one to tell them to join him at the southern tip of the Korean peninsula in Pusan.
>
> Many of his followers had turned away from him in his absence. One of his fellow prisoners had followed him to Pyung-yang, but his leg was broken. The man begged his master to flee to safety without him, since he could not move his leg to walk the many miles to freedom. But Sun Myung Moon refused to leave him behind, hoisted the man on to his back, and proceeded to bicycle the 600 miles to Pusan.

Regardless of how Moon got to South Korea after his liberation from the North Korean prison, he did arrive in Pusan and for a short time worked as a dock laborer there.

It was in Pusan, in January 1951, that Moon founded his current church, the Holy Spirit Association for the Unification of World Christianity (known in Korea as the Tong-il Kyo).

Three years later, in 1954, Moon went to Seoul and set up his church there. Moon's Korean detractors recall that the church had not been very successful in Pusan and that Moon went to Seoul hoping he'd be more successful. He had an active ministry among the students at Ewha Woman's University where his friend from high school days and ardent disciple, Young Oon Kim, was a professor. (Kim is a common Korean name. Young Oon Kim and Myung Hee Kim, who is said to have been Moon's second wife and the mother of one of his sons, are not the same woman.)

Dr. Sin writes that Moon was arrested in 1955 on charges of disrupting the social order, which came out of an incident involving eighty college students. A tract published by the Korean branch of the Royal Asiatic Society in a journal on new religions in Korea mentions Moon's arrest for "violating the social order," saying that the charges involved women followers staying overnight in the living room of his home, because they missed the curfew that had been imposed by martial law.

Dr. Sin says, however, that Moon was not convicted of the charges when the young women students involved in the incident decided to remain silent rather than testify against him. And according to the Royal Asiatic Society report, he was later released when the persons who filed the charges were unwilling to testify.

In the middle 1950s Sun Myung Moon's life became irreversibly entwined with the life of another young Korean. What an unlikely duo they made. Moon, the leader of just one of many offbeat Korean religions—one that had few members and was clouded by rumors of sexual promiscuity—began a friendship and continuing association with a young man who was a model member of the Korean establishment, Bo Hi Pak.

Colonel Pak, who today is Moon's traveling companion and translator, was a graduate of a prestigious military academy. Prior to the armistice he had served as an aid to the director of the U.S. Military Assistance Program in South Korea, and after the armistice Pak was an aide to the South Korean vice-minister of defense.

In 1958 Moon sent his first missionary, David S. C. Kim, to Japan on the first leg of what was to become a worldwide evangelistic crusade for the Unification Church. The next year he sent his old friend Young Oon Kim to the United States, where she settled on the West Coast and began proselytizing for Moon.

GURU MAHARAJ JI

Thousands of sunsets had faded behind the Rocky Mountains since a small band of acid dealers brought a pudgy thirteen-year-old Indian holy boy to a teepee on a mountainside in Boulder so he could teach them and their friends how to meditate and get high without drugs.

Since 1971 the young guru has grown into a less rotund but far richer young man. He's moved from the mountainside teepee, first to a large $86,000 house with a pool in Denver, and then to a half-million-dollar Malibu estate complete with pool, tennis court, and ocean view. He's owned Mercedes Benzes and Maseratis and has been stopped for speeding. He's had ulcers and has married and become a father. In his early twenties, he's in control of a multimillion-dollar-a-year religious business, the Divine Light Mission.

He had some trouble hanging onto his religious enterprise in 1975, after he married his tall, blonde, and older secretary, Marolyn Lois Johnson, a former United Airlines stewardess from California. Maharaj Ji's mother back in India didn't approve of the marriage, or the young man's gaudy lifestyle. At sixteen he was not old enough to marry without parental permission in Colorado, so he petitioned the court.

The judge agreed that the boy guru was old enough to marry, saying that he had an income and appeared mature beyond his years, a point confirmed by his most devout followers and disputed by others who tell of water pistol battles and legendary bouts of childish temper. The couple married in 1974 in a posh ceremony at a nondenominational Christian church outside Denver. They now live at the California estate with their two small children when they are not traveling on Mission business. The organization still maintains the Denver home as a place for Maharaj Ji to stay when he is in the city. But most of the time, premies live in the house. When their guru comes to Denver, they move out.

After his marriage, the young guru's mother, Rajeswari Devi (known as Mata Ji to premies) disowned her youngest son, saying she had made a mistake when she named him to succeed his father as head of the religious movement, and named the guru's older brother Bal Bhagwan Ji to direct the

Mission. Maharaj Ji's reaction was to fight for his place as spiritual master of the Mission, and he went to India, where he and his brother became entangled in a series of legal suits and countersuits. Ultimately the two young men agreed, in a New Delhi court, to drop all charges. Now it appears that while Maharaj Ji is firmly in control of the Divine Light Mission in the United States, his mother and brother have taken the reins of the movement in India.

The Mission's tax-free annual income, revealed by Mission spokesman Joe Anctil as about $3.78 million in 1976, came from gifts, tithings, and annual business earnings. Robert Mischler, the Mission's executive director, has said the group considers itself a religion only for tax purposes. As a religion it is exempt from taxation. Under the Internal Revenue Service regulation no part of the net earnings of a religion may go to a private individual.

Anctil says that 60 percent of the Mission's $315,000 monthly income goes to support the international headquarters in Denver, the homes around the country where the guru and the 250-member staff live. The Mission makes the mortgage payments on both of Maharaj Ji's homes and spends about $200,000 annually from the Mission coffers to support the Mission's full-time premies, its guru, and its business activities.

Michael Garson, a former premie who worked in the Denver headquarters, has a different idea. In an affidavit presented in a British Columbia court he said, "My analysis of the accounts of the Divine Light Mission indicated that approximately

60 percent of the gross receipts are directed to maintain the lifestyle of the Maharaj Ji and those close to him."

In photostats of Mission financial records submitted with his testimony, Garson pointed out an entry of $139,925 marked "special projects." He said it was money "advanced directly to the Maharaj Ji for purposes related directly to his own maintenance."

It is no secret that the Mission has overspent in its brief history and has run up some monumental debts. The guru's millennium celebration at the Houston Astrodome in 1972 left the group sadly in arrears in making payments on debts it incurred at that time. Anctil says at one time the Mission owed more than $650,000 but had been able, by late 1976, to reduce that debt to $80,000.

However, the Divine Light Mission is still feeling a financial squeeze. In selling real estate around the country the Mission has closed ashrams. With the closing of ashrams came a decline in income. When premies move out of the ashrams they no longer turn over their weekly paychecks to the Mission. It must then rely on their voluntary contributions. In December 1976, Anctil said the monthly income from contributions had dropped from a high of more than $100,000 a month to $80,000.

In response to the declining income the Mission has had to consolidate its operations. In addition to the disposal of real estate in Denver and elsewhere the Mission has sold its printing business. The business was sold to a premie who operates it in Denver and charges the Mission for printing work. The computer, which the Mission once used to keep track of its membership around the country, is gone. It was dropped when the costly lease expired.

With the printing business gone and some of the other Mission business activities shut down, premies who worked in those enterprises have had to reconsider their life's work. Many are being encouraged to go back into the world, get a job, and contribute to the Mission by tithing.

But the Mission doesn't show any signs of closing. As Joe Anctil says, "We are changing our image." It appears that the Divine Light Mission and its guru will be around as long as they can determine what the public wants and give it to them. And the guru has what looks like a long life ahead of him.

PRABHUPADA

His Divine Grace A. C. Bhaktivedanta Swami Prabhupada is clearly the spiritual leader of his religious group, the International Society for Krishna Consciousness. And he is the central workshop figure within his group. There are those who say he does not want it to be that way, that he wants the mode of the ancient Hindu god Krishna to govern the lives of his followers and hopes only to exemplify the best of Krishna for them to see. Others point out that it would be impossible for him not to see the portraits of himself that are the center of Krishna worship services in all Krishna temples. They say that if he were truly a man of integrity he would put a stop to it.

Prabhupada's role of guru, however, is a normal

and legitimate one for Hindus who often welcome avatars and holy men among their ranks, and
he followed the normal route in becoming a swami,
or religious holy leader.

When the wrinkled old man who leads thousands
of fresh-faced young men and women around the
world was himself a young man in India, he had
not yet discovered the spiritual life. Abhay Charan
De, as he was known before he became a swami,
was a student and political activist, a husband and
father. He had a successful career in business long
before he became a Hindu Krishna monk.

Born September 1, 1896, in Calcutta, Prabhupada
had a liberal education in philosophy, economics,
and English at the University of Calcutta. In his
youth he was an ardent Indian nationalist and supporter of Mohandas Gandhi, the saintly pacifist who
led India to independence.

At the appropriate time he married and settled
down to fatherhood and a career as the manager
of a successful pharmaceutical firm, but during his
thirties Prabhupada became disenchanted with
politics and turned to religion for solace and satisfaction. He met the leader of the Goudiya Vaishnava
Society (a Hindu sect which worships the god Krishna
as the supreme manifestation of the creator god
Brahman) and was initiated into the sect. Prabhupada rose to prominence within the group and
when its spiritual leader died, he was named to succeed to the sect's leadership. Abhay Charan De (Prabhupada) assumed the position through a process of
divine or apostolic succession called "parampara"
by the Hindus, although according to Stan Bernstein,

a doctoral candidate at the University of Michigan who is on the staff of the university's Institute for Social Research, Prabhupada's leadership was challenged and upheld in Indian courts.

For eighteen years he continued his life as both a spiritual leader and successful businessman. He continued to live with his wife and to help raise his children. At the age of fifty-eight, he took the third step in a program for spiritual salvation outlined in the Vedic scriptures. He left his wife and family.

In the elaborate Hindu system a man is initiated into the faith and then he must go through four life stages before he becomes a holy man. First he will be a student, then the head of a family with a wife and children, next a meditating hermit seeking enlightenment, and then in the final stage of his life he will be a homeless wanderer, renouncing all worldly pleasures, but leading others to the holy life.

When Prabhupada was sixty-two, he took the vows of a monk, assumed the saffron robes of his new status, and renounced all ties with his native society. Seven years later he became a homeless wanderer, setting out for the United States with a steamship ticket provided by a wealthy Indian woman. He was, according to Hindu stipulation, penniless. His young followers today like to tell how he arrived in the United States with only five dollars and a carton of Vedic scriptures.

Before Prabhupada's own spiritual master died, he gave instructions to spread the word of Krishna in the east and the west. During the 1940s Prabhupada began his Western mission with an English-language Krishna magazine he published in India.

The magazine endures as *Back to Godhead,* the brightly colored periodical Krishna devotees sell on the streets and in airports today. Still, his missionary zeal in India went unrewarded. The Krishna sect, one of many Hindu sects in a nation where the dominant religion allows for the worship of many gods and demi-gods, has never become a major religious force. Perhaps Prabhupada thought he would find greener pastures for Krishna in the United States.

When he arrived on American shores the Indian holy man stayed with a yoga society. The yogis told him to change his strange Indian ways, to become more westernized if he hoped to be successful. Prabhupada did not take their advice.

Perhaps as an outgrowth of the drug culture, interest in Eastern culture and Eastern religion was running high in the United States in the mid-1960s. With but a handful of followers, Prabhupada founded the International Society for Krishna Consciousness in 1966, as a successor to the Vaishnava Society he had headed in India. He and his young devotees set up a storefront mission on Manhattan's Lower East Side. He preached there and offered vegetarian meals to his prospective recruits. He gave open-air sermons in Greenwich Village parks. It was here that the media discovered this old Indian man in the saffron robes, and while it didn't make him a star in the way it did Maharishi Mahesh Yogi, the leader of the Transcendental Meditation group, still it provided the weathered swami with ample free publicity. He began to catch the attention of the young Americans who were to become his followers.

Early in his American ministry, Prabhupada offered Krishna Consciousness as an alternative to drugs. "Stay high forever," the early literature reads. In some of his sermons he promised inner peace as an alternative for the political chaos of the era.

Little by little, those he recruited then recruited others until the International Society had forty communal centers (temples) in the United States and Canada and a hundred more throughout the world. While the Hare Krishna group is not as large as it may seem, the devotees were always highly visible with their street corner chanting in the flowing robes of Indian religious men and the colorful saris worn by women.

The group seems solidly entrenched as a counter-culture haven for some young Americans, though its future is highly uncertain. Today, the Hare Krishnas are everywhere. They have set up centers all through Asia, as well as in Europe, Latin America, the Fiji Islands, New Zealand, and Australia. In Australia the Krishnas are causing the same kind of parental fury they spark here and anticult groups have been set up to fight them.

In most of this country's major metropolitan areas where they have temples, the Krishnas rent houses and buildings. However, the group owns six large farms in the United States, including the major one, New Vrindaban, near Moundsville, West Virginia. Here on the farms the Krishnas raise vegetables and nurture cattle, raising them for milk. New Vrindaban, named for Lord Krishna's home in India, is a crossroad for Krishna traveling vans, a place where devotees often stop on their travels around the country. It is here a hepatitis epidemic, a disease that has been the scourge of many communes, struck down a number of members and visitors.

Those who have visited the West Virginia farm say it is inaccessible by car and that the last leg of the journey to the farm must be made on foot, over impassable roads.

Pat McCabe, who visited her brother John there when he was a devotee, says that the place has only one tap for running water and that the devotees bathe and wash their clothes in a stream which runs through the property. "I only went for a week's visit," she says, "but the place was so bleak that I wanted to leave on the first day. I had to stay until they were ready to take me out."

The fund-raising Krishnas are on the street by 10 a.m. every day raising money for Krishna; they are persistent solicitors and their fund-raising operation is successful, but none of the reported wealth has gone to make Prabhupada a wealthy man. He continues to live the austere life of a Hindu monk, although his devotees try to keep him comfortable because of his advanced age and his revered position.

John McCabe lived and traveled with Prabhupada as the old man's secretary while he was a Krishna devotee and says that the swami is a fine, dedicated, and totally spiritual man. John blames corrupt Krishna practices, not on the leader, but on devotees who "take things into their own hands and get carried away." The spiritual master, John says, eats meagerly, sleeps but four hours a night, and spends hours each day translating the Vedic scriptures into English.

Interest in Eastern religions seems to be dying out in the United States as young people turn more and more to traditional, fundamental Christianity. Swami Prabhupada is a very old man, whose days on earth seem numbered. Most former devotees and some present ones say the movement is destined to falter when the old man dies. It is said that the argumentative, nonspiritual nature of the American devotees distresses him and that he knows that no strong leader has emerged from the ranks of devotees to replace him when he is gone. Without their strong central figure, it is difficult to see how the International Society for Krishna Consciousness can continue to exist.

DAVID BERG

Before word of David Brandt Berg's sexual proclivities caught up with him, he seemed to have a good thing going with his Children of God business. At one time, he looked like competition for the radio, television, and mail-order evangelists who specialize in proffering peace through Christ for a price. But Berg, who calls himself Moses and is the head of the Children of God cult, left the country just before the New York attorney general's inquiry into the practices and perversions of his movement was completed in 1974, and just before the report was made public. Outrage at the COG's reported practices caused him and his scruffy disciples to take a low road for a while. Moses' God business may have been a little off lately, but he has not closed up shop.

There was a time when David Berg was a respected

man of the cloth. That was back when he was the minister of a small Baptist church in Valley Farms, Arizona. In the mid-1960s Berg was let go from the charge in Arizona and never again ministered within an orthodox Christian sect. He took his family to Southern California and he started working for the television evangelist Fred Jordan. Berg took over a teen-age coffee house ministry and began a religious movement called "Teens for Christ." The charismatic minister soon developed a following and the group became known as "Revolutionaries for Christ," and then "The Children of God."

The early COGs were in the forefront of the Jesus Movement. Moses' young disciples, who looked remarkably like the young long-haired hippies who were hanging out in Haight–Ashbury at the time, were noticed and successful. He ordained several young men, calling them ministers, and consequently made them exempt from the draft. Berg made the religious life of a COG an appealing substitute for military service.

The young Children of God disciples appeared on Fred Jordan's Los Angeles television program, "Church in the Home," and solicited funds on the air for their work. Jordan allowed them to live on properties he owned in Los Angeles and Coachella, California, and in Thurber, Texas. His California ranch became known as the American Soul Clinic. The Texas ranch was called the Texas Soul Clinic.

And then Berg began to tell of divine revelation. His first major revelation concerned an impending earthquake in California. His disciples took to the streets, witnessing and imploring passersby to join the movement "before it's too late."

In spite of the theological discrepancy surrounding Berg's insistence that he alone as a representative of God on earth was qualified to interpret the Scriptures, Berg and Jordan's falling out, in October 1971, came about because of a controversy involving the administrative and financial control of COG, according to the New York attorney general's report.

When Jordan broke with "Moses," he evicted the young disciples from his property. They became wanderers, traveling about the country, setting up communes wherever they happened to be. Berg compared their nomadic adventures to the plight of the Jews when Moses led them out of Egypt.

At the time of the Lefkowitz report there were an estimated 120 COG communes in the United States. Since 1974 it appears that the Children of God have toned down their U.S. operations and are mainly witnessing from traveling communes in other parts of the world, particularly Europe, South America, and Australia.

But some COG fund raisers are still quietly working busy street corners and airports here. Most of the overseas operations are staffed by young Americans who fell under Moses' spell while he was still in the United States. Many American parents who lost children to the COG have not heard from or seen their sons and daughters for several years though they have heard they are "abroad somewhere." Others have no idea where their children are, or even if they are alive.

Still it is impossible to be sure if the group is going inactive in the United States. Testimony before the Lefkowitz inquiry reported that the COG (because of adverse publicity) were using aliases in their do-

mestic missions. Some of the names mentioned were
"Contact Jesus," "Christian Faith Association," and
"The Toronto Christian Truth Ministry."

A former COG member told investigators that
a leader of the organization had forged his name on
a letter and a withdrawal slip while they had possession of his bankbook. He said the letter to his
savings bank asked the sum of $1,050 be withdrawn
and given in a check to the New England Christian
Youth Association, for tuition and room and board
at the New England Christian Bible College. Both
of these organizations are nonexistent, apparently
dreamed up by the COG to obtain the young man's
money fraudulently.

In 1972 David Berg's son Jonathan, also known as
the Bishop Hosea by the Children of God, said his
father was "in retirement" and no longer taking an
active role in the COG.

Those who have been associated with the movement since that time say this is "entirely untrue."
Berg, they say, still controls the movement with an
"iron hand," constantly sending directives and Mo
letters to disciples, telling them how to live, witness,
and raise money.

Members of Berg's family, his wives, his son, his
daughters, and his son-in-law are the generals of the
organization carrying the commander in chief's orders to the troops.

The money raised by Children of God goes directly to the leadership. A former member of the
cult says, "The disciples send most of their donations
to the main office, to Berg's son-in-law John Tread-
well [Treadwell is known as Bishop Jethro], who is
in charge of finances."

The Lefkowitz report says, ". . . The obvious inference from testimony of ex-COGs and parents is that the moneys are directed to key leaders for their personal use and enjoyment."

COG money seems to come from members who sign over all of their worldly possessions to the group when they join and from donations and fund raising. Members of the movement are shown in a special letter-writing class how to write convincingly to their parents for money and supplies. Local merchants often give donations of food and supplies to COGs posing as Bible college students. The sale of Mo letters and fund raising where COGs ask for money for "work with young people" are also sources of funds.

Reports from some former members say that there is much discrepancy between the squalid daily lives of COG disciples and the lives of splendid opulence enjoyed by the top COG leadership. "The leaders keep their lifestyle a secret from the lowly disciples," says one former COG, "just as they keep the sex stuff away from new members."

Berg, who has reportedly been traveling around Europe for several years, was last known to be living near Florence, on the estate of Duke Manuel, an Italian supporter.

Who Gets Caught?

Barely a soul is immune to the pleas and promises of the "new" religions. The Rev. Sun Myung Moon, Swami Prabhupada, David "Moses" Berg, Guru Maharaj Ji, and the hundreds of other self-styled gurus and self-proclaimed messiahs who gather their flocks find young followers who are attracted to their cults for reasons that are as diverse as their own gospels. The religious cults choose to recruit heavily from the ranks of young people struggling to come of age in these difficult times.

The cults concentrate on recruiting the sons and daughters of the middle class, preying on the vulnerabilities of this particular generation of young adults. In our efforts to profile the cult member, we hurtled into blind alleys each time we groped for a simple solution or a pat generalization. As a group, these young disciples could be part of any crowd of idealistic college-age kids. As individuals, each is unique. Judging from the hundreds of religious cult members we have met, we can say they could be anyone's son or daughter, your best friend, the kid next door.

Religious cults do exploit youth and ought to be

held accountable for the techniques they use to convert and control their members. But the cults cannot be blamed for the cultural conditions that make today's young people especially vulnerable. Society must accept this responsibility. Religious cults do not hesitate to step in and fill the spiritual, social, and emotional voids left by many of today's overburdened institutions. The family, schools, mainline churches, and the government have contributed to the void by failing to minister constructively to the needs of the young.

Into its third century, the United States teeters, like the youth in its midst, on the brink of adulthood. Like them, this country is struggling to come of age with grace and dignity. It is a difficult transition. The buoyant optimism of the American dream has been deflated by reality. Many of today's citizens are educated and aware enough to understand that the nation can do wrong and that "God is not always on our side."

The realities of our own corruption are harsh when we read about the Army testing germ warfare in the subway system of New York City, and when we consider the inhumanity of the warfare techniques the nation employed, in the name of democracy, in Southeast Asia.

American people are having trouble believing in themselves. But the dream is far from over. The nation recently elected a peanut farmer from Georgia as President, after he promised to restore their confidence in the government and the nation. President Jimmy Carter said he had the answer and the people wanted to believe him.

Into this time of ferment come the religious cults, promising solutions for every ill. Their analgesic effect on the sick spirits of the young is obvious. Yet there are questions about their effects. Though religious cult life may not be healthy, it is attractive to the thousands of young Americans who follow unquestioningly the leaders and their ways. But since society cannot guarantee immunity, it must accept a mandate to find a cure for the malaise the cults treat so superficially.

They could have been cast in a female version of "The Odd Couple." Sylvia Buford, a pretty, tiny Texan, is a soft-spoken young woman who holds with both convention and tradition. Sylvia has been a cheerleader, a debutante, and a sorority girl.

Nini Coleman, a curly-headed Easterner, is an enchanting will-o'-the-wisp free spirit who laughed at cheerleaders, scoffed at sororities, and scorned debutantes.

Sylvia went straight through her years at Colorado Woman's College and on to graduate study in Texas. Nini is still buzzing around, trying to decide what she wants to study at the University of Colorado and where she wants to go in life. She just finished a year away from college. During her year off she concentrated on film-making, a great interest of Nini's, and now she is back in school, still searching for a life's work.

It's unlikely that these two young women, each intelligent and highly motivated, from opposite ends of the country, would ever opt for a lifestyle in common. But they did just that and neither of them will ever forget it. Sylvia and Nini were both Moonies.

As different as the two young women are, they do share many traits. Each is from that broad grouping of Americans defined by both attitude and income as the middle class. Both are white, intelligent, post-adolescents who are fighting off childhood and grasping for maturity. Each is pretty, spirited, full of questions and more than a dash of predictable naïveté. Both come from homes that were broken at one time by either death or divorce. Nini's father died when she was very young. Sylvia's parents were divorced when she was in elementary school.

Sylvia and Nini, and most of their counterparts who are still in the religious cults, were caught in that difficult transition period between childhood and maturity when each individual becomes aware of the authority in his own personality and strikes out, or rebels against, the authority figures of childhood. This transition is fraught with trauma and difficult for the strongest, as some sensitive adults remember.

Many of today's young adults have parents whose expectations were tempered by the economic depression of the 1930s and the material scarcity of the World War II years. They have been pleasantly surprised by the abundance of the past twenty-five years. They have found a formula for financial security and success that is still, many say, the guiding principle of their lives. It serves them well and they want to pass it on to their children.

The children of this newly affluent middle class grew up with expectations of boundless prosperity, never lacking material goods or financial security. Then they found that the formula of study and hard work did not necessarily guarantee success. In its own quest for identity and security, youth often rejects the values of its parents. The gap between generations is an old story. Only the label that defines the generation gap is new.

In order to mature, each person must be able to release himself from the protective environment of his childhood and begin to take responsibility for his own welfare, his own actions, and the consequences of those acts. Many of our young seem to be overprotected, guided, and controlled both intellectually and emotionally, until they reach some arbitrary age when society expects them to be mature and in control of their own lives. They are often ill-prepared for that first headlong plunge into the cold, swift waters of adult life. Testing the newfound freedom of adulthood can be a thrilling, heady experience, but it can also be a frightening time, riddled with anxieties, and feelings of loneliness. The road to maturity is a precarious route at best. Detours on the trip are to be expected.

Some young people, afraid to make the journey alone, contract for premature marriages that only complicate the problems of coming of age. Others are diverted by group membership, such as the religious cults, that promises them direction and security during the transition.

In the past, there were safe, well-traveled detours, where young people could test the waters of adulthood before they made the ultimate plunge. The Peace Corps and military service were two such detours. Today, the Armed Forces have fallen into disfavor with the middle class and fewer young men are entering today's all-volunteer army than ever before. This may be a reason that at least two out of three members in the new religions are young men. But in the cults there is little chance, as there was in the Army or Marine Corps, for recruits to sign up for a two-year hitch and then choose re-enlistment or honorable discharge.

In its heyday the Peace Corps also functioned as a useful temporary measure for those in the post-adolescent, preadult years who were not ready to make a lifetime career choice. The Peace Corps served as a constructive channel for the energy of youth while allowing a respectable, brief reprieve from complete adulthood and its responsibilities and obligations.

Even fraternities and sororities, now scorned by the antiestablishment young, were once an accepted alternative to the loneliness of college days on a large university campus. These societies were places to belong, away from home, where young men and women thought of members as "brothers" and "sisters."

Nevertheless, young travelers on this labyrinthine part of life's road often find themselves in a classic approach-avoidance conflict. The venturer wants to run back to the shelter and protection of his parents, to the warm security of childhood. At the same time he *knows* he must progress, make it alone. If an alternative, even a destructive one, comes along in the midst of this conflict it's an easy compromise. In so many ways these new ideologies are ersatz parents, offering the simple, problem-free life of childhood.

There are also specific qualities about late twentieth-century society that make it a fertile ground for unorthodox religious movements. The same cultural conditions have contributed to making the current generation of near adults even more dissatisfied and vulnerable than either their parents or their grandparents were at the same time of life.

Young people today are the first-generation products of the self-actualization bomb that exploded in the fifties and set the Western world and its inhabitants on a course hell-bent toward self-indulgence and introspection. They grew up in an environment where everyone asks, "What's best for *me?*" Many were never part of any group, even a family, where the welfare of the whole was more important than the good of the individual. A young psychiatric social worker from Boston who has worked with scores of ex-cult members and their families, helping to put lives back together after a cult experience, says that the whole generation is afflicted with copious narcissism, but that those who are lured into the cults seem even more narcissistic than their peers. The cults appeal to inflated egos with their recruiting techniques: "Gee, you are wonderful. We need someone with your special talent to help us change the world." Cult recruiters are trained to flatter, to give false confidence to those without confidence.

We in the 1970s have challenged or abandoned traditional values and institutions and are now finding replacements. Youth is not alone. Disillusioned parents have also become seekers. For every thriving neighborhood church or congregation, there appears to be an equal number of weekly meetings of Transcendental Meditation, Transactional Analysis, Erhard Seminars Training (est), astrology and occult groups, symposiums devoted to introspection, marriage encounters, and classes to both expand and control the mind. All are used to increase potential, to answer needs, and generally to make people feel better as they look deeper within themselves for the meaning of life.

Today's young adults are set apart from others by experience, and also by numbers. They are so many, these children of the postwar baby boom. Their numbers have overloaded and taxed the resources of many institutions they touched, including the schools, the courts, and the medical establishment. William McCready, sociologist and senior study director of the National Opinion Research Center at the University of Chicago, observes that "they never had their fair share of attention." The magnitude of their numbers sparked the most intensive school building campaign ever seen, but today the population explosion has petered out. School buildings erected in the past two decades are being closed, classrooms remain empty, teachers are being laid off rather than hired.

In the late 1960s and the 1970s, they glutted the labor market. Now there are not enough jobs to go around. A survey done under the sponsorship of the Federal Office of Education shows that 44 percent of the country's seventeen-year-olds aspire to professional jobs despite the fact that the Labor Department classifies only 14 percent of the national employment slots as "professional."

And so they discovered that to succeed financially and professionally another ingredient had to be added to their parents' formula for success: competition. Having to compete for jobs, advancement, and places in graduate and professional schools was tough for a generation raised with the belief that they had an unfailing formula for success. For many the victory didn't seem worth the struggle and they gave up, dropped out, or started looking for alternate routes to satisfaction. But few found easier alternatives. Their expectations were too high.

Andrew Greeley, Roman Catholic priest and contemporary social critic, observed in his syndicated column, "They grew up thinking they were going to remake the world . . . now they find it hard to get jobs, are cut off from their predecessors and successors in age groups, afraid of marriage and parenthood, uncommitted politically and religiously, filled with self-pity and turning more and more to lives of hedonistic withdrawal from the complexities of life." He goes on to say that they feel so sorry for themselves that they write off the possibility of learning anything useful from those who came before. "It's as though Vietnam and Watergate were the only bad things that ever happened in the history of the human race."

Their teachers and their parents told them, "Work hard, study well, be a success like me." They, like generations before them, look at their elders critically and aren't sure they like what they see. Since parents have become so ambivalent about values, today's youth has an especially tough time finding role models. They do "all the right things"—work hard, study well, and graduate from college like the good guys. Then they discover they can't find jobs or that they have become afflicted with incapacitating inertia, as Dustin Hoffman's character Benjamin Braddock was in *The Graduate*.

Each individual needs a workable system of values

that are his alone. To work toward a rational, productive, and successful life, the young must adopt values that can grow with them and modify to meet occasions in the ever-changing world. Guidelines, boundaries, and role models are essential. The family and our culture must provide them. But this is a time without strong role models and an era when it is increasingly difficult to see the difference between good and evil when society itself isn't clear on the issues.

Today's youth is living in the midst of day-to-day future shock. They are about to inherit a world with no clear-cut rights and wrongs. While in the keeping of their parents' generation our world has fared both very well and very poorly. Lives have been ravaged and enhanced by technological advances. To survive in and contribute to an ever-changing physical and metaphysical environment, these young people must be flexible, innovative, and courageous. No one can tell them how to make life work for them. Old formulas are not always valid. Even the ethics of today's culture are relative, rather than static. To be sexually curious or totally chaste; to marry or to live together; to have a child or an abortion; to grow long hair or to cut it short; to smoke marijuana or not to smoke are viewed by many as relative choices.

There are no shortcuts or easy answers in a world with no absolutes. There is no question that life is simpler with a set of unbreakable rules. It is this simple, no-option world that religious cults offer young people.

Religious cults, whether we are willing to face it or not, are frightening manifestations of deficiencies in our culture. The young people who are drawn to these new religions, as the poor are drawn to the tents of revivalists, would have the same needs if the cults didn't exist. They need to belong, to have friends, to be secure, and to feel important. Their energy and enthusiasm need constructive channeling. They need direction and discipline and a clearly defined purpose in life. They need to be taught how to think for themselves and to develop their own systems of self-discipline.

Our educational and child-rearing methods may be culpable, in part, for the inability and lack of desire on the part of these young people to think for themselves and work out difficult problems. Parents, who may well question the values in their own lives, want to be able to point to their children with pride and say, "Look what a good parent I am; see how well-adjusted my child is."

We have deceived ourselves into believing that childhood should be a continually happy time; that happiness is the ideal norm for childhood. Carole Klein, in *The Myth of the Happy Child,* says parents who are "cheated by the false rewards of acquisition, delight in their child's eager sense of promise."

We shelter and protect our offspring in infancy, childhood, and adolescence. Rather than handing over responsibility in small doses throughout their development, we hand over the reins to their lives all at once. At this point many of them flounder and gladly turn over their new freedom and responsibilities to new messiahs or parent figures, in exchange for continued protection from the hard realities of life. Adult life is nothing at all like this idealized childhood we have created.

Still, complex as the issues are, some see patterns in the profile of a religious cult member. Rabbi Maurice Davis of the Westchester Jewish Community Center, in White Plains, New York, has defined the cultist in general terms. Rabbi Davis was one of the first clergymen in the United States to encourage a concerted effort against the new religious cults because he believes they rob young people of their individuality and their freedom. When some young people from his congregation joined the Unification Church a few years ago, he organized Citizens Engaged in Reuniting Families (CERF), a group that has been instrumental in recruiting hundreds of families. He is a warm, articulate man who describes the cult members with empathy and compassion.

This is Rabbi Davis's profile of a cult member:

Upper-middle class, white, a boy or girl eighteen to twenty-five, someone with a great hunger for peer approval. That is tremendously important to him. Someone who isn't comfortable in a permissive society, someone who needs a strong father figure. Someone for whom the world is a little too big, such as a college freshman away from home for the first time, or a senior in college or the kid about to enter a profession he never really wanted. Someone who's had an unhappy love affair, someone who's "finding himself." The cult member is someone who has a lot of goodness in him, who'd like to see a better world, who yearns for the time when he was a Boy Scout. . . . That's the kid.

In Berkeley, California, a group of young Christians, the Spiritual Counterfeits Project, are trying to expose what they consider the perversity of the new religions, and to explain the power of the cults. They have other ideas on who a potential cult member may be: "Idealists and intellectuals who find the cult doctrines appealing as a philosophical superstructure complete with absolutes on the meaning of life and incentives for changing the world; those who have recently accepted Christ but have no biblical background; the lonely and the alienated; those with a simple hunger for intimacy."

Another characteristic of a cult member is offered by Sylvia Buford, that young Texan mentioned earlier in this chapter, who calls the problem intellectual-existential frustration. Sylvia feels that many young people are capable of understanding that man must make his own decisions, but have the existentialist's feeling that there are no rational criteria serving as a basis for decision-making. She paraphrases Jean-Paul Sartre, "Life is absurd."

Beginning with the industrial revolution and the demise of our agrarian society, the traditional family structure has been the target of assault from within and without. There has been a resultant breakdown; the extended family is dead. Generations no longer share the same homes; many children never know their grandparents. Families of corporate executives who climb the ladder of success must transfer every few years. It's difficult for anyone to have roots; it's hard to belong. But mobile executives and their families aren't the only ones affected by lack of belonging and search for identity. The postwar exodus from the cities left millions stranded in their new single-family suburban homes . . . strangers living in the midst of developments of strangers. The

churches, too, left the cities. They went to the suburbs to serve communities and, instead of communities, found shopping centers.

The mainstream Protestant, Catholic, and Jewish
faiths are losing ground as members wander off.
The clergy is worried. Only the conservative,
strongly dogmatic, traditional sects such as the
Southern Baptists and the Mormons are gaining
members.

Dean Kelley, a United Methodist minister and director for civil and religious liberty for the National
Council of Churches, says in his book, *Why Conservative Churches Are Growing,* that new members are gravitating to these sects because they get
from them what other institutions don't provide: "a
clear sense of life's purpose." These growing churches
are not "reasonable, tolerant, worldly, or ecumeni-
cal," he tells us, but rather, they are "exclusive and
intolerant." Reverend Kelley suspects the decline in
mainline religions began when they grew more concerned with social issues than with the meaning of
life. Within traditional orthodox religions the Pentecostal, Charismatic, and Hasidic movements are
experiencing renaissance and growth. These movements reach to the heart of man's search for spiritual
transcendental experience—his need for ritual and
structure.

Sigmund Freud said, "Religion is born of the need
to make tolerable the helplessness of man." Man
created gods to explain daylight and darkness, fire,
and rain. He needed faith to accept the unexplain-
able. In this twentieth century "Age of Reason,"
man has begun to understand his environment.

Behavior modification proponent B. F. Skinner

wrote in *Beyond Freedom and Dignity,* "Twenty-five-hundred years ago man understood himself as well as any part of his world. Today he is the thing he understands the least."

Contrary to the hunches of contemporary clergy, man's spiritual quest continues and, indeed, suffers from lack of direction. Father Greeley claimed, "Someone is going to have to reinterpret the Protestant, Catholic, and Jewish heritages to the inept bureaucrats, who with little faith, but lots of self-righteousness, are riding the churches into the ground."

He went on to say in his column that the children of upper-middle class Protestantism have discovered that their local church "doesn't stand for anything al all, except what the local pastor picks up from the *New York Times* Op-Ed page, the *Christian Century,* or the *New York Review of Books.*" As for the Catholic church, Father Greeley said, "It is so fouled up, organizationally, and has so many aging juvenile delinquents in high-level positions that no one at all is listening anymore."

All of these changes have affected our children. Many of them know unhappiness, though we've dignified it with the term "inner turmoil." But since parents and teachers have an increased awareness of psychological stress, many of them get help. Close to 50 percent of American youth are given some kind of psychological counseling before they reach maturity, according to the American Psychiatric Association.

Mental health experts tell us that children raised in single-parent homes have increased identity problems and one of every six children in the United States is spending some part of childhood living with only one parent. Over the last decade the number of families headed by a mother alone has risen from 2.5 million to 4.4 million, according to United States government statistics. Husband-wife families grew by less than 4 percent during the same period. The increase is explained by the divorce statistics. One of every three marriages in this country now ends in divorce and 65 percent of the single-parent homes in the United States are headed by whites. They are mostly middle class—just like the population in the cults.

Death and divorce are traumatic experiences for adults, but can be even more devastating to children who cannot understand the implications of what has happened. In *Too Young to Die—Youth and Suicide*, Francine Klagsbrun writes, "A child suffers terribly from the actual loss of a parent. Some studies have shown that if a child is not helped to handle the despair of losing a parent during the early years of life, that child may suffer severe depression and suicidal thoughts in later years."

She goes on to quote Yale psychiatrist Robert Jay Lifton, who calls the experience "survivor guilt." A child becomes angry at the parent who has deserted him and suffers guilt feelings because of that anger. He then directs the anger inward at himself. A child whose father or mother has "abandoned" him early in life, because of divorce, may also experience "survivor guilt." Not all the children whose guilt goes unattended become suicide statistics. But research showed a significantly high proportion of religious cult members come from families that had been ruptured especially by death though also by divorce. Cultists tell stories about parental deaths and the difficult times they had facing that harsh reality.

Anyone who reads the newspapers or watches television news knows that the youth of this nation has problems. Headlines scream suicide, murder, vandalism, drugs, and every parent wants to tell himself, "It's the other families. My children are okay." The National Education Association calculates the annual cost of school vandalism in this country at $600 million, a number equal to the amount spent on textbooks. And school vandalism is just as prevalent in the complacent suburbs as it is in the forgotten ghettos of the cities.

But life for some youth is so difficult that even religion or religious cults offer no alternatives. They leave life altogether. The suicide rate for young people between the ages of fifteen and twenty-four is at an all-time high in the United States. Three times more young Americans are taking their own lives today than thirty years ago. Between 1974 and 1975 alone the figure rose 10 percent. Attempted suicide victims who survive to tell their stories recount that they were depressed and at "the end of their ropes" but were also trying to punish those who had failed to love them enough.

Most of the young people in the cults say they have known psychological depression; a few of them were on a first-name basis with despondency. Nearly all of them were at emotional low periods in their lives when they met the cults. That is not to say they are abnormal. Everyone gets depressed. But they were unfortunate, for rather than finding a way out of their depressions, they met the cults and committed themselves to restrictive lives that fail to allow any of the necessary room for growth toward maturity. As Rabbi Davis says of the cult member, "If he had not met these people, he would have gone through life without these problems showing in such an obvious way."

Sylvia Buford was depressed, a potential suicide statistic, when she met the Moonies. One month before she joined the cult, Sylvia wrote in her diary:

Tomorrow I leave for Denver, maybe to stay. God I hope so. I want so much to make a life for myself. Dallas, I don't think is the place for me. For the past month I have been clenching my fist and gritting my teeth. I am angry inside. I want to end my life as an only way out from all the confusion, games, and the manipulation from people. I want to be myself and be liked for it as trivial or trite as it may sound. I want to contribute something to this world. Dear God, give me faith, teach me love for self and others, show me purpose and courage and strength. I need all the strength I can get to make it. Please give me another chance. I am a good person, I have a lot to offer and I am strong. So let me be what I already am, God, please take away my anger.

Today Sylvia is a feminine powerhouse who has a firm grasp on her life and a good idea where she's going to let it take her. Her intense interest in freeing other young people from the cults has sparked her desire to go to law school and become a forensic psychologist.

Sylvia can now sit back and quietly reflect on the sequence of events that led up to her emotional low that month before she became a Moonie. After college Sylvia had worked as a substitute teacher. "It was very depressing seeing kids in algebra classes who couldn't add. They meandered through the halls of the schools smoking cigarettes and grass." She became further depressed by a job with an employment agency that not only deceived job seekers, but "ripped me off financially." She had broken up with her boyfriend. "It wasn't a really serious relationship, but I had been honest with him and he had lied to me. After we broke up he immediately started dating the girl I thought was my best friend. I really hadn't had any close emotional ties since college."

Sylvia was open for the Moon experience when she answered a blind ad in a Denver newspaper for a "creative, conscientious individual to work for the betterment of mankind." When Sylvia responded to the ad, she thought she was applying for a job, not a lifetime religious commitment.

On the other hand, Nini Coleman and Jenny Michalsen, best friends from college days at the University of Colorado in Boulder, weren't especially depressed when they and their friend, Mike Black, met a Moonie in Berkeley, California. They'd been having a good time traveling around California for a couple of weeks after finishing summer jobs at Martha's Vineyard. "We were checking the ride boards on the Berkeley campus, trying to find a ride back East when this girl came over and tried to talk us into coming to the Creative Community Project house in Berkeley for dinner," Jenny recalls. "We wanted to say, 'Cool it, will you,' but she kept talking so we finally gave in and went to the dinner."

Nini said she was ripe for an opportunity to meet some people and to talk. "We'd been traveling and hadn't really talked to anyone but each other for weeks." At dinner the Moonies, who never admitted being part of any religious group, invited the trio to the Project's New Ideal City Ranch in Boonville, California, for the weekend. "They were really nice and showed us a lot of love at the dinner," Nini remembers. "I wanted to go to Boonville, but just for the weekend. I had a lot of commitments back in Colorado, a boyfriend, an apartment, school, and a film I really wanted to make."

Terry Coleman is twenty. She is Nini Coleman's younger sister and such an energetic person it's difficult to imagine that she is ever low or depressed. But last fall, before Terry decided to take a break from her studies at the University of Colorado and go out to Boonville to see for herself what Nini had gotten into, Terry was in an ongoing muddle about what to do with her life. The journals she kept during this period speak for her generation.

"I wish God would send an Angel through the window who would bring a filmstrip of my life. . . . I wish she would also erase 'doubt' from my vocabulary."

TERRY'S POEM

Dear Science,
You know, sometimes I really hate you. You grow like a weed. Your seeds fall and scatter like dandelions; you confuse me with your controversy.

You can't make up your mind.
You make things that break things.
You made the dentist's drill;
You made the little pill;
You made cars, planes, rocketships
    and toothpaste
    and refrigerators
    and medicine
And almost everything.
Including bombs and
    Plastic and my pen,
    which is pretty nice . . .
    and my down bag
    and beer and bicycles
Yup, you've made understanding
almost everything easier;
Except, there's one thing you can't do for me
And one thing you haven't done yet.
You can't make love!
But undoubtedly you're working on it.

Terry Coleman went to Boonville to bring her sister home. She ended up staying too.

CULT LIFE

Two Sisters–
A Case Study

When Elizabeth Albertson, Nini and Terry Coleman's mother, flew to California in the fall of 1975 to see for herself what Nini's new religious fervor was all about, she didn't have any idea that her second daughter, Terry, was also a member of the Unification Church. She thought Terry was still in Colorado going to classes, football games, and parties. Elizabeth Coleman Albertson is not a possessive mother. She didn't have any plans to kidnap, deprogram, or even remove her daughter Nini from the grasp of her newfound love. She just wanted to talk to her and find out what was so appealing about the new religious communal movement she had joined.

We were curious about Nini and Terry Coleman when we traveled to Colorado to meet them. We'd heard their mother's story of their encounter with the Moon cult—it was one of the first stories we heard—and we wondered what these two young women were really like. Did they have fatal flaws that made them vulnerable to the Moonies' enticement, or were they normal, healthy young women

who just happened to be gullible and unlucky enough
to meet a cult.

When we met Nini and Terry they were students
at the University of Colorado in Boulder, a quaint
Victorian town nestled next to a mammoth canyon
in the Rocky Mountains just close enough to Denver to be called a suburb. A crucible where the
avant-garde tries on new ideas and lifestyles, Boulder
rivals Berkeley as a mecca for nonconforming trends
and religions. It is a place where the unconventional
is the norm.

We stayed with them in an old frame house they
were sharing with other students near the center of
town. We met their friends, visited their campus,
and sat up with them into the wee hours of the morning, getting to know them and listening to their developing philosophies of life.

Getting to know Nini and Terry was a relief rather
than a disappointment. They are not melancholy or
disillusioned, frightened or distrusting. Instead they
are bursting with enthusiasm for life. They are the
kind of young women who could make the hardest
cynic wish to be young again. It was easy to enjoy
their company. Neither of them pretends to have a
problemless crisis-free existence, and neither of them
does. Each must deal with decisions and problems
that are typical for those their age. Yet each seems
to have taken charge of her life. They are warm and
loving individuals with talent, intelligence, and
beauty.

While we were there, Nini kept herself on the go
from morning to night with tennis, mountain climbing, visiting, and sewing curtains for a friend on the

portable machine that always travels with her. We began to suspect she was using all the activity to avoid reflecting on the experience that had overwhelmed her just a few months earlier. Then late one night, we saw a different side of her personality. She took us along to a party where she showed her first film—a parody on the population explosion. Then Nini opened up and talked about her life before, after, and during her cult encounter. At twentyone, Nini Coleman was all at once so proud and so insecure.

Terry, on the other hand, seemed totally absorbed in reflection. She didn't seem able, although she tried, to lose herself in a round of sports, get-togethers, and tasks. Terry is introspective, an artist who spends part of each day on the journal which is much more than a diary with its thoughts, poems, and drawings that explain her to the world far better that she can explain herself in conversation. Terry admitted that she was struggling to carve out her own identity. She was eager to talk about the struggle. She was questioning, she told us, just how much of her personality is "really Terry" and how much of it is the influence of her dominant older sister. Terry says she wants to be herself. She just needs to find out who she is.

It was not the Unification Church alone that made Terry and her sister the people that they are. These two are the sum total of all the love and experience they have known. In their lifetimes, which seem so short to us, they have known love, happiness, inspiration, and trauma. They are most extraordinary daughters of a highly unusual family.

Their mother told us that "no one in the family ever did exactly what was expected. Twenty-five years ago, I decided impulsively on a ski slope in Aspen to marry their father, who was ready to abandon his family's fortune in Chicago and begin again on his own in Mexico.

"We got married right away and went off to Mexico to establish our own life and roots and family." First a son was born to this couple and then, quickly, two daughters. Life was beautiful for the young Colemans. There were servants to help care for the three little ones, two handsome parents very much in love, days filled with laughter and sunshine and a future brimming with promise for them all. Then suddenly and without warning everything changed. John Coleman was killed in an automobile accident, leaving his widow and three young children alone in a foreign land. For nearly a year Elizabeth Coleman debated about what to do with her life and those of her children. Finally she returned to Chicago's familiar turf and to her family. She opened a small shop where she specialized in imports and spent what she describes as eight years "being both father and mother and sometimes one of the kids."

Young John Coleman was six when his father died, Nini was four and Terry was three. "All of the children were devastated by their father's death," their mother remembered, "but it was Nini who had the problems.

"Nini was obsessed with the devil, with goodness and evil. She thought she was ugly, because in Mexico the maids would tell the children they were '*fea*' or ugly if they were naughty. Nini believed she had been bad and that was why her father had died. She refused to wear the color red, because that was the color of the devil. She showed self-destructive tendencies and would point a gun at herself when she was playing cowboys and Indians with other children. One time she sat down in the middle of the street so she would be run over by a car and killed. The other mothers began to keep their children away from Nini because she was 'spooky.' "

The family bought a puppy and Nini named him Happiness. She refused to let the dog go outside, for fear he too would be killed by a car. In desperation, Nini's mother took her to a child psychiatrist and after eight months she seemed markedly improved and became a happy, carefree youngster. "We noticed a dramatic change in Nini's attitude when the dog was killed by a car after all. She drew a picture of the devil and threw it in a wastebasket and said, 'I loved my Daddy very much, but I've already cried for him. Now I have to cry for Happiness and then find something else to love.' " Nini's mother said she can't remember when her daughter ever exhibited any signs of disturbing behavior again. "The children were always well-behaved. I never really had to discipline them."

"We didn't live like ordinary people," Nini told us. The way she emphasized "ordinary," it was obvious that Nini Coleman would never use that adjective to describe herself. "We lived a kind of 'Pippi Longstocking' existence, sort of the ideal fantasy life of every child. We didn't keep regular hours, sometimes when mother was busy we would just stay up, watching television, until we felt like going to bed.

We didn't eat regular meals, at regular times. We ate when we were hungry."

Her mother reminisced, "I felt we were all in this together. One summer I packed the children into a camper and headed for Colorado to visit Aspen. I had friends and a lot of good memories there and I was a widow with no ties other than my children. We could have lived anywhere. I thought the high country in Colorado would provide a healthy outdoor life for the children and I considered moving to Aspen permanently. But I began to see that while Aspen is a wonderful place to vacation and to ski, it is an unreal world where the problems of growing up can be compounded, not alleviated. We went back to Chicago."

Elizabeth Albertson thought the Colorado high country was a nice place to visit, but she wouldn't want to live there. Each of her children has disagreed. All three of the young Colemans now live in Boulder.

Years later, Elizabeth said she felt that one can find happiness anywhere. She says she's found it in Pennsylvania with her second husband, Abner Albertson, an old boyfriend from her college days, and her family, which now includes two younger daughters.

Nini and Terry told us while the Coleman–Albertson family is intact and happy today, this wasn't always so. "We had a hard time adjusting when Mom got married again," Nini said. "We'd led a pretty unorthodox life in the eight years after my Dad died. And then, wow! All of a sudden everything changed. We had to make our beds, wash the dishes, and sit down together for dinner every night. We didn't take to the new routine easily and we were jealous because we had to share our mother with somebody else.

"Then mother got pregnant. She wasn't young and she'd had difficult births with each of us. They didn't tell us, but we overheard worried discussions about her health. I was terrified that she might die, too.

"Then we not only had to share Mom with our new dad, but with two babies—born a year apart —who vied for her attention. Still we loved the babies. The little girls are still a joy to the whole family."

After they adjusted to their mother's remarriage and to the new family additions, Nini and Terry settled into normal adolescence and happy teen-age years in the Philadelphia suburb where their family still lives. First Nini graduated from high school and went on to the University of Colorado for college. Two years later Terry followed her.

They seemed happy and comfortable with college. Their mother, who now had only the two little girls at home to look after, breathed a sigh of relief when her older children were in college and doing well. Elizabeth Albertson was complacent until her first inkling of disaster came. She got a letter from Nini, "I'm happier than I've ever been. I've decided not to go back to college now."

When Mrs. Albertson arrived in California, determined to find out as much as she could about her daughter's new life, she did not know how difficult that task would be. John Coleman, Nini's and Terry's brother, accompanied their mother on her mission.

"We were flabbergasted when we found out Terry was there too," she recalls. Mrs. Albertson admits that she had little knowledge of the situation at this point. She says, "I function on intuition. I trust it. My intuition is better than my logic. This group seemed similar to Hare Krishna and I thought that was crazy. . . . I just wanted to find out."

Elizabeth and her son, John, sensed something was really wrong because of the difficulty they had in locating Nini and Terry. "John went to the Creative Community Project's Hearst Street House in Berkeley (technically the CCP is not part of the Unification Church, but nearly everyone within the church admits that it is a recruiting arm of the church) where they told him his sisters were at the Project's farm, The New Ideal City Ranch, in Boonville, California. We called Boonville and they told us the girls were in San Francisco. Everywhere we turned, we got a runaround."

The two were further convinced they were facing some nameless disaster when they saw how afraid the two young women were of their mother. "We had always been open and trusting with each other. It just wasn't right for them to be unwilling or afraid to see me," she says now. Then, during another visit to the Hearst Street House, she saw a couple who had come to visit their own daughter. The young woman was there, in the house, but she said she didn't want to see her parents. When she finally did agree to talk to them, the mother cried and the daughter sat coolly, totally unmoved by her mother's emotional outburst.

The combination of her own daughters' fears and

this young woman's unfeeling behavior increased Mrs. Albertson's conviction that something needed to be done. By then she knew that it was the Moonies who had elicited the dedication of her daughters, so Elizabeth and John went to a local library to read all they could find about the Reverend Moon and his followers. They read and reread letters from Nini and Terry. "The letters could have been written by total strangers, they were so secretive and bland," she told us. They added to the family's already growing alarm.

When the mother learned about the polarization of good and evil in the theology of the Unification Church, she became disturbed and frightened for Nini, who had had so much trouble with this concept when she was a little girl. "I wasn't concerned that Nini had dropped out of college. She had learned to work in positive directions with her life and I trusted her. I trusted Terry too, but I also know that Terry flits from one project to another, one idea to another. I didn't fear it would be a lasting thing with her.

"I was worried about Nini and her bout with the devil. I would have left Terry to work her own way out of it," Mrs. Albertson told us a year later.

Elizabeth and John finally located Terry and Nini at Boonville and called them. "I told them not to leave, I was coming to talk to them. When we arrived at the ranch, we had to ring a buzzer at the locked gates. After ten or fifteen minutes a couple of unusually polite young people came to the gate. We asked to see Terry and Nini and we had to wait at the gate until they came. We were not even invited in," she said.

Eventually, the two young women came to the gate with big smiles on their faces and several of their new friends with them. In unison, they said, "We like it here so much, we don't want to come out."

Their mother continued her story. "When I confronted their 'guardian angel,' Ricky, and asked why we could not be alone, he said that was up to Terry and Nini.

"I said, 'Ricky, you seem like a nice boy, but this is a family discussion.'

"Terry answered for him, 'It's so wonderful that God is here and it can be proven. It is proven fact.'

"They had heard a lot about deprogramming and were afraid of it. But I reassured them I was not going to do that," Mrs. Albertson says. "I only wanted to talk to them and told them so. They didn't believe me. I was crushed. I had never lied to my children about anything in their lives; why now, in this 'godly' environment had this mistrust been spawned?" she wondered.

Later Nini and Terry explained why they had mistrusted their mother when she came to visit them at Boonville. "We thought she was being deceived," Nini said. "The people at Boonville told us that deprogrammers would physically torture us to get us to change our minds.

"They also said our mother didn't know how horrible the process was and that the deprogrammers wouldn't tell her. They said deprogrammers are all sweetness and light when they talk to worried parents. We thought she was lying to us when she said she wasn't going to deprogram us because the deprogrammer had told her to lie!"

Elizabeth and her son left Boonville after making plans to meet the girls the next day. That night she got on the phone and gathered as much information about the Unification Church as she could in the limited time available.

"I called the girls the next morning and asked them to meet me and discuss what I had learned. They said, 'Tell us on the phone.' I told them I could do that from Philadelphia, but I had come to California to spend some time with them."

The conversation ended with the two sisters echoing each other: "Please, Mama, don't take us out of here."

"I knew that going to Boonville again wouldn't help. I couldn't even communicate with them. I began to see clearly that I had to get them out of there." Discouraged and frightened, Mrs. Albertson flew home to Pennsylvania to think about things. She knew there were plans to be made.

Back home in suburban Philadelphia, Elizabeth Albertson paused for a few deep breaths and took note of the rest of her brood. Nini's and Terry's stepfather was also worried about their fate, but recuperation from a heart attack kept him from being involved in their rescue. Their mother paused for only a short time. Her mission seemed clear. She had decided to get her daughters back, no matter what.

Elizabeth remembered Rabbi Maurice Davis, who had been mentioned in a *Time* magazine article about the Unification Church and its leader, Sun Myung Moon. She called Rabbi Davis. He told her about deprogrammers who would work on cases like her daughters. She started phoning them. Ted Patrick, the best-known of the new professionals, was too busy. Joe Alexander, then working out of his Ohio home, said he'd take the case. "That was a relief." But then she thought, "How am I going to get the girls to talk to a deprogrammer when they won't even talk to me?"

At this point the situation became dramatic. Elizabeth Albertson had come to believe that her daughters wouldn't even hear the other side of the Moon story voluntarily. "How would she get to them?" she wondered. Her first plan, she recalled, was to nab them on the street.

In planning for the "snatch" Mrs. Albertson, her son John, and Nini's and Terry's closest and lifelong friend, Marian Story, left Pennsylvania for California once again. They bought a used Volkswagen van and got in touch with former Unification Church member Jenny Michalsen and her parents. Jenny, who joined the church with Nini, had been deprogrammed, and was angry at the Moonies. She was eager to help rescue her two friends.

"I thought Nini and Terry were having some second thoughts about the way they had brushed me off in Boonville," their mother remembers. "They called on Thanksgiving and sent me roses. It was their way of apologizing.

"Marian and John went to the Berkeley campus to look for Terry. The Moonies had a table on the mall there where they passed out information and tried to recruit new members. We had heard that Terry was working there. John and Marian stationed themselves behind trees, watching the Moonies, hoping to grab Terry if she showed up. I was waiting nearby in the van, ready to drive away quickly if they were able to spirit her off the campus." The plan didn't work. Terry never showed up at Berkeley.

"We had been told that Terry was in Berkeley and that Nini was selling flowers for Moon in San Francisco," Elizabeth Albertson continued. "So after the campus stake-out failed we all went to San Francisco the next night to look for Nini."

Jenny Michalsen recalled, laughing, "My mother and Mrs. Albertson were so funny. While they were staking out the San Francisco Moonie house they thought their rented car had been seen so they went to exchange it. The man at the rental agency asked them why they wanted another car. The two of them, with big sunglasses and the whole disguise bit, couldn't think of an answer and so Mrs. Albertson said coyly, 'We just like that pretty blue one over there better.'"

Elizabeth said, "This is the part of the whole adventure that sounds like a cops and robbers script from a television show." The rescue crew in addition to Mrs. Albertson, John Coleman, and Marian Story now included Jenny's mother and her brother-in-law, a young man who bears a strong resemblance to John Coleman. They sat outside the Moon house, hoping no one would notice them as they watched the comings and goings. One evening, after watching for several hours with no sign of Nini, the two young men went in. Elizabeth was elected to stand guard at the van, holding the door, waiting to slam it shut if Nini came back with the two young men. But, unfortunately, all the planning, the rehearsals, the waiting and watching were in vain. Nini wasn't there.

After the failure of two attempts to "rescue" her

daughters, Elizabeth Albertson was very despondent and searching, more than ever, for an answer. Joe Alexander, the deprogrammer who had agreed to help, if she could get her daughters in custody, told her about the two young lawyers from Arizona who had been successful in obtaining a court order, called a conservatorship, where a cult member had been temporarily remanded to the custody of his parents.

"Still, I didn't pin much hope on Mr. Alexander's offer to get in touch with the lawyers," Elizabeth recalled. "I just didn't think the plan would work."

The next day she made an appointment with a psychiatrist at the University of California at Berkeley to discuss questions she had not been able to handle on her own, whether or not her daughters were in control of their faculties, whether or not they were members of the Unification Church of their own free wills.

"The psychiatrist was so distracted by my own agitation that he avoided discussing why I had come, but rather, kept asking me if I was disturbed and wanted a prescription for tranquilizers. I was furious. I felt so helpless and so alone."

But in the meantime, Joe Alexander had been successful in his efforts. The lawyers were able to get a court order to remove the Coleman girls from Boonville and to place them in the temporary custody of their mother. The Unification Church would have to let them go. Elizabeth Albertson could now have them deprogrammed, legally.

She continued her tale, "We drove to Boonville at night. It was agreed that I would go in and meet with Terry and Nini and while they were with me the sheriff would drive up and serve the order. It was almost over."

When the sheriff appeared, Nini bolted from the mobile home where she had been visiting with her mother and ran into the dark farm fields and valleys. "She ran as though her very salvation depended on it," her mother said. While she was running, Nini fell and turned her ankle.

Then the sheriff told the Boonville authorities that if Nini Coleman didn't come forward he would check every person at the farm and leave a deputy there full time. "Needless to say, they produced Nini," Mrs. Albertson told us.

As they were getting into the sheriff's car, the girls asked that it be noted that they were entering the car against their wills. Elizabeth Albertson had her daughters, but the excitement didn't stop there.

"We knew we were being followed and weren't too sure where we were. We panicked because the court order was only effective in Mendocino County and for a few minutes we wondered if we had crossed a county line. Eventually the caravan made its way to a motel where Joe Alexander was waiting. The deprogramming of Nini and Terry Coleman took but a few hours. It involved nothing more than conversation and the reading of some material. These young women were not alienated from their family and the world. They loved and respected their mother. It could be called a simple deprogramming because they had only to be encouraged to think for themselves and had no deep psychological problems or family conflicts to deal with. Neither had they absorbed intense beliefs through months, or years, of association with zealous Unification Church members.

"The deprogrammer and his helpers found it easy to get us to change our minds because they were so nice to us," Nini confided. "We could see that the Moonies had lied, because the deprogramming was nothing at all like the horror stories they had told us. The deprogrammer asked us if we were tired, did we want to sleep, were we hungry, did we want a shower? No one tied us up or beat us or screamed at us or called us names, like we'd been told they would.

"But most importantly, we began to see how we joined the church, and why we had gotten so involved in such a short period of time. We didn't even know about the Reverend Moon for a long time after we first went to Hearst Street House (The Creative Community Project) in Berkeley. Even in Boonville, it all sounded like something very different from what we finally learned it is," said Nini.

The young women agreed to accompany their mother to Ohio, so Mrs. Albertson and her daughters flew to the Alexander home. Here the girls went through what is called "rehabilitation," a process used to reintegrate recently deprogrammed young people into society. Soon the three weeks of temporary custody were gone and the family was due back in a California court where a judge would determine whether the temporary court custody order should continue. Getting there was not easy.

A nationwide strike against United Airlines was in effect and it was impossible to use their long-standing reservations. There seemed to be no direct way to return to California. Elizabeth Albertson checked rail and bus transportation and considered renting a car and driving from eastern Ohio to California, but there wasn't enough time. Finally she chartered a plane so they could keep their appointment in court. By now the rescue and deprogramming of Terry and Nini Coleman had become a very expensive venture. Elizabeth Albertson estimates the cost at roughly $16,000. Luckily for this family, a munificent grandmother and trust funds provided for the expense.

On December 19, 1976, less than one month after they had been taken from the New Ideal City Ranch of the Reverend Sun Myung Moon, Nini and Terry took the witness stand at the hearing in California. They testified that they had been victims of mind control in the Unification Church and that they wanted their mother to gain permanent custody of them. They each said that they "wanted the security of their mother's custody and protection." The judge, after gently questioning all of those involved, agreed to continue the conservatorship.

Although both of the Coleman girls and their friend Linda Simonson testified that they had not been physically restrained from leaving the Moon ranch, Linda told the court, "They didn't want me to leave, saying lots of times people left and wouldn't come back. And I was told by my group leader, you know, that oftentimes Satan works through parents to take you away."

Other former Unification members told how their lives had been manipulated by church members and how there was no real freedom for them as Moonies.

The church, too, was represented at the hearing, both because church leaders sincerely believed they were operating in the best interests of the Coleman girls and because they were concerned that a precedent not in the best interests of their church could be established if the conservatorship became permanent.

Nini and Terry Coleman, were, at least in body, free of the Unification Church. The airline strike was over and they flew home to Pennsylvania for Christmas and began their long, uphill struggle toward independence.

"We had a wonderful family reunion and Christmas," their mother says. The younger children, Chrissy, seven, and Amy, eight, adore their older sisters and were thrilled to have them home. "And I was thankful and relieved they were finally out of the Unification Church."

But the homecoming was far from idyllic. Nini and Terry still had the task of making some sense out of what they had been through these past months. "They had never been religious before, although I had taken them regularly to Episcopal Sunday school classes when they were little. But now they began studying the Bible with a fervor I thought was reserved for biblical scholars and religious fanatics," their mother told us. "They were more interested in religion than they had ever been and somehow the word was out and every evangelizing preacher in our suburbs began calling, trying to convert the girls to his faith."

Then in March, as though they had had enough, Nini and Terry decided to put Moon and the religious experience behind them and to get on with their own lives. "It was too late to enroll in college for the spring semester, but they decided to go back to Boulder anyway. I was worried and afraid to let them go off on their own. I was afraid they might still go back to the Unification Church."

Back in Boulder, they saw old friends, made some new ones, and even visited the Unification Church center to talk with the Moonies. Nini got on with the making of her film, a vehicle for her talent as a graphic artist and photographer and her imaginative sense of humor. Terry went back to her struggle for identity, her doodles, and her diaries. She enrolled in summer school and is trying to decide on a college major that will help her to build a satisfying life someday.

Today, both of the young women are able to see a dichotomy between the dream the Unification Church promises converts and the reality of the movement. They are grateful they were rescued from the reality, and know it's a reality they would not have seen in Boonville. Nini and Terry never saw the Reverend Moon or knew of the group's political activities. They spent very little time selling flowers and recruiting members. They lived in a beautiful California ranch with a bunch of happy young people. They remember being happy at Boonville and the dream is hard to give up.

Terry talked of her life in the church. "When I got to Boonville it was late at night so I went with the group from the bus to a trailer (mobile home) where a bunch of girls were already sleeping in bags on the floor. I put my bag down and went to sleep. Can you imagine how surprised I was when I woke up in the morning next to my sister? What a re-union we had. Nini was ecstatic because she had wanted me to come so bad. She had been writing letters to me to persuade me to come.

"Nini was great, she was really gung ho but she didn't have funny eyes or a funny smile. She was the same old Nini. If I had any doubts about the place, she would erase them for me, she said.

"We'd get up at 6:30 A.M. when some girls with guitars would come in singing 'Morning Has Broken,' 'Rise and Shine,' or 'Red Red Robin.' Then we would go outside for exercises—jumping jacks, windmills, and so forth. After that we'd go to break-fast. The food wasn't bad, although we hardly ever ate meat. I don't think it was a bad diet. We had plenty to eat.

"After breakfast we'd go to lectures. I heard the same series of lectures every day for the six weeks I was there. About 90 percent of the information in the lecture was stuff I already knew and found very acceptable, about 10 percent was new information that I might have questioned if it hadn't been pre-sented with all the true stuff.

"Throughout the day we would break up into groups of about a dozen with a leader for 'inspira-tions.' " We would discuss how we were progressing with a positive attitude, for example, 'I used to feel such and so, but now I am understanding. . . .' We also sang a lot and all the songs were from the Uni-fication Church song book. Many of the tunes were familiar but the words had been changed.

"On Mondays after breakfast the new people would tell stories of their lives and how they were led to the movement. The leaders told us that there was no reason to find anything bad in another person. They said we should find the person we thought we would like the least and find out how to get along with them. They said we should do something nice for the person we didn't like.

"One day somebody made Nini's bed for her and she worried all day about who it was that didn't like her. But she wasn't supposed to think about it. They also told us to 'get out of the intellect and into the heart. The devil is the archangel of the intellect,' they said.

"I'm glad my mother kidnapped me legally from the cult. Otherwise they would have pressured me to escape from the deprogrammers. The way she did it, they couldn't bother me," Terry says.

In quiet moments Nini still allows herself to wonder if the Reverend Moon might be right.

But the Coleman girls say they are back into the mainstream of their lives. Most important to these young women, though, is how they are in control of their own actions again, as much as anyone can be during the years when many of life's most important decisions are made. They feel that even the potential problems that come with having to make decisions are an inevitable part of the maturing process.

"Never again," they say, "will we give up our independence."

Contrasts

The lifestyles of religious cults vary as much as the individual personalities of the charismatic leaders who direct them. Young people who are caught up in Love Israel's Church of Armageddon in urban Seattle live very differently from the Moonie life of study and games that Terry Coleman remembers from her days on the Boonville ranch.

Young members of the Divine Light Mission, many of whom go into the "real world" to work each day, lead lives that hardly compare to those led by the Hare Krishnas who rise in the wee hours of the morning to begin their rounds of chanting. We explore the life in these groups because each offers a definitive example of a cult life extreme.

LOVE ISRAEL

If anyone looked for the average American family of the nicest kind, with two concerned parents who appear to get along well, with bright, attractive kids who are achievers but not overly concerned with success, living in a modest but well-kept home in a solidly middle class community, Henrietta and Curt

Crampton of Redondo Beach, California, could qualify. This family, while its three grown daughters were younger and still at home, had nearly all the qualifications to be the average, textbook case, happy family.

Each of the three Crampton girls was a top student. The two oldest daughters graduated from college and went on to get advanced degrees without a hitch. The years Henrietta and Curt devoted to church and school activities and to gently coaxing their daughters into maturity seemed to have paid off.

Now there is a flaw in the appearance of familial bliss. In her sophomore year of college, several years ago, the Cramptons' youngest daughter, Kathe, became a member of a religious cult, the Church of Armageddon, in Seattle, Washington.

The group is also known as the Love Israel family. It is named for its leader Paul Erdman, a former real estate salesman with a long record of drug-related arrests (according to a police officer's court testimony), who has changed his name to Love Israel. He runs his cult with that mixture of self-avowed beneficence and stern discipline that has come to characterize contemporary religious cult leaders.

At various times the Love Israel family has been called "a wild filthy bunch" by Ted Patrick, "a loving and normal religious commune" by both a psychiatrist and a Presbyterian minister who visited the group, and "a religious cult, gathered around a charismatic leader who encourages drug use and sex" by Seattle police.

A former family member is suing to recover thousands of dollars' worth of personal possessions and family heirlooms she left behind. Present members, when they say anything at all about the group, say it is the best thing that ever happened to them.

The truth about the Love Israel family probably lies entangled in all these various opinions. The family seems to be, in many ways, typical of communal religious groups that have sprouted around the country in the past decade, focusing the energies of young converts on religious ceremonies, in a world far removed from the reality of the lives they left when they joined.

Kathe Crampton's parents are not sure how she got involved in the Church of Armageddon. Those details are probably unknown to all but Kathe and the individual family member who recruited her. Curt and Henrietta Crampton learned about their daughter's association through a series of letters that told only of a Christian family she was with. One day they received a letter from her saying, "I love you. There is no more to say. I will not write again."

And then, silence.

Henrietta Crampton continued to write to her daughter three times a week for several weeks until one day a letter was returned with a message stamped on it: "Eye to Eye, Hand to Hand, We'd Love to See You in Our Land. Return to Sender."

A few days later the Cramptons got another letter that said, "Kathe is finding her place here in the family and feels better all the time." It was signed "Kathe's brother."

A friend of the Cramptons, who knew Kathe well, made a fast trip to Seattle and returned to California with a firsthand report about Kathe. It was not good. Henrietta Crampton took the next plane to Seattle to see her daughter.

"When I got to the address on Kathe's letter and rang the bell, it was answered by a girl with long, stringy hair and sores all over her face. The biggest shock of my life came as I stood there and realized I was looking at my own daughter."

That's how the nightmare began. They still don't know how or when it will end. They have not given up hope that someday their daughter will come home again.

The Crampton story is not unusual because a bright girl from a good family got mixed up with an offbeat religious cult. It is important because it shows how one American family was victimized by bureaucracy at its worst and how this may have contributed to Kathe's present state. When sociologist William McCready says this generation of young Americans has been buffeted by institutions that have been unable to handle their numbers, he could be talking about Kathe Crampton. This young woman is typical of all those who have been let down by the schools, the churches, and the government. The story touches anybody who has ever struggled against overwhelming bureaucratic red tape and lost, who has been victimized by computer mixups or a botched credit card account. But in their bout with bureaucracy, the Cramptons lost more than their credit rating or American Express card. They lost their daughter.

The sequence of events also shows how the rights of an individual can be violated unless that individual and those around him are both vigilant and protective. Henrietta Crampton is an articulate woman, but one sentence stops her every time. "If I had it to do over again," she begins. And then she stops as her eyes fill with tears and she struggles for self-control.

In the beginning it looked to Curt and Henrietta as though their youngest daughter would sail through life with little difficulty just as her older sisters had. She was always a fine student who participated in many school and community activities. Kathe won more than her share of awards and prizes during her school years, including the *Marian Award* as an outstanding Catholic Girl Scout, and a special award for a booklet she prepared on St. James Parish, the Roman Catholic church that served her family and her neighborhood.

When it came time for her to enter the local Catholic high school, Kathe took the entrance exam and passed it with flying colors. To everyone's surprise she was not accepted. "Kathe was disappointed," her mother says. "But she was even more confused and angry when she could not get a reason for her rejection."

Still, her parents recall, she seemed to accept the fact that she'd have to go to Redondo Beach High School. "Finally Kathe decided she wasn't accepted because one of her older sisters dropped out of the Catholic high school before graduation and transferred into the public school." She complained bitterly and used to ask why the Catholic school accepted "the football players who peed in the holy water font, but not me?" No one ever answered her question.

Nevertheless, Kathe determined to excel at the

public school. Each year her grades were near the top of her class, and in her senior year she was given a special "academic achievement award" and was named a California Scholar, a state award designed to give recognition to top students in the state and to provide financial aid for college.

The Crampton family was thrilled and proud of Kathe's achievement. "Kathe felt she had earned the honor and was happy to be awarded for her hard work," her mother remembers.

If everything had gone well, Kathe would have used her scholarship aid to attend the college of her choice and again graduate at the top of her class. It didn't work out that way. Because her father earned slightly too much money, she would not be eligible for financial aid. And because she was not entitled to the funds, Kathe was not allowed to take part in the public assembly where California Scholars were recognized for their achievement.

Then Kathe Crampton got caught up in the numbers of her generation. She was a good student and had never imagined she'd have trouble getting into the college of her choice. But because it was a peak enrollment year in California, the universities instituted a system called random selection. An applicant sent in an application to the school of her choice, and if that school did not accept her, it would forward the application to the applicant's second choice, and so on, until a prospective student was either accepted or ultimately rejected. But in the meantime, precious time was lost and applications often sat for weeks, even months, before being forwarded by the colleges.

Kathe and her family could not understand it

when she wasn't accepted at her first-choice school. But when the second college also sent a rejection notice, it seemed like too much for Kathe. Somewhere along the way, one school administrator told her she could attend his university if she would major in drama or if she were an American Indian. Kathe didn't want to major in theater. She is not an American Indian. Someone suggested that she enroll in the drama course and later switch to something else. Kathe didn't think that would be honest.

When Kathe's parents helped her with her college selection, they looked for a college that was close enough so she could come home for holidays, one where there were dormitories so she could live on campus, and a school where the tuition was affordable for them. In a college catalogue Kathe found a school in western Washington state which met the dormitory conditions and tuition limit her parents had set. It was her last choice and far from home, but they thought it would be all right. So, Kathe set out for college.

Henrietta Crampton wonders if the ungraded, unstructured program at the school accounts for Kathe's apparent loss of interest in her education. "It wasn't that she stopped caring," her mother says. Calling on her twenty years as a Girl Scout leader, Mrs. Crampton says she has always believed "most young people want a certain amount of structure."

At first Kathe's letters home were filled with news of her life away from home. They were interesting, entertaining letters. During visits home, everything seemed fine. Somewhere in Kathe's second year, she had an unhappy love affair.

Soon after it ended her letters began to tell about the Christian family she had met.

LIFE IN THE CHURCH OF ARMAGEDDON

Belinda McCarthy is a pleasant-looking young woman in her mid-twenties who works for an advertising agency in New York City and spends most of her spare time studying music, taking voice lessons, and involving herself, in any way she can, in musical theater. She has a practical manner and a matter-of-fact way of discussing her own life. Belinda was once a member of the Love Israel family.

In 1970, within a few months, both Belinda's parents died of cancer. The McCarthys had provided well for their son's and daughter's futures. Both young people received substantial inheritances and Belinda was given all her mother's valuable jewelry. After her parents' deaths she decided to continue her college education. Part of a generation that moves from one end of the country to another with the ease their parents moved from a city to a suburb, Belinda left the East Coast, where she had grown up, and began studies at the University of Washington in Seattle. She was twenty years old and she began to concentrate on her studies as she never had before. She chose medicine as her future. All the while Belinda pursued her avid interest in music. In addition to her heavy academic load she continued voice lessons and tells with pride how she sang at a Russian–American hockey game in Seattle. Life was going smoothly for Belinda.

Then one Saturday afternoon as she was busily

running errands, Belinda met a young man on the university campus. The two began to talk. "He was a really gentle guy," she recalls, "very low key and, well, nice."

When he asked about her interests Belinda told him "medicine and music."

He said he lived in a house filled with musicians. Wouldn't she like to visit?

"Why not?" Belinda answered and off they drove in Belinda's sports car. Belinda went to the Love Israel house for lunch and a visit and she stayed for six months, except for one or two days when she left the commune to get her jewelry and take care of legal matters involving her inheritance.

Belinda walked away from the group because she felt she was losing her emotional and physical health. Her brother had visited and pleaded with her to leave. She was never kidnapped, deprogrammed, or forced to leave Love Israel.

Now she is suing the group for fraud and assault and battery, and she is asking for the return of thousands of dollars worth of material goods she donated while she was a member. Belinda and her attorney think she has a good case.

Belinda explains her six months' affiliation with the group simply. "I was constantly drugged." She says her first high came the first day when she visited for lunch, and she says it was *not* the result of being with a group who made a great show of love and approval. "It was drugs, and I know it since I'd had some experience and know the difference between a normal high and a drug-induced high."

Belinda wasn't with the group long before she

began to have "religious visions." She says she often saw Christ in the faces of male members of the group. She says she was so "out of it" she scalded herself in her own bath water and used to cut her feet on zippers while stomping the wash in bathtubs. Belinda says she was so far from reality that she once forgot how to iron. "I didn't realize I had burned myself until I saw a large scar on the palm of my hand. I was totally impervious to pain. I knew something was wrong with me, but I didn't know what to do about it," she says slowly.

She tells how she and other group members often left the house during Seattle's bitterly cold winters without socks or gloves, wearing only thin coats, until Love Israel gathered the group together and told them they must watch their own and each other's appearances so as not to cause suspicion that he was not caring for them well.

"I was a very spaced-out girl," says Belinda. "I used to ask if they were putting something in our food, but they always denied it. I think drugs got us through that winter—we had practically no money for food. Love told us to meditate and concentrate on each grain of rice as we ate it—to hold it up and examine it and see what was special about it before we put it into our mouths. Our big treat was popcorn, and again we could only take one piece at a time and were told to concentrate on the shape and to find something special about it before we ate it. We were starving, but we thought we could hold on until spring when we could get jobs in the fields and gardens around Seattle."

Belinda tells how one day she was out with the

group, "privately and desperately praying for manna from heaven" to feed herself, when she saw a McDonald's and went inside looking for leftovers. That night one of the group told Love Israel what had happened and he called the group to task. "We were so embarrassed at being caught doing something so sinful," she remembers. "The elders told us we must never, never do anything like that to embarrass the family again."

For a while after that, Belinda remembers getting more to eat. Still, Belinda says when she left the family she had dropped from 140 pounds—just about normal for her 5'9" frame—to 98 pounds.

"The worst thing about that group, though," Belinda says, "is the way they keep things hidden from the public. I had a hard time convincing anyone that what I was saying was true after I left. When I talked to another former family member we couldn't believe how difficult it was to communicate the horror of it to those who hadn't felt it or seen it themselves.

"The thing about the family," she says, "is that they are very smart. I know they put drugs into the food because I saw the drugs and heard all the talk about 'breaking down the walls of understanding' with chemical or sacramental substances. But they must only put it into some people's food at first, because a lot of them don't seem to respond the way I did."

Belinda believes the group decided they wanted her to live with them because they knew both her parents were dead, that she had graduated from an exclusive junior college, had her own apartment, carried an expensive guitar, and drove a jaunty sports car. "They knew I was no pauper."

She got a very good impression of the family the day of her first visit to the commune. "The houses are kept immaculately clean and everyone flooded me with love and attention," Belinda says. It was not until later that she realized that those who kept constantly filling her plate with good food weren't eating much at all themselves.

At the end of her first day with the group Belinda insisted on leaving, telling them she felt so weird and spaced out that she thought she must be coming down with the flu or something. The next day a member of the family came to Belinda's apartment and talked to her, coaxing her to return to the house. "My roommates thought I was crazy, but I told them these were very fine, good people and this is what I wanted to do." Belinda can't recall her reasons for wanting to move in with Love Israel and his family; she only remembers "a very strong pull into the group."

"We packed all my things and I moved into the house," she reports.

For weeks Belinda continued to feel the pull, the attractions to the group, but she also began to fear that something was desperately wrong with her. "I began to feel so awful and so sinful. We [the women] were not allowed to speak, unless spoken to, and I had begun to feel spacey and distant as though all of this was going on around me but that I wasn't really there."

Some months after she had joined the group, Belinda recalls looking at her body in a mirror. "I realized I had lost a sense of my own sexuality. I was covered with sores, and my breasts had shrunken so, they had almost disappeared. I could count my own ribs. I looked like a skeleton."

Soon after Belinda had come to live with the group she took part in a ceremony in which she "died to herself" and "adopted a new identity." As Belinda McCarthy's last will and testament was read, she took a new name, as all members of the Church of Armageddon do, of a virtue. She signed a form bequeathing all the material goods owned by Belinda McCarthy to the family as a group, and agreed, in writing, that in case of her death her body could not be autopsied.

"Our pasts were dead," she says, explaining that family members were not permitted to speak of either the past or the future. All mail was censored by an elder before it was given to a member, and before it was allowed to be mailed. "No one but the elders are allowed to touch money. For a member to handle money is considered a very serious sin, so we couldn't even use a dime to call someone, or to buy a stamp."

Before she left the group Belinda says she felt "like the world's most rotten person. They told me the sores all over my body (scabies caused by mites that bury themselves under the skin and lay eggs there) were caused by my own sinfulness and would go away only when I began to lead a more obedient, pure life."

During her six months in the cult, Belinda says she had only one menstrual period, the first month she was there. "I was raped by one of the elders in a graveyard near the house. He told me that it was meant to happen and that God approved of it. I was so scared and I couldn't believe it happened. But that was the only time someone forced their sexual favors on me . . . and at least I didn't have to worry about getting pregnant," she says.

Belinda's worst memories of the Love Israel Family are of the small children and the way they are mistreated in the cult. "One child repeatedly wet the bed and so they made him sleep on the floor, in a corner, with no clothing in the dead of winter," she recalls. "He cried and cried until I wanted to cry myself. It was so pitiful. One of the women gave him a blanket, but an elder came in and took it away and locked him in a closet.

"Some of the parents are very loving toward their children," Belinda continues, "but if the elders see kids getting really attached to a parent they move people around and fix it so that someone else cares for the child. And only the men are allowed to discipline them, because they can be more strict."

Belinda says she finally decided to break with the group, even though she was convinced she would be doomed to hell by leaving, because she overheard the elders plotting to give away her sports car (women are not allowed to drive). About the same time she overheard the conversation, her brother came to visit her and told her the pupils of her eyes were so dilated that he knew she was on drugs.

"I resisted and said it was untrue, but oh how I wanted him to take me away from there," Belinda now says.

Within a few weeks of her brother's visit, Belinda ran away from Love Israel, got some money from a

former roommate, and flew across the country to get
as far from the group as she could. After she arrived on the East Coast Belinda checked herself into
a mental hospital, where she was given heavy doses
of tranquilizers that kept her calm, but she says she
still felt that she needed someone to talk with
about her cult experience. After three months, Belinda says her psychiatrist told her she was "recovered." She checked herself out of the hospital.

"In the hospital I still felt like I was being
drugged. I wanted to try to live my own life without
having anyone tell me what to do. So I finally had to
plunge into the real world again."

Although Belinda continued with psychotherapy
and she believes it helped her to understand the conditions of her life and her mind before she entered
the Love Israel group, she says it was her job, her
interest in music, and her own ability to build structure into her life that helped her to feel sane and
normal again.

She says there are still many, many parts of her
cult experience she doesn't understand. "My main
question is how it all happened to me so quickly. I
left after the first day, I went home and cleaned
my apartment from top to bottom; then that guy
from the family came and I went with him. I wonder if I was hypnotized, if the drugs could have had
some effect on me that no one understands? My life
was going so well," she says in disbelief. "I still can't
understand how it happened to me. It just had to be
the drugs. . . ."

Belinda's story may seem farfetched when compared to tales of Love Israel told by others who have
observed the cult.

The Protestant minister who visited the group calls the Love Israel Family a typical religious commune, organized around a highly charismatic leader. He says he saw no drugs, no evidence of child abuse, and nothing especially unusual about this group of young people. "The children were rosy-cheeked and lively, thrilled when Love Israel came into the room," he says. "Surely if they were abused, they would not behave this way."

A young psychiatrist went into the group posing as a prospective member, rather than as a visitor. He also says he saw nothing alarming or out of the ordinary in the commune. "I felt kind of high," he admits, but says he recognized the feeling as a natural emotional high caused by the approval and affection he felt within the group. "There was no way they could have known I was a physician, or that I had any special interest in them." As for child battering he says this is something that couldn't be determined in one visit, but that he saw no outward signs of any serious illness, including skin disease. "Everyone was happy, smiling, and seemed very normal," he said.

Whatever the truth, it is doubtful that any kind of casual observer could witness what many members of the group have seen. Sworn testimony in the United States Court of Appeals for the Ninth Circuit in the western district of Washington corroborates many of Belinda's charges.

A friend of Kathe Crampton, who had traveled to Seattle for the sole purpose of seeing her, testified how he had been with Kathe on two successive days for more than one hour, but had not been allowed to be alone with the young woman. Kathe had not answered any of the young man's questions, but sat silently while the elders answered for her. During the entire visit, the young man said, Kathe and other cult members smiled vacantly and stared at him and each other with "glassy eyes." The young man said it seemed to him that all the cult members were "flipped out on LSD."

The court heard another witness say that Erdman (Love Israel) claims his teachings prohibit the use of drugs. However, the court also learned that Erdman has a police record of many drug arrests, and that he doesn't consider LSD a drug, but a substance that helps bring his followers closer to each other, to him, and to God.

Several references cite the deaths of two Love Israel cult members during a ceremony called the "rite of breathing," where members sniff toluene, a chemical substance that the medical examiner described as a solvent used industrially to break down rubber. The two men were revived, but died during the three hours that elapsed before Erdman brought authorities for help. Autopsies were not performed, in accordance with signed statements forbidding them because of religious beliefs. The Church of Armageddon's attitude toward the two men's deaths is that they were "disobedient" and died as just punishment.

Cult members responded in newspaper stories that the substance is used by God "to break down walls between us," and said of the chemical used in the manufacture of TNT that only foolish people and foolish laws would seek to prevent people with special knowledge from using this substance that God puts on earth for such purposes. One cult member described the chemical as "special atmospheric conditions."

Another part of the testimony before the court told of corporal punishment inflicted on both child and adult members of the cult. "One adult, for disciplinary reasons, was beaten with forty strokes from a two-foot stick similar in width to a pool cue. The cult elder who administered the beating later stated that it might one day be necessary to kill someone for disciplinary reasons."

Former members testified that there were incidents of extensive child abuse and the Child Protective Service of the Department of Social Health Services in Washington announced that the cult was involved in a case of child abuse.

The cult, according to information gathered by the Cramptons and entered into the court record, had an "armory of knives, bows and arrows, and sling shots which male cult members had learned to use with great accuracy."

A woman whose daughter was a former member of the cult testified that members gave all their possessions to Erdman and signed over their power of attorney to him. The woman said her daughter never had enough money to make a telephone call and that all their letters from her had been opened and censored. The woman also testified that a young child in the cult was kept apart from his mother because the elders believed "he was getting too attached to her."

A Seattle police officer familiar with Erdman and the group described them in written testimony presented to the court. "The only written material allowed the cult members is the Bible," he wrote, "which Erdman has reedited and which has his name inserted wherever reference to the Deity is made." The officer also said he knew of a young woman induced by Erdman to join the group who had inherited $50,000 worth of jewelry. (The young woman was Belinda McCarthy.)

The officer's testimony, along with others, confirms Belinda's story.

"Only Erdman and three of his 'lieutenants' are allowed to drive automobiles, and none of the members (except for the elders) is allowed to carry money or to use medicine. Those cult members who fell ill were looked down upon as weak members without enough faith to ward off disease," according to another sworn affidavit. The police officer also observed that Erdman "apparently holds a hypnotic rule over his members and very few defectors have been found."

Another eyewitness account of life within the Love Israel cult was presented to the Cramptons by a former member. "One of the religious ceremonies used in the cult involved a number of members holding hands while sitting in a circle, one of them holding metal somehow attached to the room's electrical outlet. The current was turned on, causing it to run through the bodies of those in the circle. One by one, members would leave the circle, increasing the current being endured by the remainder. The record as to the fewest number willing to prove their faith was two, both of whom became frightened when they could not release each other's hands or the electrified piece of metal. A 'religious' spectator had to remove the plug from the outlet."

DIVINE LIGHT

Meditation is enjoying an immense popularity these days and it isn't something that goes on only in the ashrams of Asiatic gurus like Maharaj Ji. It is happening in the living rooms, family rooms, and bedrooms of affluent middle-aged housewives and executives as well. Why then are these same people incensed when their children want to practice meditation?

In the case of the Divine Light Mission, the question seems to be complicated by one of the oldest questions in history: How can intelligent, rational people prostrate themselves at the feet of self-proclaimed gods or those who claim to be representatives of God? And why do human beings allow others to direct their spiritual and temporal lives?

What then makes the lives of the young premies in the ashrams of the Guru Maharaj Ji so suspect, so criticized? Do premies give the control of their lives to the group, or to their guru? Or is "knowledge" nothing more than a system to enrich and deepen spiritual lives? We went quietly into the ashrams to study the Divine Light techniques and to observe the way of life.

The house the premies chose for the ashram in one large Eastern city is a lovely Victorian mansion with leaded glass windows and intricately carved

woodwork that reflect the home's original use as the
city seat of a turn-of-the-century industrial magnate.
It sits on the edge of the city, in a neighborhood
that is "changing" and therefore affordable. The
streets are still safe enough for the area to be in-
habitable and it is well kept enough to be respectable,
bordering on one of this country's most affluent
and sprawling landscaped hospital grounds and college campuses.

The mansion has seen both better days and worse.
It was being used as a day-care center when the Mission negotiated to buy it a few years ago. They paid
a modest figure considering the building's size, location, and condition.

The interior architectural detail is reminiscent of
convents, rectories, and the manses that are often
part of church properties. There is a definite religious
feeling in this house, but instead of pictures of Christ
and crucifixes, it is now adorned with the signs of
the Divine Light Mission and the young people who
live here. In every room, including pantries and
bathrooms, there are portraits of Guru Maharaj Ji,
the premies' Perfect Master.

The young people have left their mark in other
ways. Huge bay windows now hold jungles of house-
plants. Just inside the massive carved oak and leaded
glass entrance door is a cloakroom, always filled
with shoes: leather boots and sneakers along with
high-heeled platforms and sandals. Premies, like
Moonies and Krishna devotees, do not wear shoes in-
doors. They pad around the house quietly in socks
and slippers.

On one side of the enormous wainscoted entry

hall is a staircase that leads to sleeping rooms for the fifteen permanent ashram dwellers. Premies, we are told, sleep two to a room here. On the other side of the hall are floor-to-ceiling carved-oak sliding doors that lead to the living room where nightly satsang is conducted. Here, premies meet to discuss their experiences with Maharaj Ji's knowledge to reinforce their own practice and to convert visitors to the practice of Divine Light meditation.

Beyond the hall is a dining room, with tables set for far more than the handful of premies who live here. Food is important to premies. Vegetarianism is a way of separating them from their previous lifestyles and their families. It is a factor that gives them a sense of commonality. Nearly all the meals here are prepared by Alice, the ashram housemother, and Carol, her assistant. The two are sisters. Alice is in her mid-to-late twenties and says her life as cook and housekeeper is the most satisfying she has ever had. She devotes full time to directing the housekeeping, the grocery shopping, and running the kitchen. The quality of the diet in the ashram is dependent on her skill, and one suspects the kitchen is a gathering place because Alice encourages it. Alice says that as housemother she feels appreciated and important in this group she needs and loves. According to her, the life she led before Divine Light was not a directed or purposeful one. In and out of schools, Alice says she was not the daughter her mother wanted. Although Alice and Carol's mother does not approve of the "religious part" of their premie existence, she does profess to approve of the newfound order the two young women have instilled in their lives.

Carol, too, wants an ashram life. She transferred to the East when her Midwestern ashram closed as part of the Mission's effort to consolidate their holdings. Alice, who had been the assistant housemother, took over her new responsibilities when the old housemother decided to live outside the ashram with another premie and to continue her practice of "knowledge" on a part-time basis. The former housemother now works as a secretary at a Roman Catholic college just down the street from the ashram. She still visits the ashram regularly and she is almost as involved as she was before she got her own apartment.

The day of our visit was the Guru's birthday celebration, and premies had traveled from ashrams in other cities to this big home and its day-long festivities. While Carol served lunch to a houseful of visitors, we washed dishes. And we observed the young men and women who were diligently working at cooking and cleaning the kitchen. Their own mothers would have been impressed by the dedication and concentration surrounding this "thankless" work. Not that the kitchen help was behind-the-scenes. Here, premies wandered in and out of the room, helping themselves to tea, helping with dishes and other chores. The normal isolation of the housewife and cook became a communal, everyone-pitch-in-and-help festival.

In the butler's pantry between the kitchen and dining room there was a constant supply of hot water. Spiced and flavored teas, honey, milk, and cups were set out for convenience and the pantry was, for many, the hub of the day's events.

During the visit and on previous occasions when we visited ashrams as undeclared aspirants, there was no persuasion or cajoling for us to become part of this group. We did feel a sense of calm and peace in the ashrams. Most of the premies seemed sincere and rational. They appeared to be in control of their own lives and seemed to be achieving some measure of peace as a by-product of a lifestyle they feel is constructive and healthy.

Yet one week later the Guru Maharaj Ji came to Atlantic City, New Jersey, and the same young people were there too. In their guru's presence they lost control, sobbed, swayed, and knelt to kiss his feet. They say he is their guru, not their God.

The program for the celebration said, "Guru Maharaj Ji, my life is within you. From you I was born and to you now I go. Forever I'm yours. My longing is endless."

The chubby little man, whose corpulence suggests he hasn't nearly the self-discipline he inspires in his followers, came to Atlantic City to minister to his devotees and to receive their adulation. (There is always a hubbub of anxiety when the guru is scheduled to appear, since he has often failed to show up at celebrations and festivals in his honor.)

The guru entered the ballroom of the Atlantic City Convention Hall—where the annual Miss America pageant is held—and mounted a satin throne his premies had set there for him. The assembled devotees welcomed their master with frenzied screams, sobs, and outstretched arms. The young Indian's followers came one by one to bow before him and to kiss his feet.

They heard the little guru tell them, "You cannot battle the mind. It is too complex, too sophisticated. You'll lose. To beat the mind you must ignore it." Our newfound friends were ecstatic, entranced—as though they were not the same people we'd visited a week earlier.

KRISHNA

The introduction was conducted with great fanfare. "This is Lilavahti Devi," said the temple leader with pride. "She was also a writer, but she gave it all up for Krishna."

Lila, as she is called, is a slim young woman in her early thirties, a member of the Hare Krishnas for nearly half a decade. She is vague about her former career as a writer, and when we ask if she has written articles, fiction, or poetry, she answers that she sold two pieces to a local newspaper many years ago. We press her and ask if she is being humble or evasive about her past, since she has been introduced as a prominent writer. She responds by saying that everything in her life was preparation for entering Krishna.

The young woman is calm and tranquil, with an air of remoteness and detachment about her. She seems to have trouble focusing on our conversation, perhaps because it is so "worldly," a term frequently used by Krishnas to describe things of which they disapprove. But she says she can tell by our faces that we are honest and therefore she has decided to trust us.

During this celebration of Lord Krishna's birthday, she agrees to sit with us and talk about her life

before and after she became a Hare Krishna devotee.
The West Coast temple we are in is a large and
colorfully decorated place, surrounded by a group
of barren apartments in a mildly depressed neighborhood.

Lila has decided to write for Krishna, to "show
others how we live," and she wants some advice.
She asks our opinion of a story for *Popular Mechanics* telling readers how Krishna mechanics work
twenty-four hours a day. She explains that by meditating and concentrating, a person can focus all his
attention on one subject, even while sleeping. We say
we don't think *Popular Mechanics* would buy such
an article.

She seems disappointed, but trusting, and describes
her next idea of a Krishna cooking column for newspapers and magazines. In it, Lila wants to explain
how "vegetarianism is such a good way of life," and
to tell how cow slaughter causes such bad karma
in the world. "Did you know that if cow slaughter were ended, the bad weather in Chicago would
change and the temperature would rise at least 10
degrees?" Lila senses our disbelief and continues, "I
guess that's hard to believe, but our swami told us
that and I believe it. I can't explain," she says softly.
"You have to know what bad karma is. Once my
husband shook the hand of a man in India and the
man had such bad karma that my husband felt a
terrible pain shoot up his arm while they touched."

"Is that the basis of the caste system and the un-
touchables in India?" we ask. "Do the lower castes
have such bad karma that they are virtually un-
touchable?"

Lila does not want to discuss it but says it could be so. She puts her arms around her knees and her head on her lap.

We ask her if she is a strong person. Lila looks at us for a long time before she shakes her head. "No, I am so affected by everything in life." She looks around her. "That's why it is so much easier to live here. Everyone is so nice. And the chanting is good for your consciousness." She explains that there are three levels of consciousness: ignorance and passion, goodness, and the highest, transcendental level. "We try to lead a very moral life and therefore are in the mode of goodness. It's so nice—we don't drink or anything like that. It is not a form of prejudice to say a person is very nice," she says slowly. "Everything we study is very scientific, not opinion. If a person is very nice it is because he is living a life of goodness."

Lila explains that she was raised as a Protestant, her husband as an atheist, and now they compare their lives to those lived by medieval Catholic saints. Her husband has studied how to make traditional Hindu musical instruments from contemporary substitutes for the wood, animal skin, and bone they were made of in ancient times. He is now involved in setting up the manufacture of goods for the Krishnas' own use and for sale to the public. Lila herself works as a staff member of the magazine *Back to Godhead* and spends her days at work, contemplating, and chanting.

Their only child, a daughter, lives in Dallas and they have not seen her for "quite a while." Lila says mildly, "We miss her, but we know it is for her own good to be away from her parents and to study the beliefs of Krishna with other children of devotees." Since the Krishna school in Dallas had been closed, we ask Lila where her daughter studies. She is evasive.

As for her own marriage, that took place before she and her husband discovered Krishna. Lila says they were always searching for something to give meaning to their lives. Her marriage has helped her to grow, she says, and has taught her the meaning of self-control and tolerance. She and her husband first got involved with Krishnas while they were running a boardinghouse in Canada. "Some devotees came by and I gave them free lodging. I had to move out of my own room and into my husband's room with him. He was angry about the sleeping arrangement," she says. "We both value our privacy." We ask Lila if there is any physical attachment in their marriage. Looking straight ahead, avoiding our eyes, Lila says they lived celibate lives before they joined Krishna, and have continued the arrangement ever since.

We say to Lila that while the Krishna women seem gentle and humble, the men appear to be very arrogant. She agrees and says the reason more women don't join Krishna is that they must be submissive and humble. "Swami calls the male problem with the traits of humility and gentleness the 'broad-shouldered mentality. It is a great impediment to the humility of our men.'"

And then we meet Lila's husband, a sarcastic young man who makes a futile attempt to hide his hostility. We ask if he has found peace in Krishna and he says, "Yes. We began to see how really bad things were in the world when we joined, and how our own marriage was not together and how no one else's was either," he tells us. "Now when I look around the world and I see how disturbed everyone is, I know how much better off we are here."

It is a challenge the Krishnas frequently toss out: "We're okay, you're not."

We respond and say, "Things are not always so bad." Then we ask if he would like to meet our husbands.

He becomes even more sarcastic. "Oh, I see what you mean. You think you are really together. That's what they all say. Nothing is wrong with us. It's always the other guy."

He tells us how his wife let some people come and stay in her room and she was forced to move in with him. The six-year-old memory makes him even angrier.

As we say goodbye and tell Lila we would like to talk with her again sometime, she is looking off into the distance and only weakly says, "Goodbye."

We understand now what she meant when she told us how marriage has taught her so much, especially self-control and tolerance.

This story seems almost too harsh in the retelling. It is only fair to note that this couple seems to carry some of the more notable Krishna traits, the anger and hostility to the world, for instance, to an extreme. Because of this, they are among the most memorable Krishnas we have met, like caricatures that are unfailingly accurate because they are so vivid.

Give Us This Day

This chapter looks at the lives led by cult members within their groups through the day-to-day experience of fund raising and personal relationships. It also examines some cult diets, the system of marriage, and cult attitudes toward education.

FUND RAISING

Most cult members look forward to fund raising with what looks like stoic resignation salted with religious fervor. Selling peanuts, candy, literature, flowers, or candles not only raises cash for the cause but also "strengthens the will," they say. Only reluctantly will they tell outsiders how they really feel about airport, street corner, and door-to-door sales work.

When pressed they sound like the man who, when asked why he was pinching himself, responded, "Because it feels so good when I stop."

They say, "People are so thoughtless and so selfish, such an accurate representation of America, that we're relieved to get away from them each evening when we return home to our group." The fund raising of the Moonies and the Krishnas not only deep-

ens their sense of mission but also widens the gap
between them and the world they have left behind.

There are questions about fund raising that can't
be answered in an interview or a conversation. We
were determined to go along to learn more about the
process. How do cult members react when they are
verbally abused by a public that disapproves of their
religion or their leader? How has negative publicity
affected their capacity to coax buyers into parting
with precious dollars? Do they really raise the huge
sums their critics claim they do? What emotional
and physical repercussions do they suffer from
pitting themselves against the world and the elements, as they work outside in fair and foul weather?

They only fund-raise to keep their individual centers going, they say. Reports of million-dollar operations are gross exaggerations, according to the fund
raisers.

When we asked if we could accompany them fund
raising, they couldn't believe anyone wanted to.
Then they had excuses. "Fund-raising teams build
a special rapport and we worry that an outsider will
disturb it" was the most reasonable. But finally,
after a friendly Moonie convinced church leaders
that we were attempting to write a fair analysis of the
movement, we were grudgingly allowed to come
along. Not for interviews, they specified, but to see
them in action.

The team we would accompany goes fund raising
every Saturday and devotes weekdays to witnessing
for new converts at a campus near their church
center. It consists of three women and a male group
leader.

And so, we report at mid-morning on a bright fall Saturday. The big Victorian-style house, close to an Ivy League campus in an Eastern city, was nearly empty. The other teams had begun their work and had a head start. This changing neighborhood is racially mixed, in an area that has seen more gracious times and is now "coming back." Here houses that appear abandoned sit side by side with others that are being restored painstakingly to former grandeur. One of the nation's highest crime rates comes with the high-ceilinged Victorian splendor of this neighborhood. Those who live here, mostly middle class white and black families, have banded together to patrol their blocks on dark winter evenings so neighbors who are on the streets during rush hour can get home safely.

It is here, on a busy side street, where squirrels dart out of tall, old trees into the huge store of peanuts in a corner of the porch, that we stand in a tight circle while the team offers a prayer of hope for a successful day. Dick, the young group leader, leads the prayer, asking for "help in raising funds for Heavenly Father's work to further love and peace in the world, in Jesus' name. . . ."

Then, with a cheerleader yell, "Let's go," Dick leads the way. Balancing cardboard boxes filled with bags of roasted-in-the-shell peanuts on our hips, we walk toward a main street where we will board a bus to take us into a nearby all-black residential neighborhood. They say the blocks closest to the Unification center have already been "worked" by church members and the ten-minute bus ride will take us to fresh territory. A church member confides she prefers to go into black neighborhoods because the people are friendlier, contribute more easily to the cause, and so the days of doorbell ringing seem to pass more quickly.

It is decided we will spend the morning with Dick, the leader. He encourages us to "try your hand at raising funds, so you can get a real feel for the process." As he begins, we watch. Dick runs up the steps to each of the homes in this blue- and white-collar neighborhood and says to everyone he meets at front doors, on the street, fixing cars, or standing outside stores or bars, "We're raising funds to continue our work with young people in our church, and we're asking for a donation of one dollar for a bag of peanuts." If his prospect pauses, Dick fills the silence with chatter, always about his peanuts. "They're awful good," he injects, and sometimes adds laughing, "fresh from Jimmy Carter's peanut farm. . . ."

Dick is neither timid nor self-conscious when he pushes for a sale. If the prospect pauses even slightly, he knows there is a chance for a sale. Only those who bluntly say no escape his vigorous sales pitch. He sounds like the caricature of the natural salesman as he raves about the quality of his peanuts. He keeps his association with the Unification Church to himself, never mentioning the Reverend Moon's name while he's trying to make a sale.

The morning is uneventful. It is amazing to watch how readily black homeowners, here where their own spotlessly neat homes are sprinkled among groups of abandoned shells, give both time and money to these white strangers. Some ask why they should pay one dollar for a few ounces of peanuts in a partially filled lunch bag.

Dick quickly answers that the money will help in his church. A few want to know where the church is located. Dick offers the street name, nothing else. Most of the men and women who answer their doors and show any initial interest will disappear back into the dim inner recesses of their homes and return with a dollar bill and a wish for "good luck" or a "God bless you."

Dick is the first real super-salesman we have ever watched in action. Even after years of opening our own front doors to young people selling raffle tickets and candy or adults hawking vacuum cleaners and magazines, we still find his enthusiastic sales pitch an embarrassing process to witness.

In the meantime, between running up and down steps and climbing quickly over the low fences that separate row houses from each other, Dick tells us his philosophy. "We're giving them an opportunity to give. Giving is so powerful that these people are blessed by having a chance to give to our church. We're allowing them to open their hearts to us. Giving is a wonderful way of getting God's blessing."

As we walk together, he tells his own story. This young man with the old eyes is twenty-seven. He was part of the back-to-nature movement, married with one child, when, he said, he and his wife found the Reverend Moon and his Divine Principle. When they joined the church, he says, they saved their foundering marriage. Their new relationship is based on love of the Heavenly Father, and on "purity" (a word he uses several times).

Dick and his wife no longer live together. She is working for the church in another city several hours away by train or car, and their child is with her. But they manage to see each other "whenever our work allows." Dick will not be specific about his marriage. He is evasive about how often he and his wife meet, but says that their work in the church is important to both of them and that it is their work that keeps them apart.

Dick is not a particularly reticent young man. He discusses most of his thoughts and feelings openly. Yet when we ask if his emphasis on the word "purity" to describe his marriage means that his relationship with his wife is nonsexual he either does not hear us or ignores the question. We are not surprised. Most Moonies either avoid questions about sex or answer them with platitudes.

We've heard many Unification Church members call themselves Moonies, but when we use the word with Dick, he says it is disrespectful. He spits out the word "Moonie" as though it is a disgusting piece of spoiled food. We say that Christians were named for their messiah, as Buddhists were called after Buddha. We press him about the Christ root of "Christian" and ask what followers of the Reverend Moon ought to be called. He won't answer.

Dick continues to ring doorbells and sell peanuts with a fervor that goes beyond enthusiasm. "God has meant for us all to be high on love," he says when I comment on his attitude. Dick says he is sure that God has a hand in his ability as a salesman. He says he simply loves his work and tells how cynical he used to be. In the face of silence, he defends his new-found enthusiasm and his ability to coax the last dollar out of a prospect. He tells with pride about a man in a bar who gave him every cent of his money.

We'd heard stories of "heavenly deception" from former Moonies, who say they lied and deceived the public in order to bring in dollars for their church. According to the frequent allegations, the programs young disciples claim the money they are raising will be used for are nonexistent, such as drug rehabilitation or other social problem areas where the church has no programs. A young student at the Barrytown seminary admitted that she had lied because she was feeling so low, so backed into a corner that she would say almost anything to help her get money for the church. Former Unification Church members report they were encouraged to "say whatever is necessary to bring in more money," and tell how they conditioned themselves not to consider it lying. One young man said he always told people he was raising money for a "children's home." He rationalized, "Well, the center is a children's home, of sorts."

After about an hour and a half of door-to-door selling, we arrive at a corner where we had arranged to meet the other team members. Between us, we have about $30. We are a few minutes early for the rendezvous so Dick plunges into a tiny corner pharmacy. At the noon hour it is filled with customers and Dick approaches each of them with his peanuts. An efficient young woman at the cash register is ringing up sales at a brisk pace. We wait in line with Dick until it is our turn and he asks the sales clerk if she would like to contribute to work with young people in his church. She asks the name of the church and Dick tells her, "Unification."

"You're followers of the Reverend Moon," she

retorts. "I've read a great deal about your church and I don't want to contribute to it." She turns away but then turns around and says, "And I notice you never identify yourself with the church name."

Dick responds with a friendly offer of literature about the Reverend Moon which she curtly refuses. As we leave the store Dick is smiling. Outside Dick's apparent affability explodes into rage. We decide this is a good time to ask why he hasn't been identifying himself as a Unification Church member. Now while his emotional level is high and his guard is down we may get a candid answer. Wouldn't he be doing the church good by letting people know they are meeting Moonies face to face?

"The point is not to convert while you are fundraising, or to get into long conversations about the church. The point is to raise as much money as possible," he says in a condescending tone of voice. "We can't concern ourselves with the hopeless cause of trying to correct the . . . the . . . ," and he pauses, "filth and lies the press has spread about us."

We offer to show him our copious files of newspaper and magazine clippings about the Unification Church. We challenge him to point out the "filth and lies" in these news clippings.

He isn't listening. "The press has done it. They have turned the country against us. They have turned the country against the Reverend Moon." Dick's outburst is beginning to take on the appearance of a full-scale temper tantrum as his voice rises to a near shout. Bystanders turn, curiously, to watch. In the distance we see the two team members returning, dragging empty boxes at their sides. Seeing them, Dick quickly regains his composure. His anger cools as quickly as it appeared, and again he assumes the role of the enthusiastic fund raiser.

"She was the champion fund raiser," he tells the young women, pointing at one of us. We're astonished, since it is clearly not true. Amidst murmurs of approval, there is no mention of the argument.

Back at the church center, after a hastily prepared lunch of vegetable soup, sandwiches made from meatloaf, lettuce, cheese, and tomatoes, milk, tea, imported Canadian cookies, and the ever-present bowl of fruit for dessert, we discuss the morning's work.

We raise the issue of identification as a Unification Church member, and the young women say they always identify themselves. They have raised a few more dollars during the morning than Dick's team, since they separated for the entire morning and we did not.

After lunch we borrow a car and drive to an all-white neighborhood in another part of the city. Here the row homes are nearly identical in size to those in the morning's neighborhood. There are no abandoned houses. There is none of the active street life we observed in the black neighborhood. Here everyone is behind closed doors that are often marked by Knights of Columbus stickers. Statues of the Virgin Mary grace many of the tiny front lawns along the narrow streets.

We change partners and are teamed with Penny, a gentle young woman who says she found the Unification Church just when she was wondering about the meaning of her own life, during her sophomore year in college. She is intelligent and attractive.

Her round face and softly curling, unstyled hair give
her an almost angelic appearance.

Penny is a quiet young woman, but blessed with
wit. She makes an immediate apology for her lack of
super-sales skill, saying she feels the human contact
of selling is as important as the actual sale. "I can't
sell like Dick does," she says, but then quickly, as
though she's afraid she sounds negative about her
Moonie "brother," she adds, "I wish I could."

At every door Penny says nearly the same thing.
"I'm raising funds for the Unification Church, to help
in our work with young people." Sometimes she adds,
"missionary work." She is always polite, and makes a
studied attempt to inject enthusiasm into her voice.
Generally, she is able to carry it off and sounds as if
she is focusing all her energy on this sale. But occasionally her requests sound rehearsed and hollow.
Penny is not pushy, but dignified and low-key in her
sales approach.

The city dwellers we meet in the afternoon are
not as open and trusting as those we met in the
morning. No one slams the door, but frequently they
open the doors just a crack, peer out defensively, and
abruptly cut us off with a terse, "No. I give to my
own church," as they point to a gray stone complex
of buildings topped by crucifixes that occupies a full
city block nearby.

Sales are depressingly slow. We do not separate
and Penny does not press us to "swallow blocks," the
term used when two fund raisers take opposite sides
of a rectangular block of homes and meet on the far
corner of their starting point. "We don't have to if
you don't want to," she offers. We stay together.

The sunny fall morning has turned into a bleak, cold afternoon as we go about the lonely work. There is a pinched feeling about this neighborhood. Only one woman offers any sign of friendliness, and she is overly friendly as though she hasn't seen another human being for weeks. We shy away from her offer of a few minutes of warmth. We are thirsty. Penny says most people will offer a glass of water if you ask for it. We don't ask.

"Fund raising is so good for you, it really develops will," Penny says. We don't respond. Then she confides, "Fund raising is really best for the person who can turn off his mind, just take a yes or no answer and then go on to the next house. The simple-minded type."

We mull over Penny's remark and then decide to give her our honest reaction. "You mean like Dick?"

She is startled. No one ever says anything negative about church brothers and sisters, and we have. Then she laughs. Her honest laughter says she agrees. Quickly, though, she reverts to her Moonie self and says, "Oh, I used to just hate Dick when I first knew him. I mean really hate him. But then I began to try to understand him. And now I know that he has a very deep heart."

"He may have a deep heart, but it is combined with shallow intellect," we say.

She looks shocked but says nothing. Still, she is silent for a few minutes. "I think it really improves a person to find it in her heart to forgive someone or understand a person they think they do not like," she replies lamely.

We promise ourselves to bring up the subject

later, when there's more time and when she has had
time to think about it and not feel as though she has
betrayed this brother with the deep heart.

After what seems like endless hours of having
doors shut in our faces, we return to the appointed
spot to meet Dick and his workmate. We still have
more than a dozen bags of peanuts to be sold and
decide to "blitz" some nearby shops and bars.

Now we run into our first real rebuffs of the day.
In a bakery a man pulls a dollar bill from his pocket
but before handing it over asks "Are you with the
Reverend Moon?" We answer yes. He vigorously
shakes his head no and puts the money away.

In the first bar, a color television blares to a
nearly empty room. Everyone is sitting quietly, and
the owner herself buys a bag. We leave several
dollars richer. In the bar on the next corner, we run
into a happy volleyball team, young men in their
early twenties with team shirts on. They are laughing, drinking beer, and either celebrating a victory
or drowning a loss. They are curious about our
group, and a few of the young men cluster around
the two attractive female church members. Then
one of the ballplayers asks if we're with Reverend
Moon. "Don't buy anything from them, they're
Moonies," he yells to the crowded barroom. He is
playing a pinball machine game, but turns away
from it for a minute. "I've studied your Reverend
Moon and I could talk to you all night about him.
But I won't." He turns back to his game and says,
"He's making asses of all of you."

Most people are kind, willing to give the benefit
of the doubt. As we walk around the U-shaped

bar, we sell peanuts to at least half of the men
sitting and drinking. They are clearly embarrassed
by the young man's outburst and although no one
mentions it, the further away we get from the
volleyball team, the more peanuts we sell. As we
return to the door, our last bag of peanuts sold, the
young volleyball player looks up from his pinball
machine again and says, "You poor suckers. . . ."

Dick, who has just come in, yells back, "We'll
be the judge of that."

Later we get back to asking Penny questions
about her friends in the movement. After spending
time in the company of religious cult members there
is a tendency not to speak candidly, to assume
an artificial reserve as one would when speaking
with nuns or clergy. It is a form of condescension,
but the unwillingness to face life's harsher realities
is so total in most religious cults that it is easy to
blend into the bland, colorless atmosphere. The need
to conform is alive in each of us.

Moonies especially play down the rational thinking part of man's nature and instead concentrate on
what they call "the feelings of the heart." They have
coined a word for this phenomenon, "heartistic,"
and they use it often to describe a variety of senti-
ments. We notice a forced friendliness among these
young people; at first we think it is staged for our
benefit. But then we see it in their own group relationships. "How are you?" is always answered with
"Great." No one can always feel terrific, we say to
ourselves.

With all their talk of heart, the Moonies seem so
forlorn, so superficial. The women appear less in-

dependent than others their age, and the men somewhat more intent on being "leaders" than young
men outside. There is always tension around
Moonies. They are nervous, what used to be called
"high strung." Their abundant prayer does not appear to be effective in calming postadolescent
anxieties.

The next day, while we are visiting a museum
with our families, we meet one of the young men
from the center with his mother and father. We stop
to chat. The young man asks if we are coming to
the "great movie" at the center that night. We explain we are going to spend the evening with our
families and introduce him to them. He shows almost abject disappointment. We decide then and
there not to patronize him and bluntly ask him why
he would think we would come away from our own
families to see an old movie that has been on television several times. He seems embarrassed, but
responds in typical Moonie fashion, "It's a really
great movie and I'd really like you to be there
and share it with us."

Later we ask Penny why everyone adopts this
"simple-minded" Pollyanna approach to life and
question how she plans to avoid becoming like them.
She admits that many of the kids in the church are
not very intellectual, but warily avoids our second
question. We talk generally about a blend of intelligence and sensitivity that enables humans to
function well. We theorize about how conversations
always seem to fall to the level of the least intelligent person in a crowd, and ask Penny if she has
seen this happen in the church. We express the hope

she will not become so "deep-hearted" as those she has to learn to love, at the expense of her own intellect and personality. She listens and is silent.

Some warmth has grown in our relationship. She says she feels we are honest and we say the same to her. We talk of spending another afternoon together. She is evasive.

We do not see Penny again.

Penny may continue her fund raising and never have an experience more disconcerting than the rebuffs we experienced the Saturday afternoon we spent together. But other young women who fundraise are not so fortunate. Narrow escapes or threatened rapes only reinforce the fervent belief of the Moonies in the Unification Church.

In a letter to a friend on the outside, one young woman Moonie writes of her disappointment that he is involved in anticult activities. "Judge not, and you will not be judged; condemn not and you shall not be condemned; forgive and you will be forgiven," she quotes from the Bible. Then she admonishes her friend for not being more Christ-like, and says that "terrorizing" Unification Church members is not a way to make them leave the church. As an illustration of her point, She writes of her own experiences with terror: "I was fund-raising in Fort Wayne when I was forcibly taken from my parking lot by two young men with a gun. These guys did it because they wanted fun and were 'tired of masturbating.' They put a gun to my head and asked if I'd rather be shot or raped. I told them to go ahead and shoot me. They didn't touch me. Finally, they got so drunk or stoned (they indulged in both) I jumped out of the window of their apartment." She concludes, "This experience has only made me more determined to fight for God."

What she ignores is that she would not have been in the parking lot alone if she had not been fundraising for her church. Young people working on a mainline church project managed by thoughtful adults would never be encouraged, as Unification Church members are, to solicit under such extreme conditions.

Unification Church members, both men and women, are often seen alone on street corners or in bars, at all hours of the day and night, selling their candy and peanuts under what police officers often describe as "extremely hazardous" conditions. Many stay out far into the night so that they don't have to return to the center with unsold wares. A young former Moonie in California tells us that in his center members were ridiculed if they weren't able to sell everything they were given each morning.

Hare Krishnas, who are often harassed and derided when they fund-raise or chant publicly, are reinforced in their feelings of separation from the world at large when they are abused by members of that world.

Stanley Bernstein tells how van loads of Krishna devotees follow the sun and the tourists to Florida during the winter and spring vacation season. And he tells how they are arrested en masse and charged with disturbing the peace. "Can you imagine being arrested for chanting and fund-raising during the height of the tourist season in Florida?" he asks. "It is difficult for me to believe that they are the only noise makers, the only revelers," he adds.

Anyone who has ever been to Fort Lauderdale during the spring college vacations would have to agree.

Krishnas have been taken to court and moved from shopping centers and street corners because they deliberately flout American values with their costumes and strange chants, not because they break any laws. Bernstein says he feels they compound their insult to the American public by never attempting to justify themselves. People don't take them seriously.

"It would be demeaning to answer them," the Krishnas reply.

In many cities and towns the Krishnas have been denied solicitation permits while traditional churches and Little League teams fund-raise unrestrained. Several American Civil Liberties Union chapters say they have no case histories of mainstream religions being denied access to public fund raising. In Dallas when merchants asked that the Krishnas be enjoined from chanting and dancing on a shopping mall, the judge reminded the complainants that they never brought similar complaints because the First Baptist Church choir was making noise singing Christmas carols on the mall, or because of parade music from the Longhorn Marching Band of the University of Texas. In the Texas judge's opinion religious discrimination was clearly implied.

Still, city councils and local governing bodies have the right to set up solicitation permit systems to control the number of groups who raise funds by selling. The permit system is to protect the individual from fraudulent businessmen and fund raisers and to control the number of door-to-door solicitors in a community at any one time.

In the view of counter-cult activists, such regulations should put the burden of proof of community-oriented work on the shoulders of fund-raising groups. But the administrative burden of proving "intent" and the issue of fairness has kept most communities from setting up restrictive solicitation permit laws. In general, solicitation permits require only identification and a minimum of information about the group that benefits from funds. Still, Mobile Fund-Raising Team Moonies say they occasionally spend a night in jail because they failed to get a solicitation permit in a community that demands rigid compliance with its laws.

Religious persecution? The Moonies say yes. But community members say they have the right to know where and how funds are being used. If fund raisers either cannot answer their questions satisfactorily, or solicit without permits, they are breaking the law and are subject to prosecution, say members of government.

FOOD

Sara Bontempo is worried about her son. This trim and youthful mother of six, who lives in upstate New York, is concerned about the long-range psychological effects of her son Brian's association with the Unification Church. But she finds the day-to-day life he leads as a member of a Moonie Mobile Fund-Raising Team (they're called MFTs) even more alarming.

Mrs. Bontempo's fears center around the eating habits and lifestyle of the MFT Moonies. She isn't the only parent worried about the way a son or daughter eats while in a cult. Many parents and some doctors find religious cult diets cause for concern.

Brian Bontempo has been a Moonie for three years. Currently he heads a seven-member fund-raising team, traveling in the Midwest selling goods to raise money for the Unification Church. The seven young people in Brian's team, he's told his mother, live in an unheated van and they spend $130 per week on food. The team's average weekly take is close to $7,350, according to figures Brian gave his family, but the young Moonies send more than $7,000 a week to church headquarters.

One night a week, sometimes two when it's bitterly cold outside, they check into a cheap motel for a night, then they bathe, and spread out on the floor to sleep in their sleeping bags rather than in the beds. Brian's mother says her son is so used to sleeping bag comfort he avoids beds even when he comes home for a visit.

Brian says that the team starts each day off with a cold breakfast. Since members have been complaining of gaining weight, Brian encourages them to eat cottage cheese for breakfast, rather than the more typical cold cereal and milk. For lunch they buy cold cuts and bread at a grocery store and make sandwiches in the van. For their evening meal, the one hot meal of the day, they visit a McDonald's, or another fast-food hamburger chain. Although the fast-food franchise operation is part of the American way of life, even McDonald's stockholders would agree that a steady diet of hamburgers,

French fries, and milk shakes is pretty shaky nutrition.

Anyone who eats one meal a day at a fast-food franchise store may get most of his daily protein requirement from that meal, more than enough carbohydrates for a day, and almost half of the calories he needs. A McDonald's meal contains 1,100 of the 2,700 recommended daily calories for an adult male, according to a leading consumer magazine. But if he eats the way Brian Bontempo tells his mother he eats, he will be missing a number of other essential nutrients in his diet. The vital nutrients missing in a fast-food diet, the magazine states, "are biotin, folic acid and pantothenic acid"—all part of the watersoluble B vitamin complex which is essential for healthy nerves and skin. A sustained deficiency of folic acid can lead to the formation of abnormal red blood cells and pernicious anemia.

Vitamin A is found as the provitamin carotene in green and yellow vegetables (a provitamin is a substance which enables the body to manufacture the vitamin) and as a vitamin in the meat of fish and animals. According to suburban Philadelphia dermatologist Pascal J. Imperato, M.D., a vitamin A deficiency could account for the skin rash that seems to plague so many Moonies. The vitamin also helps to keep the lining of internal organs strong and healthy and is important in bone development. A Vitamin A deficiency often shows up first in night blindness—a lack of vision in dim light and blindness upon sudden exposure to light. The body uses the vitamin to make a pigment in the retina of the eye which is an important component in the complicated photochemical process of sight. That magazine warns, "If you eat at a fast-food chain regularly, it would be wise to make sure that your other meals include such nutritious foods as beans, dark green leafy vegetables, yellow vegetables, and a variety of fresh fruits." That should overcome the nutritional deficiencies of fast-food meals.

There doesn't seem to be any question that the Moonies who live in communal centers and at the Unification Church's seminaries and training facilities eat a more wholesome diet than their more mobile counterparts. Still, one young woman, who was a member of the church at the Boonville, California, ranch, charges that the ranch diet is deliberately designed to play havoc with the emotions of the Moonie converts who are recruited and study there.

She claims the diet at Boonville is intentionally low in protein and high in carbohydrate content, the kind of diet she says can bring on emotional highs and lows by fouling up the body's blood sugar level. She says the daily schedule of lectures, exercise, and sharing sessions is arranged around the meals, with the mood-elevating lectures taking place when the groups are experiencing high blood sugar elation and the guilt-inducing sharing sessions saved for when the young recruits are suffering from anxiety associated with low levels of sugar in the blood.

The same young woman says the Boonville Moonies used the "sugar trick" when she was trying to get away alone to see her mother in San Francisco. "I told them I was going to see my mother. And I told them I was going to see her alone.

"The leader said, 'Okay, but we'll drive you to San

Francisco.' We got up early in the morning and they
wouldn't let me have my breakfast before we went.
I stole an apple from the kitchen. But on the way
the leader stopped the van at a roadside stand and
bought everyone a soft ice cream cone, smothered
with M & M's. What a strange breakfast, I thought.

"Feeling a nice sugar buzz as we continued the trip
south, I wondered if they had planned it this way.
Was I supposed to feel good and happy on a
'sugar high'? Would I dissolve to tears of anxiety
when the buzz wore off? I wondered."

The Boonville Moonies don't get much meat, but
they do eat quantities of cheese and peanut butter.
They are also served fruit, vegetables, cereals, bread,
milk, and occasional sweet desserts. The ranch has
its own bountiful crop of fruits and vegetables, but
meat must be purchased.

The daily breakfast rations of oatmeal or granola,
fruit, milk, and sometimes hot chocolate are not very
different from the breakfast millions of Americans
eat each day—if, that is, they bother to eat breakfast
at all. The ranch lunches of peanut butter and jelly
sandwiches on whole wheat bread with a cookie and
an apple are no better or worse than the lunches
many children carry to school across the land.

The evening meal at the ranch differs from traditional fare because it seldom contains any meat.
A typical Boonville dinner, according to several
young people who have lived at the ranch, is a vegetable casserole, usually eggplant, zucchini, or broc-
coli, rice, and whole wheat bread. On Sundays a
meat casserole—spaghetti or chicken à la king—is
served along with a dessert, perhaps brownies. The

main meal of the day at Boonville almost always includes a tossed salad. During a visit to the Moonies' Barrytown, New York, seminary, we ate a lunch of dry sandwiches made of gristly cold cuts and bread, an apple, washed down with water that was provided in pitchers on the table. Dinner at Barrytown was hamburgers made with large meat patties on sesame seed rolls, French fried potatoes, and a mixed vegetable tossed salad. Dessert was fresh grapes, apples, oranges, and pears from the ever-present bowl of fruit.

Elizabeth Albertson remembers that she was amazed at the robust appearance of her daughters when she first visited them in Boonville. "Although both of them appeared to have gained weight" (a fact neither Terry nor Nini contests, saying they ate more bread and starches at Boonville than they usually do), "they were blooming with bright eyes, suntans, and a generally rosy glow."

Terry and Nini were basking in the warm California sunshine at Boonville and eating regular meals, but the Moonie mobile fund raisers who go on prolonged missions (some fund-raise for as little as six months, others keep it up for two years or more) often appear wan, pale, or plagued by a complexion rash. Dr. Imperato says the disorder, typified by an overall facial rash with tiny pin-headed lesions that give the complexion a chapped, red, rough appearance, is probably caused by a vitamin A deficiency.

At the Moon rally at Yankee Stadium in June 1976, we met a cheerful young woman who caught our attention in a crowd of Moonies because she showed spirit and had a robust, healthy appearance. Three and a half months later, when we saw the same young woman at Moon's Washington, D.C., rally, she looked like a different person. She had been roving the country in a van, fund raising for the church, she said. Her clear skin had turned rough, red, and pimply, her once-bright eyes were dull, and she seemed lethargic. The personality that was so appealing in June had dimmed by September along with her natural beauty.

The vegetarian diets of the Hare Krishnas and the Divine Light Mission premies alarm parents, who say they feel helpless as they watch once-sturdy sons and daughters fade into shadows of their former selves while adhering to restrictive dietary laws.

Some parents, of course, are irrationally afraid of the unorthodox diets. Vegetarian diets with milk, cheese, and other dairy products are not necessarily debilitating when practiced sensibly. Jim Locke's parents found this out when he came home for a visit.

When Jim went home to Connecticut to visit his parents at Christmastime in 1976, the twenty-seven-year-old Divine Light Mission member appeared so tired, slept so much of the time, and had lost so much weight from his once-strapping 6'4" frame that his mother insisted that he visit the family doctor for a checkup. The doctor gave Jim a clean bill of health after a physical examination and a careful blood chemistry study. Jim's mother says she is glad she insisted on the checkup because the results give her "peace of mind."

But parents like Dee Dee Fischer are not overreacting when they become concerned about the physical condition of their sons and daughters. Dee Dee's son, Michael, was so malnourished while he was a Hare Krishna that he had to be hospitalized and fed intravenously.

Other conditions besides the diet can contribute to poor health in the cults. A common feeling among young cult members is a mistrust of hospitals, medicine, and the medical establishment, accompanied by a great faith in God as cause and cure of all ills. Winnie Swope lost the sight of one of her eyes while she was a Moonie because she was discouraged from receiving prompt medical attention when her sight began to fail, according to her father, Dr. George Swope.

Peter Boyle tells of a young man, a leader at the Boston Hare Krishna temple, who is debilitated from tuberculosis but is not under a doctor's care. Instead, Peter says, the young man rests most of the day and drinks an Indian potion that is supposed to cure him.

The potential danger with the vegetarian diets the premies and Krishnas follow is not based on what the young people are prohibited from eating. A vegetarian diet is potentially wholesome. The danger lies in eating too little or an insufficient variety of the limited foods allowed. Some devotees simply can't stomach many of the exotic Indian recipes and other vegetarian dishes they are served. Others simply never get enough to eat, or suffer vitamin, mineral, or protein deficiencies because the cooks at individual Krishna or Divine Light communes are not knowledgeable about nutrition. It requires more skill and planning to prepare a well-balanced vegetarian meal than it does to provide a balanced meal that includes meat.

The primary challenge in planning a vegetarian diet is to provide adequate protein. Nutritionist Dr. Jean Mayer calls protein the "basic, primary components of life." There are literally thousands of proteins, all of which are made up of smaller parts called amino acids.

In a complete protein there are twenty amino acids. Some of them are referred to as *nonessential* amino acids, because under the right conditions the body can produce them itself. But there are eight amino acids that the human body cannot synthesize. They are called *essential amino acids*. Basically only meat, eggs, and dairy products have the eight essential acids in the right proportion to qualify as *complete protein foods*.

In his book, *A Diet for Living*, Dr. Mayer explains that the human digestive system breaks down the proteins one eats and puts them back together to build body tissue. "These proteins are broken up by stomach acids and enzymes into fragments, and in the intestine they are broken down even further into amino acids. Then they're reassembled into human proteins."

A diet that includes meat is not essential to good health. But Dr. Mayer emphasizes the importance of adequate, or complete, proteins in the diet. "So long as you eat enough protein . . . your body can manufacture them." Certain vegetable foods, such as dried beans and rice, are high in amino acid quality and quantity and when combined properly in a meal provide adequate and complete protein for the body to function. (Frances M. Lappe expands on this information in her book, *Diet for a Small Planet*.)

Yet it is not protein deficiency that is the nemesis of vegetarians. Dr. Mayer says that the greatest risk run by a vegetarian who eats beans, nuts, whole grain cereals, and plenty of fruits and vegetables is a vitamin B 12 deficiency.

The vitamin is contained in animal source foods exclusively—meat, poultry, fish, eggs, and dairy products. In the body, B 12 is a necessary enzyme for the synthesis of nucleic acids (a nucleic acid is one of a group of complex acids that are components of cell nucleus proteins). It is also necessary for the production of healthy red blood cells in the body. Dr. Mayer says a person who persists in following a vegetarian diet without meat, eggs, milk, or cheese should have a daily vitamin pill containing B 12.

In the foreword to *The Hare Krishna Cookbook* compiled by Krishna Devi Dasi and Sama Devi Dasi, Kirtanananda Swami describes the devotees' diet as a "yoga diet." The diet is designed, the swami says, "not for him who eats too much or for him who eats too little." It is "designed to supply the body with all necessary nutrients, without pandering to the whims of our changing senses. The principle of regulation is strictly adhered to, and the daily fare is almost unchanging. This is very important for a *brahmacari* or celibate student (the young devotee's status in Krishna) for if the tongue is agitated for sense enjoyment, all the other senses follow." The devotees call their meals "prasadam." There are only two meals a day for Krishna devotees. The food is never tasted during its preparation, and it is always offered to Krishna in a religious ritual before it is eaten by the devotees.

Daily Krishna fare hardly ever varies, and those who don't develop a taste for dried bean mush and raw chick peas (garbanzo beans) may not eat enough protein to remain healthy.

Here is a sample menu:

—Morning prasadam: raw chick-peas (they are soaked overnight, and the cookbook recommends ½ cup of beans as adequate for a family of four), cream of wheat (farina), sweet milk, raw ginger root (chewed by the devotees as an aid to digestion), and fresh fruit (usually apples or oranges).

—Noon prasadam: dahl (many varieties of a bean dish that is prepared from a bean mush made by soaking and boiling beans until they can be mashed), chapatis (a flat, round breadstuff prepared from whole-wheat flour and butter and fried quickly on both sides until it puffs up), rice, and a curried vegetable. The cookbook contains many delectable vegetable recipes, but those who have eaten regularly at Krishna temples—for meals other than Sunday feasts—say a weekday vegetable entree is likely to be something like tomatoes mixed with farina.

—Bedtime snack: hot milk. The Krishna recipe for milk includes up to a third of a cup of sugar per quart of milk. It is unquestionably sweet.

Sunday prasadam at a Krishna temple is a celebration feast for devotees and guests and it has a far more varied and elaborate menu than weekday meals. This meal includes, in addition to a variety of dahl and vegetable entrees, desserts, or sweets, as the Krishnas call them.

During the week devotees eat from waxed paper, but at the Evanston, Illinois, temple we ate the Sunday vegetarian feast with our hands from paper plates. The meal included a spicy sautéed curry made with zucchini and fried noodles similar to Chinese noodles, and another dish with eggplant, green beans, onions, celery, and peppers in a curry sauce. Chapatis were served along with fried bean dahl. For dessert we had a flavorful but glutinous blob of farina which tasted like grits mixed with honey and blanched almonds. The beverage was a watery tropical punch that tasted as though it had been spiked with peppery sauce. Possessors of fairly adventuresome palates, even we found the fried beans loathsome and understood how young devotees can become malnourished even when they are offered a balanced diet.

But the Krishna birthday celebration in Los Angeles that was billed as a sumptuous feast was sorely disappointing. A long table was spread with more than 100 dishes of food served in what appeared to be plastic half-gallon milk containers that had been sawed off below the handles. The elaborate feast could be best described as a variety of bowls of cream of wheat, each tinted a different color. In the whole array we noticed only two vegetable concoctions. All of the birthday party delicacies were sorry affairs, hard and dry around the edges as though they'd been prepared days ahead of the celebration and left to sit, uncovered, in anticipation of the event.

If a Krishna devotee gets enough to eat and if he can stand to eat the food that's prepared for him, he may remain healthy and strong on the Krishna diet.

However, if the temple does not provide enough to eat for its devotees, or if a devotee cannot stand to eat some of the concoctions, he may, as Michael Fischer did, develop some serious nutritional deficiencies.

The eating habits of the Divine Light Mission premies—those who live in ashrams and those who eat in their own homes—are not as rigidly prescribed as those of the Hare Krishnas. While the injunction against eating meat, poultry, fish, and eggs remains the same, premies are not told specifically which foods to eat nor are they told when or how to eat.

Premies drink coffee and tea. They have three meals a day. Full-time ashram premies are more worldly than the Krishnas since many of them go off into the "real world" each day to work, carrying a vegetarian bag lunch prepared for them by the ashram housemother. The lunch is provided, not because premies are forbidden to eat in restaurants, but because it is less expensive than eating out.

The premie cuisine is not limited to a selection of Indian recipes that are favorites of the spiritual master, as in Krishna. Housemother Alice Charles says she finds many different vegetarian cookbooks useful in her work, preparing food for a houseful of premies. Alice particularly likes the *New York Times Natural Foods Cookbook*. Her kitchen is replete with an array of spices and food stuffs that would be out of place in most middle class households. Alice prepares a lot of salads and Japanese-style dishes that use tofu (a spongelike soybean curd) and miso (a soybean paste). One lunchtime meal was a salad prepared from fresh spinach, cauliflowerets, radishes, and bean sprouts. An array of dressings was set out on the table. One was a creamy avocado guacamole and another was made from a spicy bean paste. For dessert the premies ate a cheesecake made without eggs in a graham cracker crust.

One bitter winter day Alice prepared an evening casserole meal of tofu, spinach, onions, and mushrooms, seasoned with Tamari (a soybean sauce). Since her fellow ashram-dwellers were complaining that day of colds and flu symptoms, Alice explained she was also making a hot soup, using the miso bean paste as a base.

Milk, cheese, and other dairy products are allowed in Divine Light, although milk is not a staple of the premie diet, as it is in the Krishnas' programmed fare. Alice says she prefers to "stay away from milk myself."

Her premie friends attest to her cooking ability and Alice concedes, "I guess I have a natural talent for cooking." She takes her job seriously and has schooled herself in the finer points of good nutrition. The premies who eat at her table seem to be getting an adequately balanced diet.

Other Divine Light devotees, those in ashrams not fortunate enough to have a dedicated and innovative cook like Alice and those who live on their own and cook for themselves in a haphazard fashion, may be fooling themselves into poor health. Religious conviction is no substitute for good nutrition.

MARRIAGE

With its obligations, responsibilities, and the likelihood of children, marriage means permanence and a commitment to a life many hope will not be a young cult member's final choice. For these reasons, parents of cult members fear cult-blessed marriages more than almost anything else.

When a rumor surfaced in late 1976 that the Reverend Sun Myung Moon was planning another mass marriage ceremony, many parents of Moonies were nearly frantic with worry. Cause of their fears, they say, was not just the increased possibility of the cult life as a permanent choice, but also the way mates are selected and the kind of lives couples in the Unification Church lead after they are married.

Everyone, it seems, both within and outside of the cults has a strong opinion on what constitutes the ideal marriage and family. Cult members claim that they alone have the answer to America's family problems which, incidentally, they see as nearly insurmountable. With one of every three marriages ending in divorce, it is difficult to make a convincing argument that the family, as a basis for our society, is in good health.

And young people, especially those who claim to have found "salvation" in religious cults, are harsh in their criticism of the American family. Unschooled in the art of compromise, they are severely judgmental on the subject of marriage and the raising of children. Most say their own upbringing was a series of mistakes, however well-intentioned. They are even more critical when judging their parents' marriages. The majority say bluntly that the marriages they saw were bad. Parents, particularly those who had enjoyed close relationships with their sons and daughters before they joined a cult, are hurt and baffled.

Raised with high expectations of marriage, they often find it difficult to defend themselves. It can be helpful to remember that few adolescents have the experience to understand the struggle, compromise, and energy that goes into sustaining a marriage and family, into making them work. And because their goal is nothing less than perfection, cult members' limited tolerance totally disappears when they discuss marriage.

Most religious cults have their own definition and stringent rules governing sexual contact. Others' rules are so flexible that "marriage" is an inappropriate description. In the Unification Church marriage is a sacramental rite. It combines the rebirth aspect of baptism with the union of two members approved by the Reverend Moon and dedicated to producing "perfect, sinless children" through the "blessed union."

In Hare Krishna, with its denunciation of sensual gratification, sex outside of marriage is forbidden, and within the Krishna marriage it is prohibited except for one day each month, when the wife is ovulating, only for the purpose of procreation. The Krishna cult considers the male orgasm "damaging" to brain cells and a waste of vital energy. The female orgasm is ignored.

In Krishna, "If everything is done for Krishna, and not for sense gratification," devotees say, "marriages are pure and work out very well." They say it again and again, and look upon the world outside of their cult as a source of potential sexual problems since it is in the hands of Maya, the goddess of sex. According to a former Krishna, "Sexual thoughts, or fantasies, are to be especially avoided and male devotees tightly bind their genitals in a diaperlike cloth to avoid sexual stimulation." They also take several cold showers each day "to discourage lust."

In those groups with strict rules governing premarital sex, much emphasis is placed on marrying "one of our own." In the other, kinkier groups, the desire for gratification alone is sufficient justification for sexual intercourse.

A former top leader of the Children of God told the New York attorney general's investigation into the activities of the group about his personal experience with the casual marriages, or "betrothals" in that cult. He said, "The persons involved would not know beforehand. . . . There might be four betrothals in that same night, but only one couple knows ahead of time that they are going to be married. . . . After the first couple comes forward and all the catcalls come and the colony leader presides over that, then they would state, 'Is there anyone else that wants to be betrothed?' At this time a brother could stand up and call out just about any girl who is single and ask her to come forward with him. . . . There is an extreme amount of pressure at these events and it's pretty hard for the girl . . . even if she does not love or like the guy. Thus there have been many betrothals where the following morning or the following week the wife or husband woke up to find they had truly made a big mistake."

He adds, "Marriage, or these types of betrothals, are sometimes registered legally and sometimes are not, depending upon the age of the individuals and whether or not the parties involved are remarrying without having a . . . legal divorce already enacted from their previous marriages outside of the Children of God movement or from someone who has left the Children of God movement."

The Moonies have a far more conventional view of marriage. Many Unification Church members call sex "the root of all evil" and mix guilt for past sexual experimentation with a pastel, candy-coated picture of marriage as a "partnership" existing solely to foster the growth of "sinless" children.

"Of course people do fall in love," says one longtime Moonie, "but they try to keep their emotions in check with the hope they can be united with the Reverend Moon's blessing."

The Unification Church leader has some very specific ideas about his "blessing." His attitude toward the Christian sacrament of matrimony is explained in the transcript of a sermon he once gave. "Jesus explained that no one is married in Paradise. There is no married life in Paradise, but there is in the Kingdom of Heaven. A husband and wife do not have marital status in the spirit world until they are spiritually blessed in marriage by the True Parents. The first marriage recognized by God is the marriage of the True Parents, which is mentioned in Revelation as the marriage of the lamb."

The Reverend Moon says this about the choice of marriage partners in his group: "The Leader favors individual desire but he applies the Divine Principle in matching suitable types. If this is violated, then the marriage will not be harmonious and the children will not be perfect. When a couple is perfectly matched, then the children will be potentially perfect. Do not expect the Leader to personally find you a mate."

The system of arranged marriages in the Unification Church seems to be similar to the custom practiced in the Far East, parts of the Middle East, and Latin America. In those places, parents watch among the sons and daughters of friends and acquaintances for potential mates for their own offspring. They arrange for the young people to meet, in one of the homes for instance, and then wait and see how things develop. In this way, the young people have the opportunity either to approve or to veto the choice, but the parents have ensured the potential mate's acceptability.

Of course, if a young man or woman cares for the potential mate in a way we describe as "love," all the better, but if he says, "She's very good and a nice person, but I don't love her," he's apt to be told, "We're not talking about love, we're talking about marriage."

In our contemporary society a marriage that is not based on romantic love is anathema to many. And yet, the somewhat insular American upper class has always encouraged its young to marry within the class by assuring that young people meet "their own kind" at dancing classes, debutante parties, boarding schools, and through the exclusive social clubs at Ivy League colleges, and they can hardly be accused of "arranging marriages." It is impossible to say whether the success or failure of such marriages in this country and abroad, in or out of cults, is affected by the system of "arrangement."

Most former Unification Church members admit

they knew very few married couples in the church. Married couples in the church often live apart for reasons that are never clearly explained.

Giovanna Wood, who was a member of the Moon church for many years, says that members who are married are discouraged from having children until they are thirty-five. "Babies slow down fund raising, and abortion is condoned by the church," she says. Holding her own baby daughter on her lap, she continues, "An abortion can (morally) take place anytime during a pregnancy since, according to church doctrine, life does not begin until a child has taken its first breath."

From one long list of marriage partners issued by the Unification Church, it is clear that, either by accident or by intention, more than half of those marriages took place between Americans and foreign nationals. The church says international marriages are a way for furthering the goal of world unity. Former members note, "One of the best ways to get a permanent resident visa in the United States is marry a foreign member to a United States citizen."

Many Unification Church members claim the discrimination they experience as Moonies is rooted in racism, not only because their Master is an Asian, but also because he approves interracial marriages, since according to his plans all men will one day be unified and clearly defined skin colors and races will disappear.

The Korean evangelist does, however, have definite opinions about the type of persons who should be united in marriage. "If the man is hard as rock and the woman is soft as cotton, they are not properly matched and the woman survives with great difficulty. A tiger and a house cat cannot marry because they are of different species and are natural enemies." Because, says the Reverend Moon, some people have the "inherent probability of marrying twice," he will make them wait until later in life so that they have only one marriage. But, he says, when a man and a woman are ideally matched, they can marry early in life.

In Krishna, former members say that adjusting to married life seems to be a very difficult transition for both men and women. Several former Krishna women say they knew of many married women who stopped menstruating when they wed, and who were visibly upset by the male assertion of superiority within the union.

According to Stanley Bernstein, many Hare Krishna men believe they must serve as "models" for their wives, and therefore are very stern and strict. One young woman who was a Krishna tells how some of the married women showed her bruises and marks they received when their husbands beat them.

Bernstein's doctoral dissertation for the University of Michigan touches on the Krishna conversion experience but centers on interaction within the Hare Krishna temples. He had observed the temple life firsthand and has information gathered from confidential questionnaires he distributed to Krishnas. Bernstein is fond of the Krishnas, as many outsiders who have come to know this group of quarrelsome, arrogant, strong-minded individuals are. But his attitudes toward Krishna marriages are tough-minded.

"Marriage in Krishna is a very shaky institution.

There are a great number of extraordinarily unhappy relationships," he says. Explaining how the movement works against success in marriage, Bernstein states, "With men who are conditioned to believe that women are a drag on them [there is, everyone admits, a strong antiwoman bias in Krishna, though there are some very strong, capable, and interesting women in the movement] there is a feeling that wives can be a threat in the advancement of a man within the hierarchy of the movement."

He says that more frequently than one would suspect couples are separated, living and working in different cities. Still, every religious movement is conscious that it must be fruitful and multiply, and so procreation is, for the Hare Krishnas, a "necessary evil." Bernstein points out that in one temple, the president kept track of each couple's "day of procreation" and made sure that they did engage in sexual intercourse on that day. Although marriage partners are not excused from their required fifty rounds of chanting on this day and must also do extra rounds plus their usual chores, other devotees often help them with their work so they will have time for their sexual "duty."

Frequently, married Krishnas sleep in temple dormitories with members of their own sex and join their mates in some private spot for their monthly conjugal visit. But even the Krishnas are adaptable. When leaders begin to sense difficulties developing in marriages, they encourage couples to move out of the temple and into an apartment of their own. Outside the scrutiny of temple life, the householders are often better able to cope with the intricacies of married

life. However, in smaller temples this system is not
financially possible.

"When the Krishna marriages do work out, it is a
marvel to see them. They have had to work through
so much that the marriages are very, very sound,"
according to the University of Michigan social scientist.

In some of the smaller, offbeat religious cults that
are centered around a strong leader, his opinion of
marriage and sexual attitudes is often treated as sacred. According to accounts of life in the Love Israel
cult, members of the group "bond" for the purpose
of having babies. They also "unbond." No former
member of the cult recalls any sort of legally registered marriage ceremony conducted by Paul Erdman
(Love Israel), though he claims to be able to unite
couples "in the eyes of God." Several say they are
sure that bigamous relationships exist in the cult since
some of the members who were already legally married when they joined were "bonded" to someone
else in the Love Israel Family.

SCHOOLS

When it comes to the matter of schooling—how and
where their own young childern are to be educated—
cult members often defer to the opinions of the cult
leader. If the leader is in favor of public education,
cult members' children attend local schools. If he is
not, members either carefully evade truant officers
and give their children an informal education within
the cult community, or they set up cult-sponsored
educational systems.

School-age children of Unification Church members in the United States (there aren't many, since the church's membership is so young), attend public schools, according to church spokeswoman Susan Reinbold.

In Japan and Korea, where the Moon church has been established longer, members' children are educated in the public school systems. Susan Reinbold tells of a nursery school play group operated by the church for members' preschool children and says that some members harbor a dream of Unification Church sponsored schools for school-age children. "But," she says, "I doubt the Reverend Moon would go for it. He's not in favor of that kind of separation. He is in favor of public education."

The Hare Krishnas, who prefer to keep their children away from worldly influences, eschew the public schools and have tried, in Dallas, Texas, to establish a boarding school for children of devotees. It is now closed.

The Divine Light Mission premies usually send their own children to public schools. However, in Denver, Colorado, the site of the Mission's international headquarters, the group has established an elementary school for premies' children. It is an alternative to public education, on the order of the independent, progressive, and secular school.

Religious cults that avoid public education often cite, as justification for keeping their children away from school, a Supreme Court decision that gave Amish parents the authority to stop their children's schooling at the eighth grade. This was done because the Amish believe further learning is not only unnecessary for their agrarian way of life but also threatening to Amish religious beliefs.

The case, *Wisconsin* vs. *Yoder et al.,* involved parents who refused to send children, aged fourteen and fifteen, to school after the eighth grade. Wisconsin law compels children to attend school until they are sixteen years old. (The Amish traditionally operate their own schools up to the eighth grade.)

The parents were found guilty in local Wisconsin courts, and their conviction was upheld in a Wisconsin Circuit court. However, the state supreme court reversed the lower courts' decisions, confirming the defendants' claim that their First Amendment right to free exercise of religion had been violated.

A United States Supreme Court review of the case affirmed the Wisconsin high court's ruling, agreeing that the Amish parents had amply supported their contention that enforcement of compulsory higher education for their children would endanger, if not destroy, their right to freedom of religion.

The reasoning of the United States Supreme Court opinion is based on a principle penned by Thomas Jefferson. "Education is necessary to prepare citizens to participate effectively and intelligently in our open political system if we are to preserve freedom and independence. Further, education prepares individuals to be self-reliant and self-sufficient participants in society."

The federal court found little reason to question the ability of the Amish to raise their children to be self-sufficient and self-reliant. The jurists said, "Aided by a history of three centuries as an identifiable religious sect and a long history as a successful and self-sufficient segment of American society, the Amish have demonstrated the sincerity of their religious beliefs, and the interrelationship of belief with their way of life."

Another point in the Supreme Court opinion confirms the Amish mode of vocational education as satisfying the established minimum requirements of compulsory secondary education. Chief Justice Warren Burger writes, "There is nothing in this record to suggest that Amish qualities of reliability, self-reliance, and dedication to work would fail to find ready markets in today's society." The court had no fear that the children of Amish parents would become burdens to society or statistics on unemployment and welfare rolls.

But the self-sufficiency of many modern religious movements has yet to be proven.

The Hare Krishnas, particularly, seem to sense this and have so far avoided a legal conflict. When the Texas state department of education ordered the Krishnas either to modify their Dallas school or to close it, the Krishnas chose to shut down the school rather than fight the decision in the courts.

At the "Gurukula" (Krishna boarding school) the sons and daughters of devotees, toddlers through early teens, were taught exclusively from Krishna prayer books and Vedic scripture texts. The children were not taught to read or write in English, but in Sanskrit. English was spoken in the school, but it was not taught as a subject. Neither was geography, mathematics, or any history other than Hindu religious history.

The subject matter taught in the school fell short

of meeting the state's minimum requirements, and
state authorities also found fault with the school's
living arrangements for the children.

When the school closed, the young Krishna children were dispersed to farms and communal Krishna
centers around the United States and elsewhere. An
attempt to buy a new school property in Alido, Illinois, was foiled because of public sentiment against
the Hare Krishnas in that community. But Hare
Krishnas still avoided public education for their
children.

The Divine Light Mission's Unity School in Denver is fully accredited by the state and is open to
children of premies and any other children whose
parents choose to send them to it. Unlike the
Krishnas' Gurukula, the Unity School offers a practical and progressive elementary education, based
on the Waldorf teaching methods inspired by the
Swiss educator Rudolf Steiner.

According to the Mission, Guru Maharaj Ji's
teachings are not part of the school's educational
format. Mission spokesmen explain, "His teachings
are not teachings in the normal way. Rather it is an
actual experience one has."

It seems obvious that the U.S. Supreme Court
opinion in the Amish case would not be supportive
of all religious cult schools. Unlike the farming ap-
prenticeship of the Amish, many of these schools
would include little more than training in streetbeg-
ging or fund raising by the selling of goods.

However, it also seems that if the precedent were
to be applied to contemporary cults, their right to be

different would not be in question. The court opinion carefully spells out: "A way of life that is odd or even erratic but interferes with no rights or interest of others is not to be condemned because it is different."

But the opinion also explains that an individual's activities, even when religiously based, are subject to regulation as part of the government's right to promote the health, safety, and general welfare of the people.

Brainwashing or Enlightenment?

Americans easily understand the concept of physical coercion or torture but have a hard time accepting the ideas of mental coercion or brainwashing. The American public holds an image of itself as a strong, self-reliant people and shrinks from the notion that one of its number can be forced to conform to alien actions or beliefs by any means other than physical coercion. A jury will acquit anyone who can prove he acted illegally because someone was pointing a gun at his head. But juries, like the public they represent, find it nearly impossible to understand that a person's actions can be controlled through a definite process of psychological mind control.

The Western world was late accepting the conditioning theories of the Russian scientist Pavlov. "After all, he is working with dogs, not men," said English scientists when told of his work. Soviet revolutionaries, however, saw the possible long-range implications of Pavlov's theories and they encouraged his research. It was because of his work that techniques of psychological coercion were developed, refined, and used by Communists in China and North Korea, according to William Sargant, author of *Battle for the Mind: A Physiology of Conver-*

sion and Brainwashing. Knowledge of these advanced methods of coercive persuasion was brought vividly before the American people by casualties of North Korean prisoner-of-war camps, so it is surprising that twenty years later they still don't understand.

The use of sleep deprivation in eliciting confessions, both true and false, was long recognized as more effective than physical torture by unscrupulous police officers, until the Supreme Court insisted that prisoners' rights must not be violated. The night Patricia Hearst was convicted, we saw Americans scrambling to newsstands to buy newspapers with accounts of the decision.

"Don't tell me she was brainwashed. There's no such thing," was a statement heard over and over in one urban corner grocery store where neighbors gather and chat as they buy the papers. "She was never tortured. She couldn't have been brainwashed in that period of time. She'll get what's coming to her." We overheard newspaper buyers make statements like these as they scanned the Patty Hearst headlines and stories.

Dr. Martin Orne testified as an expert witness for the defense at Miss Hearst's bank robbery trial. The psychiatrist, who has studied hypnosis and coercive persuasion techniques, says, "She was convicted because no one could be convinced she was actually brainwashed." Dr. Orne believes that Miss Hearst was converted by her abductors and adopted their Symbionese Liberation Army philosophy, and like the victims of brainwashing in China and North Korea, she began to identify with her captors.

"If she had been able to return to society suffi-

ciently repentant, public sympathy would have been
with her, but there she was lifting her fist in a ges-
ture of defiance," he says. When finally arrested, she
did not "snap out of it." She continued to identify
with her captors. In the company of SLA member
Emily Harris, Miss Hearst had a witness for her
"heroism," as she continued to act as a member of
the group that had controlled her. Without Ms.
Harris, chances are that she might have come out of
it sooner.

We weren't too different from most Americans
when we started this book. We could see that young
people's minds and actions were changed significantly
by religious cult membership, but we had trouble
believing cult critics who told us: "Thousands of
young 'Manchurian Candidates,' brainwashed American young people, are running around this country
carrying out the orders of malicious false messiahs
who have programmed them and robbed them of
their minds."

Parents who feel they've lost a son or daughter to
a religious cult often want desperately to believe their
offspring have been unwitting victims of insidious
plots to separate them from their real personalities.
But, fantastic as the allegations may seem at first
hearing, experience supports some fears about social
coercion and brainwashing.

The process is not nearly as dramatic as the term
and all the mystery that surrounds it suggest. Though
the results may be cataclysmic, the mechanics are
subtle, and victims often don't even know they are
being manipulated. The change is gradual and it be-

gins when a recruit *starts to behave,* long before he
starts to believe.

But the conditions of ego destruction and coercive
persuasion—milieu control, mystical manipulation,
the need for purity, confession, the separation of the
group through the aura of sacred science, the development of a new language, and the belief that all outsiders are unworthy and unfit for salvation—must all
be present, in order for the subject to be brainwashed, according to the classical definition given the
process by those who have studied it.

Rick Heller, a college student from Dallas, told us
how he surprised himself when he started behaving
like a Moonie. Rick went to spend a night in the
Unification Church at their center in Austin, Texas.
His older brother was a member of this group at the
time, and Rick thought he might like to be one too.
"I was in my sleeping bag on the floor of a room
with about twenty other guys. At about 5:30 in the
morning this guy comes in with a guitar and starts
playing and singing 'You Are My Sunshine' and I
thought, Oh, brother. I rolled over, buried my face,
and tried to go back to sleep.

"But all of a sudden I realized all the other guys
were singing and rolling up their sleeping bags. It
was weird, like a private production of *Hair* or something. I thought, They're crazy, a bunch of fanatics.
But then I realized that I was the only one in the
room who wasn't singing, so I started to sing too."

Rick explains that then he had to rationalize and
justify his behavior to himself. "I had thought they
were behaving like fanatics. But I was behaving just
like them. Either they weren't crazy, or I was. So I

decided that they were okay. I was behaving like a Moonie before I knew what hit me," he says.

Brainwashing? Hardly. But, like Rick Heller, we attended Unification Church group workshops and experienced and observed the process of conversion. Our inside look at what can happen during the initial contact with religious cults convinced us that the common sequence of events that precedes these "conversions" is similar in many ways to the coercive techniques used by the Chinese Communists during their revolution and the North Koreans in their prisoner-of-war camps. The issue of brainwashing in religious cults cannot be totally discounted.

Still, there are differences. Religious cults neither imprison their subjects nor threaten them with death or bodily harm. The results of the conversion process, in China, Korea, and in some new religions, are the same. The subjects ultimately embrace a new set of beliefs, and adopt a new code of behavior. The question may not be whether all the elements of the process of mind control are used, but whether the groups need to employ all the techniques.

Cult recruits have already volunteered their time and presence to the groups. Unlike the independent businessmen, landowners, and others who opposed Chairman Mao's takeover in China, or the Allied soldiers in Korean POW camps, they don't need to be threatened. These young people are idealistic and are frequently searching for a goal, a purpose, and a sense of community, so the promises of the cults appeal strongly to them. Many are willing, even anxious, to be persuaded.

Religious cults don't incarcerate their subjects for two reasons: It is illegal, and it isn't necessary. Unrelenting group pressure, combined with a young subject's inherent need to conform, produces the same result as imprisonment. The potential convert's complete and undivided attention is in the hands of those who wish to control him.

During their indoctrination programs, the groups use various techniques to heighten the emotions. *The Book of Highs* is a classic among young readers, many of whom are already familiar with drug- or alcohol-induced highs. It outlines a variety of ways of getting high without benefit of drugs or alcohol. Being high is a state that is valued and sought by today's youth, just as it is sought by the older cocktail-a-day drinker, or the partygoer who uses alcohol as a means to relax his inhibitions.

Some adults who smoke marijuana know how their own feelings of well-being and joy sometimes "rub off" on their children, who begin to sing, dance, and have a good time simply from being around a group of intensely happy people who have been smoking grass. This is called a "contact high," and it is a generally accepted fact of the youth and counterculture. Those who once enjoyed a few social drinks but have quit drinking and switched to soft drinks talk about feeling a "contact high" while at a party where everyone else is drinking.

Creating a "contact high" is one way a religious cult manipulates potential members. Here is how it can, and often does, happen: The potential recruit is administered a heavy dose of love and peer approval. The amount of attention he receives might be considered highly inappropriate in the outside world. But in this new world, where everyone is acting kind and loving, it feels good. Often a member of the opposite sex is assigned to a new recruit, told to look after his new charge and to shower her with attention and flattery. In dozens of cases, young people with a strong need for intimacy say they mistook the initial interest for personal or sexual attraction.

In retrospect some young people say they thought the constant attention and overly nice behavior was "sort of weird, or square." Others say they felt sexual attraction and a sense of infatuation for their sponsors. But since they were never allowed to discuss their feelings with anyone outside this new group, or with other new recruits, they eventually went along with the program and allowed the group love and individual attention to wash over them like the waters in a baptism-by-immersion.

"I suspected I was the oddball, since everyone else seemed to be having such a good time," is a line we've heard over and over again. At the same time, visitors to the cult centers are permitted much less sleep than they are used to, often no more than five hours a night. They are served a high carbohydrate, low protein diet that is frequently vegetarian and filled with the strange tastes of exotic recipes. While the diet is not harmful in a short-term situation, it is nevertheless unfamiliar and contributes to a sense of distance or removal from ordinary life.

In some cases, new members are secluded from all but other full-time members. The centers usually have no newspapers, no radio, no television, and the only music is that performed by group members. The recruit is given little time for showers and personal hygiene and seldom allowed to be alone.

Tremendous energy is devoted to group activity, especially singing. "That threw me too," a former Moonie said. "I knew all the music, but the lyrics had been changed. Everyone else was singing at the top of his lungs, so I tried to learn the new words as fast as I could so I'd catch on. It took a lot of concentration just to fit in and sing along."

Still, this hardly adds up to brainwashing, in any sense of the definition. In fact, people vacation in strange and foreign lands, where they are just as shut off from friends and family, so that they can have the sense of removal, or distance, from their everyday lives.

But religious cults go further. Adding to the recruit's growing feeling of disorientation and this high emotional pitch is the group's implicit disapproval of the young person's "worldly life," whatever that life may have been. With group-sharing sessions, or confessionals, cult members are able to gather information about the recruit's former life. When they have details, they frequently hone in to arouse feelings of guilt and anger in the recruit.

At the same time, they make cult life look increasingly safe and attractive. "Parent or family problems? None of those here," the recruit is told. "Financial worries? We take care of our own. Sex-related anxieties, or worries about relationships with members of the opposite sex? We live lives of purity. All premarital sex is wrong, and so your worries are over, the problem never comes up," say members of most new religions. Other groups, those with free sexual mores, tell recruits, "Promiscuity? There is no such thing. Don't worry about it, just do what comes naturally." In either case the problem of sex, and the accompanying guilt and anxiety, is washed away by the cults' moral attitudes.

The second stage in adopting the belief system of a religious cult is the *increased suggestibility* of the mind. Now the recruit is "softened up" and is high on both emotion and the idea of adopting lofty new goals. Dr. Virginia Jolly of Texas Women's University is a psychologist with a special interest in hypnosis and altered states of consciousness. These altered states of consciousness are not nearly as "frightening" as one may think they are, she says, explaining that every individual passes in and out of such states in his daily existence. Some of the altered states of consciousness everyone is familiar with are when a person daydreams, in the few minutes before he drops off to sleep at night, or in those few dreamy, half-awake minutes in the morning before he is fully awake.

According to Dr. Jolly, a person is far more open to suggestion when he is in this state than when he is in a normal, wakeful state. "Dancing, chanting, prayer, singing, and meditation can alter the state of consciousness just as surely as hypnosis or drugs," she says. "When the cults get a recruit to chant or meditate, or do any other things that change his state of mind, they can then easily implant new ideas, new realities, and begin to control the thought processes."

While the mind is suggestible, *new beliefs are introduced* to supplant old ones. Religious cults differ from each other greatly here. Some claim to be compatible with Christianity and Judaism. Others immediately point out the differences between their own doctrine and that of mainline religions. But in each group, it is during this stage that the new material, much of it the kind that might have been questionable and unacceptable before, is taught. It is in this stage that all cults instill a fervor for not questioning. "Skepticism is negativism. We must think positively. Since you don't yet completely understand our teachings, you must trust and rely on those who know more to guide you," is a philosophy heard again and again. Since partial knowledge is, according to the cults, the cause of major life problems, the recruit must admit how little he knows and accept the stricture that he may not question or analyze what he is told. If questioning is discouraged, critical analysis is impossible. And so beliefs must be accepted as they are presented, in dribs and drabs.

In the final stage of conversion, the new convert's *mind is controlled*. During his conversion, his behavior has been changed, his consciousness has been altered, and ultimately his mind and his behavior are controlled by the cult, by members who have themselves undergone the identical process and have become true believers.

Yet, not all the people who are intrigued by the members' approaches and the group promises are vulnerable enough to become victims of cult-indoctrination techniques. Some of them are simply too willful, too self-actualized to conform, as even Rick Heller did in the beginning. Others have demanding commitments on the outside—schools, jobs, careers, marriages, love affairs that make it impossible to leave their lives behind. Some are just not interested in changing the world, as most religious cults dedicate themselves to doing. (Rick Heller was spared from further Unification Church indoctrination because he was called home by his parents to witness and to participate in a deprogramming of his brother by Ted Patrick.)

Russ Beauchene, one of the founders of Eclipse, a West Coast anticult organization, got interested in his cause after attending a recruiting weekend at Boonville, the Unification Church and Creative Community Project's New Ideal City Ranch. Russ says the weekend indoctrination was nearly irresistible. "If I hadn't known—maybe because I'm older than most of those kids—that there is no single answer to life's problems and that perfection is not only impossible, but ridiculous, I might have stayed," he says, shaking his head. "It was one fantastic emotional experience, and it wasn't until later that I realized how 'high' I'd been during those few days. I came home so confused. Very scary," he emphasizes.

Here the issue of cult control of an individual's life becomes complicated. Are an adult's rights being violated by a group if that adult consents to allow the group to manipulate his mind and his life? Does a religious cult ever give a prospect enough information to make such a decision? Although many of the young people who go through a cult's indoctrination process have the advantage of knowing with whom they are dealing (for not all of the groups withhold their identity as the Moonies do in some recruiting centers), others simply do not have the maturity or the knowledge to suspect what the total price of commitment to cult life will be.

Russ Beauchene, in his thirties, had the advantage of maturity and at least an inkling of what membership in the Unification Church might cost him. He also suspected the price of cult membership because he was an aware adult who had been observing religious cult operations in the San Francisco area, not because the Moonies told him.

An adult may know the identity of the group that is attempting to convert him. He may know that the desired outcome of his indoctrination is conversion to total commitment. But do members of any group ever tell a prospect, "We are going to manipulate you, so that you will agree with us; we are going to use mind control techniques on you to secure your conversion"?

Attorney Richard Delgado has been working for several years, first on a fellowship at Yale and now as a faculty member at the University of Washington in Seattle, on an analysis of religious cults. He has attempted to answer the broad philosophical and legal question "Should society exercise a role in controlling religious cults?" In his analysis, Delgado plans to show that there is something going on in cult indoctrination and membership that produces clear-cut psychological anomalies such as neurosis, arrested maturation, and impaired decision-making processes. He is also investigating the idea of constitutional interest-balancing, questioning whether the constitutional protection the cults enjoy as religions inhibits the individual freedom of the persons who join.

"Even if cult membership is proven harmful, can

a cult member consent to be harmed?" Delgado asks. He suggests that if consent to cult membership is not full consent, but is obtained piecemeal, society must determine just how harmful membership itself may be. He points out that manipulation of conditions, even consent to possible harm, is present in many accepted areas of society (such as military basic training) where a person consents to being manipulated in order to achieve some clearly defined end.

With Yale psychiatrist Robert Jay Lifton, Delgado has drawn up a scale of totalitarianism, outlining thirteen conditions of control that were present in the Chinese Communist prison camps. "Basic military training," according to Delgado, "has ten of the thirteen conditions. "The Unification Church uses twelve of them."

"Central to the notion of a person's consent is his ability to realize what influenced him," Delgado says. He points out that although a cult member may consent to possible harm, the question of just how voluntarily his consent is obtained is an important one. He emphasizes that most of the groups he has studied (generally, the same ones we are writing about) never tell a convert the outcome of his decision. He says, "Each step in the conversion process may be consented to, but full consent is obtained in stages." To emphasize his point, he gives an analogy about a surgeon and a patient.

The surgeon first asks his patient if he can examine her leg. The patient consents. Then the surgeon says there seems to be slight infection and tells her he wants to apply an antiseptic. Then, since the leg is clean, he decides to examine it further and asks if he can anesthetize the wound area, and she consents. Now he tells the patient that the wound needs to be probed. Again, she consents. The surgeon finds cancerous tissue and suggests that since the leg is already anesthetized and germ-free, he should remove the malignant growth. The patient is frightened but she gives further consent. Ultimately in this obviously exaggerated sequence of events, the patient consents to having her leg amputated.

"The patient might never have consented to all of these steps, if she had been told the final outcome of her office visit before the beginning of the process," Delgado suggests. It is doubtful that any surgeon would be part of such an action. There are, after all, laws and ethics governing how consent must be obtained. It must not be exacted bit by bit. Everyone knows he should read a contract before signing it. But what if the contract is an unwritten one, and what if the group deviously hides the outcome of the chain of events that begins with conversion? What then?

All the young cult members we have met vehemently assert they are willing members of their religions. But most former cult members say they did not understand either the process or the principles that "converted" them. Many Moonies say they did not know for several days, often several weeks, that they were involved with the Unification Church. Others say that the sexual practices of the Children of God and the sexual abstention and ascetic lifestyle of the Hare Krishnas were not made clear to recruits until after they became members. If the identity of a group is hidden, as we saw it was at the Unification Church's Creative Community Project in Berkeley, and group practices are veiled or clouded, full consent to membership is clearly impossible.

Here is the story of one young woman who became a Moonie before she ever learned about the Rev. Sun Myung Moon. Mariellen Howe had been on a cross-country trip with some friends. The foursome, two young men and two women, lived in a van while traveling from their Midwestern homes across Canada and down the West Coast to Berkeley. Mariellen was somewhat undecided about her own future. She felt she wanted to get away from home, which was in the same city as the college she had attended. She wanted to become more independent. Mariellen and one of her friends thought they might look for jobs in California or transfer to a college from the vast Midwestern university they had been attending.

Fresh from the corn belt, they were fascinated by the Berkeley scene. For many young Americans the streets of this campus-centered community in the shadows of the Golden Gate Bridge and the California mountains have become a Mecca. In Berkeley everyone seems to do his own thing. There is a rich mixture of international and academic influences and a blanket acceptance of lifestyles ranging from very freaky to completely straight. It is in Berkeley, where thousands of backpack-toting young Americans visit and often hope to settle, that the Unification Church gets its greatest number of new recruits. (There is some disapproval among East Coast Moonies, who claim that they are more honest than the West Coast disciples, who use deceitful recruiting tactics that should not be allowed.)

Mariellen and her friends met the Moonies in front of a Creative Community Project bus, parked just off Telegraph Avenue, the main street of Berkeley. The Moonies identified themselves, not as members of the Unification Church, but as part of a volunteer project run by young people, and they invited Mariellen and her friends to come to their house in Berkeley for dinner. ("Lots of kids who go there never come back," a young Berkeley cop told us.)

"A girl and a guy came up to us and started talking. I wanted to say 'cool it,' they were coming on so strong," says Mariellen. "They invited us to dinner and we said we might stop by, but then we sort of forgot about it. But that night three of us decided to go. I wasn't hungry, but we figured we'd stop in to see what was happening.

"We got there after they had eaten. I had taken off my shoes and put them in a nearly filled rack by the door when this John Davidson type, all smiles and gushiness, took me by the arm—gently—as if I was his grandmother or something, and led me into the dining room. Everyone was sitting on the floor. They had just finished dinner and were eating fruit from big bowls in the center of each low table. I was separated from my friends, who had been led to other tables. Everyone was talking about going to a farm for the weekend, and I wondered why they would want to leave such a great town.

"Someone explained that people are so uptight in the city, they can't see things clearly or accept change as readily as we all can when we're close to nature

in the beauty of the countryside. They talked poeti-
cally about the beauty of their farm, with fields of
vegetables and fruit orchards, in the solitude of a
mountain valley north of San Francisco.

"Then we all got up and went into another room
for entertainment. We sang some rah-rah songs and
some regular rock songs with the lyrics changed to fit
the ideals of the project. Very square, I thought, but
I joined in because everyone else was singing and
clapping and having a good time. Anyway, I had
never been as hip as I had pretended. I am really
pretty square and I've always liked corny music.
Like John Denver songs," she says laughing.

That night Mariellen and one of her two friends
decided to go to the farm for the weekend. They returned to the van, got their sleeping bags, their
money and cameras and a few personal items, and
they returned to Creative Community Project, where
a bus was waiting to take them and the others to the
farm. The cost of the weekend trip would be $18,
they were told. Mariellen says she paid it from her
dwindling travel fund, thinking she would soon re-
plenish it with a job or be sending home for more
money. After nearly a four-hour bus ride, they
arrived at the farm.

The young people were hustled into sleeping quar-
ters, where they spread out their sleeping bags and
quickly drifted off to sleep. One evening and the long
bus ride was enough to tell Mariellen that "You Are
My Sunshine" was a group favorite. But she still has
a look of disbelief when she tells the events of the
next morning, a story that has, for us, become familiar. "At some ungodly hour that seemed like about

two hours after we arrived, a girl with a guitar came in the trailer where we were sleeping and began to sing that song. I tried to ignore the commotion and go back to sleep." But Mariellen, like Rick Heller, soon realized that she was the only one who wasn't singing along. "Everyone was singing, I thought it would lift the roof off the trailer. I was the only one who was still in her bag. I felt like I was on stage in *West Side Story,* standing immobile front and center while everyone else performed." Mariellen got up and sang.

Then after a quick face wash the group went in to breakfast. "I saw my friend, but she was sitting at another table and I had just a minute to say hello." Breakfast, Mariellen recalls, was cereal and fruit, juice, and milk. Then the whole dining room of young people trooped off for a lecture. "There was more group singing and lots of talk about how good it was to be there together, how beautiful the mountains are and the power of love and goodness. Again, we sang popular songs. With new lyrics.

"The lecture was given by one of the members of the community, a guy about twenty-six who manages a maintenance company the group runs in San Francisco. He was one of these super-serious guys who tell dumb jokes to prove they're with it . . . not my type at all. But there at the farm with a big approving audience who laughed at his jokes, he seemed okay. Later, he confirmed my worst suspicions about him when he played the violin, very badly. But by that time I was trying so hard to concentrate on only positive thoughts that I was ashamed of myself for judging him. I tried especially hard to like him."

In the lecture the young man covered subjects that
Mariellen says she had been thinking about seriously
before she met the group. "He talked about the concept of inner self, the conscience. Giving to others is
good, he said, but most people stop giving when they
see that no one gives anything back to them. But, the
lecturer claimed, if everyone gives to everyone, an
endless progression of giving begins and conflict
stops. Everyone in the group was "high on love" he
said, because "we all care so much about each
other."

Mariellen had recently been through the pain of
ending a long relationship with a young man. She
now says that she "needed to be loved," and this
made the lecturer's statements even more appealing
to her. "They made it all sound so realizable, so
good," she says.

"After the lecture, we all went outside to exercise
to 'keep our minds alert for some more good stuff in
the afternoon.' Someone suggested we run to the top
of a nearby hill. "It looked like a mountain to me,"
Mariellen recalls with a laugh. "We all collapsed
when we reached the hilltop. It was a great experience. After we had caught our breath and looked at
the view, I began to feel so close to everyone, so full
of love, just the way they told me I would.

"I went to talk to my friend who had come along,
but my 'big sister,' the girl who had been assigned
to look after me, said I should talk to her instead
because as an older member she would have a greater
understanding of how I was feeling. We all talked
for a while, in small groups, about the content of the
morning lecture. Even though I knew it was simplis-

tic, it sort of made sense. I had started to wonder how we could get this epidemic of loving and giving started.

"After lunch we got ready to go to the afternoon lecture. Everyone was sort of draggy and tired, but we sang together and did a big circle dance to liven ourselves up. The afternoon speaker was a really neat-looking guy in his late twenties. He wore a narrow gold band on his left hand, and I was told that he was married to a woman who was working in the East. The lecture was vague. I can't remember much of it, but it dealt with skepticism. He said that skepticism is often the result of partial information and told us that we see things only through our own experience, that we don't learn to share our experience in order to realize the whole truth. That's when he told the elephant story. It was the first of many times I would hear about the Moonies' elephant. . . .

"Four blind men come upon an elephant. Each man touches part of the animal. One touches a tusk and thinks he's found a sword. One touches an ear and thinks he has found a fan. Another feels the tail and thinks surely it's a snake. The fourth man bumps into the side of the elephant and calls it a wall. The four all get together and argue and argue. When they return to the elephant, each touches all the parts. When they get together this time and pool their information they realize that what they've found is an elephant.

"After the lecture, we broke up into small groups for sharing sessions. Each of us told about what made us most unhappy in our lives. I talked about not knowing what I wanted to do with my education, not knowing what kind of a job would make me happy. I didn't feel that my education had prepared me to live a decent life, and I didn't want to have the kind of life my parents had. I didn't think they were very loving toward each other, or toward me either, for that matter. I said I was tired of playing sexual games and that I was relieved that the guys here didn't 'come on' the way I was used to on the outside. The group leader told us how important it was to live lives of purity and goodness. He said we could all help each other by not tempting sexually. We should all live clean, honest, and open lives of goodness. God was mentioned, but only as an influence of goodness, nothing more complicated than that.

"We went back to our trailer, and I was really anxious to talk to my friend to see how she felt, but I couldn't find her. So I talked with my big sister, who was now calling herself my spiritual adviser. I put some of my doubts into words. 'This seems almost too good to be true,' I said, and asked about where they got their money, how they financed their work.

"She said they sold things—just small items like candy, candles, and peanuts—and while they were selling they told others about their work. Frequently they got new members while they were raising funds, she said.

"I hadn't heard very much about the Reverend Moon, but something about the selling rang a bell in my head and I said, 'You're not Moonies, are you?' She was shocked and sort of faltered. Now that I think about it, I know she didn't want to lie to me. She tried to evade the question, but finally said, 'No, we're not.' I believed her and so didn't press it.

"We had only about a half an hour at the trailer before dinner, and I missed taking a shower that day because I got involved in conversation with my 'big sister.' That's the only time of day I had at the farm to take care of personal things."

Mariellen recalls that dinner was a very good vegetable curry with rice and coleslaw. The vegetables were fresh from Boonville's fields, and a group member said they were giving away crates of vegetables they couldn't use to the poor in Oakland. After dinner, they went to another lecture and afterwards sang until about 11:30. Again, Mariellen wanted to look for her friend, and again her big sister talked her out of it, saying she ought to get some sleep since another full day was planned tomorrow and she would see her friend then.

"The next day the whole routine began all over again, but that day we formed threesomes (trinities) and we spent all our time together when we weren't doing something else. We played dodgeball, and I felt victimized because I was hit by the ball several times. But I felt I had to act like a good sport because everyone else was having such a good time. There were more lectures, and an idea, one I liked a lot, was introduced. It was the concept of the perfect family."

It was, Mariellen recalls not so happily, accompanied by a dash of anti-Semitism. "They said that Jesus had come to rescue mankind from sin, but he was rejected (by the Jews, whom he loved) and through his death had failed to save mankind. If Jesus had lived, he would have married and fathered a perfect family of man. But his death allowed Satan to claim all of mankind. And the kingdom of heaven is one with God, not just free from Satan. Freedom from Satan would not be enough for us; we must try to be one with God and keep God's love foremost in our hearts. The part I liked was that, because of our love, we would be able to create strong, healthy families."

By the time Sunday night came around, Mariellen says she was prepared to return to the city. She was intrigued by what the group had been telling her, but too much had happened in a short period of time. "I thought I neded time to think over everything they'd told me. I finally had a chance to talk to my girlfriend. She was planning to stay."

Still, Mariellen planned to go until about an hour before the bus was to leave. Her "big sister" and a young man she had gotten to know and like took her outside and talked about her doubts. They tried to convince her that her worries weren't major, that she was only concerned because she thought what she was seeing was "too good to be true." They said they knew they could dispel her doubts if only she gave them a chance. Maybe, said the young man, we haven't loved you enough. That was all she needed. She says she really "dug this guy, and there he was, talking about loving me."

Mariellen stayed. She knew by then that she was involved with a religious movement, but they claimed to be nonsectarian. She remembers being afraid she was caught in a group of fanatics, but says, "They didn't seem like fanatics at all."

After this gentle young woman told us the story of what had happened to her that weekend, we asked her how she feels about the experience in retrospect. She says that now she believes she was deceived. "Later, when I found out that the group was directed by the Reverend Moon, I almost lost my breath. Me? A Moonie? But by then I was so convinced that the group was doing all the right things, that I was part of 'God's Chosen Few,' and so charged up about saving the world that I doubt if I would have ever left on my own."

Mariellen did leave the Unification Church after a month. Her mother went to California to see her and convinced her to leave the farm for a day in the city. Together they visited a woman who lives nearby and has studied the workings of the Church. Mariellen's mother says she was fairly easily convinced that what she was involved in was not right for her, and within a day or two they had returned to her Midwestern home.

Mariellen was told by the woman things about the Moonies that she would never have learned in Boonville. One of the standard materials used in deprogrammings, or debriefing such as Mariellen's, is chapter 22 of Robert J. Lifton's book *Thought Reform and the Psychology of Totalism: A Study of Brainwashing in China,* which explains the conditions present in mind control and ego destruction.

Does she think she was brainwashed? Was her ego destroyed, her mind controlled or altered? Mariellen, along with many former religious cult members, has read everything she can find on the subject of mind-altering techniques. She sees definite parallels in her own situation and what is described by Dr. Lifton and also by Joost Meerloo in *Rape of the Mind*.

"Everything about my world was changed or altered in a very short period of time. The food was different. We didn't sleep much and we ran like crazy all day long. Everything was on such a high emotional plane, which is probably why I slept for a week when I first went home. During the time I was there," she says, "I asked about getting a newspaper and they told me, 'No. Newspapers are full of negativity and are not useful in our life.' I thought that was ridiculous and I said so, but I didn't argue, because it wouldn't have mattered.

"Now I realize that the division between good and evil is preposterous. As they present their ideas, they make a certain sense, but everything is on the level of a fifth-grade mentality. I never totally accepted the idea that absolute perfection is the only positive goal."

Mariellen now says she feels that anyone who claims to have "the answer," the single and only solution to life's problems, should be viewed with suspicion. "I used to love to argue about issues, but I found I couldn't argue with the Moonies, because they would analyze my every word and then caution me about 'being negative.' Their trust is absolute, and if I didn't understand it I should study harder and try to learn more. The believed, they said, that I could become a good church member, but I would have to guard against my natural skepticism, since I didn't see the whole picture and was prone to ask too many questions from partial knowledge. Everyone was so severely judgmental that I was afraid of them. Now I think my fear was silly.

"Was I brainwashed?" she echoes the question. "I just don't know, I definitely know that I was 'high' most of the time I was there and that I was doing things I didn't believe were right . . . like fund raising and saying anything to get money for Moon. The thing that worries me most is not knowing for sure if I would have stayed if my mother hadn't gotten help to talk me out of it. I never completely bought their whole package. I never cut my hair, although they wanted me to. I might have left on my own," she says tentatively.

Mariellen Howe may not be able to decide if she was subjected to classic brainwashing techniques, but the conditions of her training at the Creative Community Project's Boonville ranch correspond with eight conditions set down by Robert Jay Lifton in his book *Thought Reform and the Psychology of Totalism.* Lifton says of his title, "In this ungainly phrase, I mean to suggest the coming together of immoderate ideology with equally immoderate individual character traits—an extremist meeting ground between people and ideas." Dr. Lifton says that the tendency toward individual totalism exists to some degree within everyone.

Meerloo, in his early classic on the subject of mind control, writes of an unexpected discovery among the victims of concentration camps. "Often those with a rigid, simple belief were better able to withstand the continual barrage against their minds than were the flexible, sophisticated ones, full of doubt and inner conflicts. The refined intellectual is much more handicapped by the internal pros and cons."

Meerloo continues, "The more isolated the group, the stricter the [emotional and mental] conditioning

that takes place in those belonging to the group."
Young people, who are searching for a peg for their
lives, while they may not be intellectual sophisticates,
are nonetheless open to suggestion and are prime
candidates for an ideological change in gear. Meerloo
goes on, confirming what cult leaders have known
all along, "The mind that is open for questions is
open for dissent." Therefore, some groups allow no
serious questioning.

Mariellen says she does not know of a single person who left Boonville for any *specific* doubt. "Those
who left just didn't feel right about staying, but they
couldn't pin their doubts on any single thing. Now
that I think of it, they left because they trusted their
instincts and their instincts said 'go.' "

This confirms her own suspicion that those who
stay do so because they don't have enough knowledge
to formulate serious, intelligent questions. That fact,
coupled with the heavy discouragement against questioning "partial knowledge," indicates to her that
their thought processes have somehow been altered.
The effectiveness of Lifton's chapter 22 in helping
young religious cultists decide to leave their groups
may be due to the way it seems to be written about
today's religious cult recruiting and indoctrination
practices instead of some far-off Oriental prison
camp.

Lifton's eight conditions present in ego destruction begin with *Milieu Control*. This is the purposeful
limitation of all forms of communication with the
outside world (newspapers, radio, books, television),
along with sleep deprivation, a change in diet, and
control over the people whom the person being controlled can see and talk to.

In a speech on coercive persuasion in religious cults that he gave for a parents' group, Dr. Martin Orne, the authority on hypnotism and suggestibility, explained, "One of the major ways to disorient a person is to remove all props that support an individual's conception of who he is. If you remove clothing, the car, the house, the job, whatever . . . from this person, it dehumanizes him." Dr. Orne uses an example of a visit to a large hospital for an X-ray. "You get dressed in this johnnie gown that never fits, and you stand in line with twenty-seven other people, and you begin to feel like a nothing in no time. It is very easy, with very little effort, to make a person feel like nothing, just by removing his props. But by the way," Orne continues, "if one of your friends comes along —one of the doctors—and says 'Oh, hi, how are you?' even though you're dressed funny and feel disoriented, you begin to feel human again."

In religious cults, communication is controlled and the new members are often forbidden or strongly discouraged from visiting with friends who came to the group with them, or others at their own level of understanding. And there is little or no possibility of a chance encounter with a friend that might reestablish the cult recruit's sense of identity or normalcy.

An afternoon in a Hare Krishna temple is one of those disorienting experiences. With our identities as reporters intact, we feel comfortable going almost anywhere, as observers, and during our first visits to Krishna temples we ostentatiously clutched our pens and notebooks. But even with our props, the atmosphere of a Krishna ceremony is both unnerving and highly stimulating. The Krishnas jump and wave and dance, while incense and perfumed oils scent the air.

They appear to be in a trancelike state as they pay homage to brightly painted and exquisitely dressed large-doll-sized deity statues. At the center is a lei-draped portrait of their leader, Swami Prabhupada. The sounds reverberate off the walls of the room and, near the end of the service, a holy flame is passed to be touched.

The parents of Krishna devotees and Unification Church members often visit their children and bring their bedroom slippers to wear inside, since removal of shoes is customary. It is easy to see that going barefoot is something that makes them uncomfortable. The shoe is one of their props. For some, to remove one's shoes is to relax one's dignity.

The second of Lifton's conditions is *Mystical Manipulation,* and it is evident in nearly all religious cults. Here the potential convert is convinced of the higher purpose within the special group and is shown his individual responsibility in the attainment of that goal. He must be convinced that he is of those chosen by God, or the group leader, for this work for the greater glory of the world.

Never is this condition more apparent than in a satsang lesson of the Guru Maharaj Ji. He has told his devotees, "So whatever extra you have got, give it to me. And the extra thing you have got is your mind. Give it to me. I am ready to receive it. Because your mind troubles you give it to me. It won't trouble me. Just give it. And give your egos to me because egos trouble you, but they don't trouble me. Give them to me. So whatever extra you have in your mind, or your mind itself even, give it to me. I can bear it. It won't affect me. So just try to be holy and try to be a good devotee, a perfect devotee of the guru, who is himself perfect, who is really perfect."

An overwhelming urge that is planted in the new-comer's psyche, and reinforced by those who sow the seed of the thought, is a tremendous *Need for Purity,* the third condition on Lifton's list. Only by being good, pushing toward perfection, as the group views goodness, will the recruit be able to contribute to the well-being of the world. Along with this urge comes a sense of guilt and shame for the "impure" acts performed before joining the group. Since part of everyone's psyche is bogged down by guilt and shame, the drive for purity will in most cases add to the burden an individual already carries.

Jenny Michalsen, a former member of the Unifica-tion Church, is a lovely young woman with a quiet but direct way of expressing herself. Yet she was the victim of her own guilt while she was a Moonie. Jenny bought a box of doughnuts for a friend who had joined the church with her. "Mike never got enough to eat, so I got him something to snack on. Then I began to wonder if along with my concern for him I might not be having impure [sexual] thoughts about him. Since impure thoughts are the gift of Satan, I worried that the doughnuts were also impure. So I threw them away." While listening to this young woman talk, it is difficult to imagine how she could have been so removed from her own well-developed sense of propriety and generosity. Jenny can't explain it either.

After the invocation of guilt and shame comes the next condition on the psychiatrist's list: *Confession.*

In all religious cults, public or semipublic confessional periods are used to get members to verbalize and discuss their innermost fears and anxieties. Parents of cult members worry about family skeletons leaping out of tightly closed closets during these sessions. And well they might. Fresh from one such sharing session, a young Moonie told us about incest in her family and reflected that her mother's life and her own had been under a heavy burden of shame because her grandfather had forced her mother to have sex with him. The young Moonie told us she was planning to confess the secret to church members in order to free herself from the burden of carrying it. Counter-cult activists claim that some religious cults keep dossiers on members and their families—the more secrets the better—in order to use the material as emotional blackmail if the members should decide to leave, and tell of cases where this has happened.

The next condition of the eight-part list is the *Aura of Sacred Science* that surrounds the belief system. Because the core of the religious cult system is sacred, it is beyond questioning. Lifton writes, "The ultimate moral vision becomes an ultimate science; and the man who dares to criticize it, or to harbor even unspoken alternative ideas, becomes not only immoral and irreverent but also 'unscientific.' " Implicit in this concept is the idea that the cult's resulting laws of morality are absolute and therefore must be followed automatically. Many of the groups, especially the Hare Krishnas, say their beliefs are based on science. They say, over and over, "All our beliefs can be scientifically proven," an allegation that must leave any thoughtful person in an uneasy state.

Terry Coleman told her mother at Boonville, "God is here, and it can be proven."

Anyone who has spent much time with a Unification Church zealot, a Hare Krishna devotee, a Child of God, or a Divine Light premie can spot the group lingo in the condition Lifton calls *Loading the Language*. In each case a new vocabulary is invented, confusing well-known words with their own new meanings.

In the Unification Church the language becomes constricted as ideas narrow. The Moonies place far greater value on feelings than on intellect. They constantly refer to their hearts, speaking of "heartistic feelings, opening their hearts, deepening and strengthening their hearts."

When the Moonies ask if one has "received the blessing," they are asking if one has been married by the Reverend Moon.

When a premie asks if one has received the "knowledge," he is inquiring if one has been taught to meditate by Guru Maharaj Ji.

Each religious cult has created an entire new language and teaches adherents meaning of words in their language. A strange patois can only help to create an additional aura of mystery and separation for believers. Many members of religious cults use a style of speaking that would challenge the talent of a cliché artist. They build entire philosophies on clichés. It is this narrow style of speaking, which suggests an equally constricted way of thinking, that distresses parents of cult members when they see

formerly articulate men and women turn into religious zealots with fifth-grade vocabularies and fifth-
grade logic.

And while young cult members spit out clichés
with the authority of rock-station disk jockeys, they
tell converts that past experience is of no value in
interpreting the new morality. Lifton refers to this
condition as *Doctrine Over Persons*. It teaches that
doctrine always takes precedence over everything a
person has learned in life and it becomes the new
reality in which to function. The value of an individual member is insignificant compared to the value of
the group, its work, and its doctrine, according to
this belief.

Lifton's final psychological principle, *Dispensing
of Existence,* is the sharp line a cult draws between
those who will be saved, the cult members, and those
who are doomed to hell, the rest of the world. While
some of the most arrogant (and perhaps insecure)
cult members accept this concept at face value, others
believe that individuals in the rest of the world outside the cult may be saved "a little" if they cooperate
with the cult with tolerance and contributions, or if
members of the "chosen few" pray for their salvation.
This concept polarizes them into "we and they" and
helps to set the cult member apart from the rest of
society.

When attempting to relate these conditions to any
belief system, it is wise to remember that many apply
to everyday situations in everyone's life. When someone attempts to manipulate a person into buying
something he is selling, accepting something he
wants him to believe, or doing what he wants him

to do, he is imposing some of these conditions. But when many or all of the conditions are present at the same time, and in a group with intentions that are deliberately kept unknown to the potential converts, then the conditions are a scale against which such systems can be measured. Not all of the conditions are present in all religious cults. Each group must be examined individually before any judgment on the degree of destructiveness and social perniciousness can be made.

The most insidious element in the mind-control process that we believe is used in some religious cults is the total defenselessness of the young people who become devout followers of today's self-proclaimed messiahs and prophets and who then continue to work on other newcomers. Why these young people are so easily deceived may be a much more important question than how the groups deliberately set out to do so. Still, when there are no clearly defined dangers, who but the most jaded and cynical sets up defenses?

Politics and
the Unification Church

The motives behind the smiling cherubic countenance of Sun Myung Moon remain an enigma. Where will Moon go from here—onward to Europe and back to his native Asia as a beneficent, theocratic ruler of the world? Or back to Korea in disgrace after being exposed as the perpetrator of an international scheme to defraud the American people?

The questions rage. Is the Unification Church connected with and acting in the interests of the despotic Korean government headed by Chung Hee Park? Is the Reverend Moon, therefore, an unregistered foreign agent? Are his believers working in political channels contrary to American laws guaranteeing separation of church and state? Was the Reverend Moon's Mission in the United States sponsored so that he could be a positive influence on this country's continued support of Korea? Are his theocratic theories a mere cover-up for more immediate political aspirations that lead directly into the halls of Congress? Who sponsored his initial and very costly swing through this country?

The allegations of political connections and intrigue lead counter-cult activists to the final and perplexing questions: Since all of Moon's followers pledge to fight for him in the land of his birth, are they unwitting dupes in an international conspiracy? Is Moon's religious movement merely a cynical cover for a political organization aimed at protecting both South Korea and its tyrannical leader?

These questions have enough substance to have inspired an investigation in the House of Representatives Committee on International Relations, Subcommittee on International Organizations. Under its chairman Donald Fraser (D., Minn.), the investigating arm of Congress has been conducting an inquiry into "alleged ties between the South Korean government or the Korean CIA and certain persons or organizations associated with Sun Myung Moon."

In order to understand where Moon's movement might be headed, it is important to know where this self-proclaimed prophet has been and to grasp the nature of political charges leveled against him.

In 1960 two significant events took place in the life of Sun Myung Moon. He married his current wife, Han Hak-cha, who was then a beautiful seventeen-year-old high school girl and who in the next seventeen years presented her husband with nine children. It is said they plan to have one for each of the tribes of Israel. Also in 1960, the government of Syngman Rhee was toppled in a student uprising that put a short-lived government in power. The next year that government was overthrown by a military coup headed by Chung Hee Park. To this day Park governs South Korea with an iron hand.

Shortly after Chung Hee Park took over the reins

of the South Korean government it became apparent that Moon's doctrine of Korea as "hallowed ground," the New Israel, birthplace of the Lord of the Second Advent, was in line with Park's righteous nationalism. Moon began preaching that communism was Satanism and predicting that an apocalypse between the Godly forces of anticommunism and the forces of Satanic communism would take place in the form of a war in Korea. The Korean president, who had already begun limiting the freedoms of traditional Christian clergy, and Moon, the messiah of an offbeat religious movement, made another pair of strange bedfellows.

It is Chung Hee Park's obvious favoritism toward Moon and his religion which has caused a number of Korea-watchers to observe that the two must be tied politically. Donald Ranard, former director of the State Department Office of Korean Affairs, told the Fraser subcommittee, "I would find it hard to understand how the Unification Church would seem to exist completely beyond the control of the Korean government."

He elaborated, "Anyone with a sense of feel for Korean affairs would know that when someone sticks his head above the line, as Moon has done, he isn't a maverick. Moon's organization doesn't exist in Korea without a connection to the government."

Edmund Kelley, an analyst in the Office of Korean affairs, noted in a newspaper, "No one can be as financially successful in Korea as Moon and be offending anyone in the Park government."

Jai Hyon Lee, a former Korean embassy official

who has renounced his connection with the Park government and currently teaches journalism at Western Illinois University, told a congressional hearing, "There seems to be a curious working relationship between Park's dictatorial regime, the Korean Cultural and Freedom Foundation, 'Little Angels' [a group of Korean children who perform under the auspices of the foundation and the direction of the Reverend Moon], Moon's Unification Church affiliated organizations, and the [Korean] CIA, let alone dictator Park's patronage of Moon's multimillion dollar ventures in South Korea."

"Today in Korea, a land in which the free expression of religious conscience is often met by the government with charges of treason and sedition, Moon and his lieutenants enjoy a kind of diplomatic immunity," Alan Tate Wood reported to the congressional investigators.

Shortly after Park's takeover in South Korea, the Reverend Moon's associate Bo Hi Pak, that well-connected military school graduate and intelligence community member, was assigned to the Korean embassy in Washington as a military attaché. Pak divided his time in the United States between his diplomatic work and work for the Moon cause. He resigned from government service in 1964 to begin the Korean Cultural and Freedom Foundation.

In 1961 the Holy Spirit Association for the Unification of World Christianity had been incorporated in California by Ms. Kim and in McLean, Virginia, by Colonel Pak and Jhoon Rhee, another long-time supporter of Moon who currently operates karate parlors in the Washington, D.C., area.

According to Elizabeth Darling, a private citizen who has made a study of the Unification Church, "Jhoon Rhee first came to the United States from Korea in 1954. He worked teaching American soldiers karate at a military base in Texas. Rhee is said to be no longer a member of the Unification Church. Still his name appeared on a list of supposed Moon associates that was sent by Representative Fraser to the Comptroller of the Currency in 1976, asking that the Comptroller's office investigate the possibility that Reverend Moon through these associates secretly controls the Diplomat Bank, a Washington, D.C., bank chartered in December 1975."

The Moon church seems to have always wanted and never secured the support of mainline Christian orthodoxy. When the group applied for and was refused membership by the Korean Council of Churches in the land of its origin, the council head, Kwan Sukkim, denounced Moonism, saying, "We consider it a pseudo-religion more evil than Satan."

Still Moon and his faith have achieved both numbers and influence in South Korea. Korean Christian clergy say, in a near-echo of their American counterparts, that Moon's following in the country comes "mainly from disenchanted intellectuals and college students who find it hard to obtain meaningful employment within the Korean economy." Instead of struggling with professions, they say, the sophisticated intellectuals who become Moon-followers opt for menial labor in his factories. They seek a chance to be part of his "higher-purpose," working to unify all the world's faiths, suppress communism, and achieve recognition for Korea as the new holy land.

The Moon faith claims to have 1,000 churches and some 360,000 members in South Korea. That is not a large following, considering that the 1974 census reported a population of 33,959,000.

While some industries have faltered under the iron-fisted rule of Chung Hee Park, Moon's Korean business interests have thrived. Unhampered by government intervention, and restriction, they receive instead government privilege. The Moon businesses also prosper because they don't have to contend with unions or wage demands from church members who staff and operate them, taking very small stipends or no salaries at all. This enables Moon to undercut the market in whatever his product happens to be: air rifles, ginseng tea, titanium, pharmaceuticals, or stone work.

Another sign of the special role enjoyed by Moon in his homeland is an academy the church operates near Seoul, where the government regularly sends military and administrative personnel for seminars to increase their anticommunist fervor.

The question of where the seed money for the first "Moon-swing" in America came from is an important one. Did Moon get the money from his own Korean businesses? Did he get it in the form of a loan from his church in Japan? Did he get it from right-wing Japanese industrialists? Did it come into the United States illegally through sacrosanct diplomatic channels? Or, as many Americans now suspect, was the Moon American campaign financed by the Korean government or the Korean CIA?

By the time of the crusade, Moon's disciple

Young Oon Kim had started a few American communes of the Unified Family, as the church was known in its early American days, but she lacked the financial resources to get the movement off to a spectacular start. Ms. Kim's groups, to whom she taught Moon's Divine Principle as she had translated it into English, were totally spiritual, devoted to Moon and his philosophy. But they weren't yet, as Alan Tate Wood recalls, "the hard-working mercenaries that latter-day Moonies are known to be."

Charles Babcock reported in a Washington *Post* story that friends of Moon's associate, Jhoon Rhee, said, "In the past before Moon came to this country he had no money and Rhee provided him with a plane ticket."

And yet when Moon came to America in 1971, he had money. He had more money than his tiny band of American followers could have provided him with and more money than he could have skimmed off the top of his Korean investments. "At the time there were no more than 250 Moonies in the United States," former Unified Family member Wood recalls. Other early members of the Unified Family confirm this number.

There have been reports that the initial Unification Church barnstorming crusade, the Day of Hope tour in 1973, was financed by a loan from the Japanese branch of the church. That theory seems unlikely since Moon's brand of religion never really caught on with the masses in Japan, where the influence of Christian missionaries is not so strongly felt as it is in Korea, or in Vietnam. The Korean scholars report that the Unification Church in Japan has 40,000 members, most of them in rural areas of the country.

Since the overwhelming religious leanings in Japan are toward Shintoism and Buddhism, there was never more than a remote chance any substantial following could be found for Moon's interpretation of Christian theology. However, the evangelist's anticommunist rhetoric did inspire a following in Japan among wealthy right-wing businessmen and industrialists. Moon's church, particularly his church-sponsored International Federation for Victory over Communism, has received financial support from some of these men such as Yoshio Kodama, a central figure in right-wing politics in Japan, and Ryoichi Sasagawa, a powerful figure and avowed anticommunist who has achieved recognition as an ultraconservative multimillionaire industrialist in postwar Japan.

Sasagawa reportedly told a West Coast journalist and correspondent for the Manchester *Guardian* and other newspapers that it was he who supplied Moon with the money for his first big American crusade, to the tune of between $1 million and $2 million.

In 1974, Sasagawa formed the World Karate Federation and became its first president. Coincidentally, Jhoon Rhee, the karate school operator in Washington who was an early associate of Moon in the Unification Church, is reported to have been one of the federation's first officers.

Some "Moon-watchers" are beginning to suspect that the Korean evangelist's mission in the United States was not launched without the knowledge and

the approval of the United States government and
the United States CIA. One astute observer told us,
"While it is possible that the government understood that Moon would try to raise the stature of
South Korea with the American people, it is doubtful that officials could have even suspected the
devastating effect his religion would have on American youth and their families."

Before Moon ever stepped foot on American soil,
his friend Bo Hi Pak had set up the Korean Cultural Foundation. The foundation had the support
of the Korean government through its ambassador
to the United States at the time, Pak's former boss,
Yan You Chan. The first honorary chairman of
the foundation was Kim Jong Pil, founder of the
Korean CIA. One of the original directors was an
American, the late General Andrew Curtin, who
had been assigned to Korea in a military intelligence
capacity.

Expanding on the connection between the intelligence services, Robert R. Roland, an acquaintance of Bo Hi Pak's (whose former wife and
daughter are Unification Church members), told
the Fraser subcommittee that Pak explained his
military attaché duties to him (Roland), "Pak noted
that he served as a liaison between South Korean
and U.S. intelligence services."

Ranard, the former State Department official and
Korea expert, told us that it is "Moon's association
with Bo Hi Pak, whom I know a great deal about,
and a couple of other things which I am not free to
mention, that make me *sure* there is a connection
btween the Unification Church and the Korean
CIA."

The Reverend Moon was the focus of suspicion for some time even before the Fraser subcommittee presented a forum for investigating his dubious connections with the Korean government.

Although Pak had ostensibly severed his direct relationship with the Park regime when he resigned as military attaché, he maintained, according to Jai Hyon Lee, a curious relationship with the ambassador and the embassy for one who no longer worked there.

Lee testified that Colonel Pak enjoyed access to the embassy's direct communication channels to Korea as late as 1971, years after he was no longer attached to the Korean diplomatic corps. Lee told the investigators that he was present when Korean Ambassador Kim Dong Jo approved the sending of a message from Colonel Pak to Seoul over a cable that was reserved for secret correspondence. "One day I was discussing a matter with the ambassador in his office. In the middle of our conversation one of the embassy's communications officers walked in, and he imparted to the ambassador a message from Colonel Bo Hi Pak and this message was to be sent to Seoul. The ambassador turned to him and listened to his report and simply nodded. It seemed so casual. Bo Hi Pak was president of the Korean Cultural and Freedom Foundation at the time."

Lee testified that he had never seen anything like this before in his career as a foreign service officer. "No private person has access to diplomatic pouches or diplomatic cable channel. No, sir!"

As he recounted his own reasons for suspicion of the Moon movement, Lee told the Fraser investigation that Moon's Freedom Leadership Foundation (a youth organization whose membership is made up almost entirely of Unification Church members and which is affiliated with Moon's International Foundation for Victory over Communism) "maintained contact with KCIA agents in the Korean embassy while I was still in the embassy.

"I remember at least three American secretaries in South Korea's Washington embassy had been hired upon recommendations of the Freedom Leadership Foundation, which furnished candidates at the request of the embassy's KCIA agents." Lee said one of the agents brought the practice to his attention when he was in the process of hiring a new secretary.

Lee's conclusion that the Unification Church must be in cahoots with the Park government is reasoned this way, "The KCIA is involved in virtually every aspect of Korean life. Therefore, it is entirely unthinkable that the omnipresent CIA simply overlooked Moon's movement. On the contrary, the KCIA would be most interested in putting some Korean like Moon, who supports all its goals, in a position to work and lobby for the Park regime's position on the American political scene."

If Lee's and other Korea experts' assumptions are correct, they could account for Bo Hi Pak's reported presence at a meeting that took place in the Blue House, the South Korean executive mansion, in 1970 before Moon came to the United States to live and work. The meeting is said to have included Korean President Park, Colonel Pak, and Tongsun Park, the dashing Georgetown University graduate who fled the United States rather than remain to face sure questioning and possible prosecution because of his alleged influence-buying on Capitol Hill.

The men met to "plan a multimillion dollar campaign of propaganda, influence-buying, intimidation, spying, and bribery aimed at assuring the U.S. continued support for his [Park's] regime," Saul Friedman and Vera Glaser of the Knight News Service reported in late 1976.

The United States government has not commented on reports that information of the meeting was obtained through electronic surveillance. However, the South Korean government in December 1976 demanded through its minister of culture and information that the United States "clarify in public" whether it had bugged President Park's office. (Richard Mauzy, an investigator for the Fraser subcommittee, told us that details of the meeting were revealed in Ranard's secret testimony and word of it was probably leaked to the press by a government official who had access to a classified transcript of the hearing.)

Subsequent to the reported meeting, the Korean president sent a letter on official government stationery to some 60,000 prominent Americans soliciting contributions for the Korean Cultural Foundation's current project, *Radio Free Asia*. That letter led the State Department, several months later, to ask the Department of Justice to investigate whether *Radio Free Asia* was a legitimate American organization or an agency of the Park government.

Under the Foreign Agents Registration Act, all

operatives and operations of foreign governments must be registered as such with the U.S. attorney general. According to this piece of legislation, "Anyone who acts at the order, request or control of a foreign principal, or a person any of whose activities are directly or indirectly supervised, directed, controlled, financed, or subsidized in whole or in any major part by a foreign principal is an agent." Those who engage in political activities within the United States for or in the interests of such a foreign principal, or "who may solicit, collect, disburse, or dispense contributions, loans, money for a foreign principal," are also required to register.

Those who engage solely in religious pursuits, such as Moon ostensibly does, are exempt from registering. Unless, of course, they also engage in political activities. The Justice Department found enough cause to recommend that the State Department undertake an investigation of *Radio Free Asia*. The State Department subsequently began, and then dropped, the search when it could not confirm allegations by "competent evidence."

Moon's evangelism and his doctrine seem designed both to recruit new followers from the ranks of American youth and to influence American public and legislative opinion in favor of South Korea and its government. According to Alan Tate Wood, early efforts of the Unification Church, through association with the World Anti-Communist League, were directed toward making President Chung Hee Park understand that "Moon was his strongest ally and supporter."

Park's acceptance of the Moon movement was essential, Mr. Wood recalled for the Fraser investigation. "In those days, we were often told that there was some danger that Mr. Moon might be assassinated by agents of the South Korean government."

In 1974 at a Parents Day speech he delivered in Jackson, Mississippi, Moon told his assembled disciples, "America has so much to give to others. Therefore a victory in America is not just a victory for America. This is also a victory for Korea. In winning America, Korea is already won. . . . This is a prophetic statement. Someday in the near future, when I walk into the Congressman's or the Senator's offices without notice or appointment, the aides will jump out of their seats and go to get the Senator."

Moon also told his young followers that day, "If we can turn three states of the United States around, or if we can turn seven states of the United States to our side, then the whole of the United States will turn. Let's say there are 500 sons and daughters like you in each state. Then we could control the government. You could determine who became senators and who the congressmen would be. From the physical point of view, you can gain no faster success than this way."

Later, in a training address, Moon told his disciples, "When senators are linked with our Master, the Centers' Directors [Unification Church Centers] and senators will be close. If the top level leaders are united with the Master, then all the people will be united with our church. Because of the work

Master needs much money. Also Master needs many good-looking girls—300. He will assign three girls to one senator—that means we need 300. Let them have a good relationship with them. One is for the election, one is to be the diplomat, one is for the party. If the girls are superior to the senators in many ways, then the senators will just be taken by our members."

It appears that Moon's plan of 300 girls working Capitol Hill never materialized, although Neil A. Salonen, president of the Unification Church in America, confirmed in February 1976 that the group's mission in Washington had, at times, up to twenty women who circulated among the congressional offices to witness "God's revelations to the leaders."

Salonen's statement appears to have been prompted by a column Jack Anderson wrote on Moon's Capitol Hill activities in December 1975. Anderson made one of the young Moon ladies, Susan Bergman, a doctor's daughter from New York, "famous" when he reported that Miss Bergman had a "special" relationship with the then speaker of the House of Representatives Carl Albert (D. Okla.). "The hazel-eyed Ms. Bergman sits in the House gallery, often in the special section reserved for congressmen's families, where she watches the Speaker in action almost every day," Anderson wrote.

"Earlier in the day, she usually greets him in the hallway outside his office and presents him with flowers. Often she brews him ginseng tea in the small kitchen just down the hall from the

Speaker's office," Anderson also reported. Albert insisted, Anderson wrote, that the young woman "never lobbied him on any political issue."

The evangelist himself is not mute on political issues, however, and, according to Anderson, Moon told his followers, "Whenever America withdraws or cancels or stops her foreign aid to the land of Korea, the United States will decline and perish."

Ms. Bergman's relationship with the former speaker of the House of Representatives appeared to be innocuous, and many church critics considered the Anderson column "overstated" at best. But Ann Gordon, a former Unification Church member who worked on Capitol Hill and left the church after being deprogrammed, said in a sworn statement that Ms. Bergman sent postcards ahead to each hotel on Albert's itinerary when he was touring Europe. "She had gotten [the itinerary] from his secretary. . . . When Albert returned, he called long distance to Barrytown, New York, to ask, 'Where is my friend, Susan?' " Ms. Gordon added.

Explaining Moon lobbying aspirations in her statement, Ms. Gordon said, "Public relations members [the young Moonies assigned to Capitol Hill] were to make gradual acquaintances and friendships with staff members and aides and eventually Congressmen and Senators themselves, inviting them to a suite in the Washington Hilton rented at $54 a day (the normal rate should have been around $120 a day), where dinner and films or short lectures on Moon's ideas and accomplishments would be presented. All this effort is sort of an ongoing program by Moon to get political support for himself and the Chung Hee Park dictatorship in South Korea. We were told to be 'somewhat' vague when dealing with Capitol Hill contacts in order to protect our presence there, but we were to try to influence our contacts to support Moon and South Korea."

According to Ms. Gordon, the Moon lobby has not always been in vain. "Since I have been out of the Unification Church, I have read a State Department communiqué about the United States need to continue protection for South Korea and thereby for Japan—in nearly the same exact wording we were told to use to influence our contacts on this issue."

Alan Tate Wood claims that he and another young man, Charles Stephens, helped set up the *American Youth for a Just Peace* to be a legitimate and partisan political lobby organization to carry out pro-war activities. As a representative of AYJP, Wood and several other young Americans visited Vietnam, during the heat of fighting there, to bolster waning American support for the Vietnam war effort. Mr. Wood said he believes the funding for the trip came from the South Vietnamese government. While Wood and the eight other young Americans were in Vietnam they were filmed and later shown on American television, voicing their support for the war at a time when most young Americans were demonstrating against it.

The Foreign Agents Registration Act and the Internal Revenue Service code both require that religious organizations refrain from direct involvement in political campaigns and significant propagandizing.

In September 1976 Chris Elkins, another former Moonie who had been active in the Freedom Leadership Foundation, told the Fraser subcommittee that as a Moonie he had been enlisted to work on a congressional campaign for Charles Stephens in New York in September 1974. Stephens, who was at the time in the midst of an unsuccessful campaign against Richard Ottinger, was the same young man who had helped Alan Tate Wood found AYJP. Elkins said he had been directed by Neil Salonen, who was the president of both the Unification Church and the Leadership Foundation, to go to New York and assist Mr. Stephens with his campaign. Elkins said he did not know Stephens, but "I knew the name Charles Stephens. I knew he had been working with the FLF and I had heard we were working on his campaign."

Elkins said he and other church members who worked on Stephens's campaign were not paid by the campaign. "We stayed on church property, the church facilities at Tarrytown, New York. I received maybe a meal or something like that while working for Charlie Stephens, but I was not paid by Stephens to work with the campaign."

The young man also told the inquiry that Unification Church members had been active in a congressional campaign in New Hampshire that same fall—a campaign in which the church-endorsed candidate, Louis Wyman, lost. However, prior to that defeat Elkins said he had been promised a job with Wyman's Washington staff if Wyman won.

"I understand that the Unification Church there [New Hampshire] gave quite a lot of time and effort as far as his [Wyman's] campaign was concerned and he said he would give a position on his staff to a member of the church because of their participation."

Elkins said he was the church member who had been designated to fill that position.

In late 1973 and early 1974 the Unification Church spent a reported $72,000 on a campaign in support of President Nixon, whose credibility was at an all-time low because of the Watergate crisis. Moon had visited Korea in November 1973. He returned to the United States and said that while he was in Korea God spoke to him and told him to support Nixon. In December Tricia Nixon Cox, the President's daughter, came out of the executive mansion and posed for pictures with a band of young Moonies who had been demonstrating in her father's behalf in Lafayette Square, across from the White House.

In answer to a question posed by Congressman Fraser concerning the Moon church's involvement with the Nixon impeachment charge, Elkins answered, "Moon issued a statement. I think he called it the Watergate statement, that we should forgive Nixon and stand behind him until he was proven guilty. Of course, at that time we were absolutely, I would say almost absolutely, the only ones supporting Nixon. We were quite outgoing about it . . . in every State we had rallies and here in Washington also. . . . I know I went to Chicago and Nashville because the President was going to show up there.

We were going to pro-Nixon rallies there when he was there."

Elkins also recalled a political incident in late August or early September 1974, after Nixon had left office. Elkins said he was told by Neil Salonen that he [Elkins] and four others were going to throw eggs at the Japanese embassy "and perhaps catch the Japanese ambassador."

He explained to the congressional inquiry that there was considerable antipathy between Japan and Korea at the time, since it was shortly after Mrs. Chung Hee Park had been killed by a Japanese radical's bullet that had been meant for the Korean president. "It [the egging] was to be," recalls Elkins, "a foretaste of what would happen when Japanese Premier Tanaka visited a few weeks later."

However, Elkins said, "The egging was called off after Mr. Salonen spoke, by telephone, to the Reverend Moon. Moon told him that President Ford had agreed to make a stop in Seoul, Korea, on his way to Vladivostok, in which case that would show more than enough American support for South Korea and the egging would be unnecessary." It seems, if Elkins's memory is accurate, that the Reverend Moon had advance information on Ford's travel plans. His trip to Vladivostok was not announced publicly until October 26, 1974. Ford did visit South Korea in November 1974 on his way to the meeting with Russian leader Leonid Brezhnev.

Following Elkins's testimony, Neil Salonen issued a press release, denying that an egg-throwing plot against the ambassador of Japan was ever planned or carried out. "Our demonstrations are well-known for their lawful and orderly character," Salonen said.

Michael Runyon, who was serving as a spokesman for the Unification Church at the time, told the Washington *Post,* in an attempt to discredit Elkins, that he is "a nice guy, but a little immature and unstable." Elkins later said Runyon wouldn't be able to pick him out of a crowd, since they had never met.

According to Elkins, the Freedom Leadership Foundation also engaged in massive letter-writing campaigns to members of Congress whenever a military appropriation bill for Southeast Asia was about to come before the legislators. Elkins explained, "Support for our 'American' efforts in Vietnam was very shaky then, so any time there was an appropriation concerning Southeast Asia it was very doubtful it was going to go through. Many of these package deals involved Korea and we were particularly interested in the solvency of South Korea."

Elkins said he remembers sitting up all night working at automatic typewriting machines, "making these letters so we could send them out in time. Of course the stuff didn't go out on FLF stationery. They knew there was a restriction as far as their corporation was concerned."

Often the FLF joined with other youth groups, such as the Young Americans for Freedom or the Young Socialists, on these mailings, he said. "You know, it depended on what we needed as to who our association was with at that time. . . . We were in pretty close association with those who could lobby." The other youth groups were often members of the American Youth Council, a group whose funding and purpose has also been seriously questioned by those concerned with the Moon issue. One theory connects the AYC with the American CIA.

The American government, in its effort to defend the free expression of religion, never defines a religion or a religious institution by its beliefs. Rather, religious groups in this country are governed by other laws, which apply to other groups as well. Religions are regulated particularly by laws which have to do with taxation and exemption from taxation.

The Internal Revenue Service code specifies that churches and other nonprofit groups are exempt from taxation. In order to secure this privilege, however, which even excludes churches from filing income tax returns, the group must behave in a certain way. For example, the code states, "No part of the net earnings of the group can inure to the benefit of any private shareholder or individual, no substantial part of the activities of the group can be carrying on propaganda or otherwise attempting to influence legislation and the groups cannot participate in, or intervene in (including the publishing or distributing of statements) any political campaign on behalf of any candidate for public office."

When Chris Elkins was telling the congressmen how he had been directed to participate in Charles Stephens's political campaign he also said that he picked up his train ticket to New York from Salonen's Washington office.

Arnold Brush, Internal Revenue Service agent

who is an exempt organizations specialist, explains
how a religion or other tax-exempt organization
could participate in the political arena. "Let's say
a church has one million dollars in income—it can
transfer money to a political group, and that's not
illegal." However, the group cannot spend the
money itself in the cause of a political campaign.

"For instance," Brush continued, "when the
Sierra Club, a tax-exempt educational organization
[which conducts a viable lobby for ecology] moved
into the legislative arena because the work it wanted
to do could be done by working with legislators, it
had to change its status to an organization operating
solely for the social welfare. Its net earnings are still
tax exempt, but donations to the Sierra Club are not
tax deductible.

"If a church transferred funds to a political organization and if it was proven that the church was
the sole source of support of the organization and it
could be shown that both the groups intended to
defraud the government, there could be a problem," Brush said. However it must be noted that
the intent to defraud the government would have
to be proven and that the government hesitates to
intervene in religious affairs.

"Religious legislative activity is hard to define
because it is not absolutely prohibited by the law.
The burden comes in proving what is 'substantial activity,' " Brush told us.

Both the Unification Church and the Freedom
Leadership Foundation enjoy complete tax exemption privileges, meaning their net earnings are free
from taxation and those who make contributions to

these groups may claim the donations as tax deductions. The Unification Church is incorporated as a religion and the FLF as a nonprofit educational organization.

Neil A. Salonen, president of both groups, claimed in a 1974 statement to the Internal Revenue Service that the FLF has no relation to the Unification Church except for the fact that the organizations have some members, offices, and directors in common.

But Alan Tate Wood, who was president of FLF before Salonen, told us the foundation was initially funded entirely by the church and the FLF members are almost exclusively members of the Unification Church. Other former members of both organizations have told us they were cautioned not to mention their church membership when engaged in political activities with FLF.

Dan Feffernan, who is a member of the Moon church, and who conducted the day-to-day activities of the FLF as secretary-general of the foundation until 1976, agrees with Wood that the foundation is almost exclusively staffed by church members, but he denies that the church supports FLF. Feffernan says church funds account for less than half of the foundation's operating budget. The source of the rest of FLF's funding, however, still remains a mystery.

The Internal Revenue Service will not admit they are conducting any investigations or audits of Moon-related organizations, although many complaints have been lodged by disgruntled parents and suspicious taxpayers. IRS policy forbids dis-

cussing investigations, even if they are in the works.
But several parents of present and former Unification Church members say they have been visited
and interviewed by IRS agents, who are, obviously,
compiling information on Moon's church.

It is known, however, that the United States Immigration and Naturalization Service and the Unification Church have been playing a cat and mouse
game since 1974. In September of that year the
immigration authorities, acting on complaints, ruled
that nearly 600 of the Reverend Moon's international followers sought to extend their stays in the
United States under an illegal pretext. During 1974
the service decided that these young Moonies who
had come into the country on tourist visas were
spending their time fund raising rather than sight-
seeing.

The church, through its legal counsel, tried to
have the visas of the foreigners extended by changing their status to missionary trainees. The immigration service, after an investigation, declared that
the missionary program "was designed primarily
for fund raising rather than training purposes."
Since the young people were requesting not im-
migrant status, but missionary-student visas, the
service said it couldn't be done. "We regard such
extensive solicitations as productive employment,
both in violation of nonimmigrant visitor status and
beyond the pale of trainee classification." The 583
visitors whose visas were in question were ordered
to leave the United States when their visas expired
or face deportation proceedings.

Some parents of Moon followers fear that the

marriages the Korean messiah arranges for his followers are another way the church tries to skirt immigration laws. One list of Moon-arranged marriages showed that over half the marriages were international matings, leading to the charge that the evangelist marries young American men and women to foreign nationals, thus securing permanent visas for the aliens.

Since it is incorporated and recognized by the government as a bona-fide religion, the Unification Church does not have to file an income tax return. However, immigration service investigators found conflicting reports of church income when they examined official church statements of operating income in 1973. One statement listed the 1973 operating income at $11.17 million, and another said the 1973 operating income was only $2.1 million. The immigration authorities, a spokesman said, "found the church's credibility very much in doubt."

The Unification Church has at various times claimed a nationwide membership of 30,000 adherents and 7,000 hard core members. Modest, and perhaps more realistic, observers say the Church has about 3,000 members. Yet there is no question that with only 3,000 members the Unification Church today is a very successful financial endeavor. From our own experience with a fund-raising team, we are certain that a Moon fund raiser, working an eight- to twelve-hour day can fairly easily raise $100 a day—and in some cases much more. Members and former members report earning $200 and tell us the group puts great emphasis on "producing."

Assuming that no more than 1,000 Moonies work the streets, bars, and shops every day (a very modest assumption), selling peanuts, flowers, candy, and candles, and that each earns no more than $50 a day, the income from these efforts alone would reap more than $18 million a year for the Moon cause. The ability of devoted Moonies to raise money for their church has never been in doubt. The financial questions center around where the seed money came from to finance the initial American Moon crusade and what becomes of all the money the group raises now.

The Unification Church tells all who will listen that the Reverend Moon is not a wealthy man—that he owns nothing in his own right, all that he has is owned by the church. Yet Sun Myung Moon seems to have a lot, and some of that appears to be in his own hands.

In the first two years of Moon's residency in America, the movement chalked up some monumental real estate acquisitions. One Westchester County, New York, taxpayer who watched while the Moon forces picked up one choice suburban New York parcel after another commented, "It looked for a while like they thought Westchester was a Monopoly board and that they had to buy it all to win the game."

By 1974 the Unification Church had purchased its sixty-acre Belvedere Estate on the Hudson River from the Bronfman family of the Seagram Distillery fortune for reportedly "more than $2 million." In 1974 the church also bought the nearby twenty-six-acre estate of the brassiere tycoon who owned

Exquisite Form—"Exquisite Acres"—for Moon's personal residence. The selling price of the twenty-five-room mansion and its grounds and antique furnishings was $675,000. Moon rechristened the place "East Garden."

Another Moon purchase in Westchester is a forty-six-acre tract adjoining the Belvedere property, which the church bought from the Robert Martin Corporation, a real estate development firm. Some Westchester taxpayers fear that the church is taking all this prime suburban land off the tax rolls while it appreciates and that the Moonies will eventually resell it for real estate or condominium development. The total Moon holdings in the affluent county are valued at $8 million, and some of Moon's Westchester neighbors are angry enough to have encouraged local authorities to question the church tax status. When the properties, which had contributed substantially to the tax coffers when they were owned by private individuals, were taken off the tax rolls, the remaining taxpayers had not only to make up the deficit, but also to pay for additional services required because there are large numbers of Moonies living in what were before private homes.

In financially hard-pressed New York City, where every tax dollar counts, officials are also questioning the tax-exempt status of the Unification Church's real estate tax exemptions on the former Columbia University Club near Times Square, which the Moonies bought for $1.2 million, and the forty-two-story Hotel New Yorker, across from Madison Square Garden, that the church purchased in the summer of 1976 for a reported $5.6 million. A knowledgeable New Yorker says he's no longer surprised at anything that happens in New York City and doesn't think the city's quest to extract tax money from the Moonies will be successful. "There's never been a case where any group claiming to be a religion has been denied tax exemption in New York City."

Another major Moon purchase is the 258-acre Barrytown, New York, Moon seminary, a Roman Catholic Christian Brothers seminary before the Moonies took it off their hands for $1.56 million. The rural property, perched high on a cliff overlooking the Hudson River in upstate New York, is also a focus of controversy, for the State Board of Regents has still not acted on whether or not it will accredit the seminary as a graduate school of religious education.

There is no question that Sun Moon lives a life of affluence. His young followers, who live severe lives of self-denial, deny their master nothing. Moon has a fifty-foot yacht cruiser, the *New Hope,* for fishing and leisure. His school-age children attend exclusive, and expensive, private schools. There is some question, however, whether all of Moon's luxuries are indeed owned by his church. And not all of his followers live in the abject poverty that has come to typify the existence of a Moonie. The top Moon aides live in sumptuous style while the masses of his following sleep huddled together in sleeping bags on the floors of rooms that are barren of all furniture, or in unheated vans.

One former Moonie, who traveled with a Moon Mobile Fund-raising Team, said she and her team lived out of a van, checking into a cheap motel once a week so they could get a bath. "We dressed in church hand-outs, ill-fitting out-of-date clothing that looks as though it's purchased by the trainload from a warehouse clearance, while the young men and women who work in public relations for the church are encouraged, and given the money, to amass fashionable wardrobes. . . ."

Colonel Bo Hi Pak, Moon's translator, traveling companion, and confidant, lives in a $115,000 home in the Washington suburbs. Ooni Durst, a middle-aged Korean woman, who with her husband, Dr. Martin (Moses) Durst (a professor at Laney College in Oakland, California), heads the West Coast Moon activities, lives in a home that is said to be sumptuous and expensive. A young woman who worked with Mrs. Durst when she was a member of the Moon cult, and who is currently on the staff of a rehabilitation center for ex-cult members in Arizona, says, "I was told the home has . . . a sauna and a swimming pool." According to the young woman, Ooni Durst dresses in custom-made dresses, mink coats, and diamonds.

Around the country the church owns a number of less impressive properties, valued between $50,000 and $100,000, that serve as church-commune centers in major cities and college communities. The Unification Church Center in Boulder, Colorado, is a modern building of interesting architectural style that was sold to the church by a fraternity which found itself no longer able to afford it when the fraternity movement at the Colorado university hit rock bottom a few years ago. Ann Gordon told how she arranged to "borrow" $7,000 from her parents to help the Moonies make a $17,000 down payment on a $65,000 house in Tulsa, Oklahoma, that was to serve as the Unification Church's state headquarters.

In Berkeley, California, the New Educational Development System, a group which operates the New Ideal City Ranch in Boonville, California, and which is the most successful recruiting arm of the Moon Church—yet which still claims that it is not a Moon organization—is housed in Berkeley in the former William Randolph Hearst mansion, valued at $225,000. Farther north the group owns a ranch on 680 acres of prime farmland in Boonville and has recently purchased a recreational site in the lush Napa Valley. In southern California the group has a large house in the Westwood area of Los Angeles and operates a training center at a former Y camp in the San Bernardino Mountains.

In other places, where the church has no established centers, fund raisers often rent property on short-term leases so that they can have a base of operations while they blitz a town with flowers, peanuts, candy, or candles before moving on to greener pastures.

Church-operated businesses, while they don't seem to be the financial mainstay that the fund raising has become, are operated in several cities. They include a maintenance and cleaning business in the San Francisco area, a ginseng tea house and restaurant in Washington, D.C., and Christian Bernard, a jewelry business the Moonies operate in Paris, France, which has a showroom in New York City and in the Midwest.

The Tong II Fishing Company, of New York, a

Moon-operated business, has attempted to capture a substantial part of the East Coast tuna fishing trade. The dark meat of Atlantic Ocean tuna is not a favorite with Americans, who prefer the white meat of the Pacific tuna, but to the Oriental taste it is choice. Moon fishing interests ship the giant tuna from eastern waters, packed in ice, to Japan, where it brings three times the price it would in the United States. The church has also purchased a fishery in the Norfolk, Virginia, area.

And the Unification Church International has entered the newspaper business in New York City. The Moon newspaper, *The New World,* is aimed at young adults and is being sold initially in New York City. The paper's business manager, Tom Miner, said the venture is being financed by the church, However, the newspaper will be autonomous. "We want to make it very clear that this is not going to be an organ for the Unification Church in any way," Miner said. The young newspaper publishers cited the Christian Science Publishing Society in Boston for "setting a precedent with their highly regarded *Christian Science Monitor* for a religious group putting out a newspaper that is totally aside from their religious point of view." The Freedom Leadership Foundation in Washington has published an ultraconservative, anticommunist newspaper, *The Rising Tide,* for several years. Alan Tate Wood says he doubts the paper has ever been financially successful, but it did bill itself "the fastest growing newspaper in the United States" at one time.

Records of the Diplomat Bank in Washington, D.C., which was chartered in December 1975, show

that Moon and others whose names have been linked
with his control the majority of the stock in this bank.
The eighteen Moon associates listed as stockholders
in the bank include Bo Hi Pak and Mrs. Moon's translator, Won Pok Choi, as well as Jhoon Rhee and
Tongsun Park.

The Fraser subcommittee, in a letter from Congressman Fraser to the Comptroller of the Currency,
asked that the Currency office investigate whether
money from foreign sources was used to establish the
bank, whether any such funds came into the United
States illegally, and whether any stock in the bank
is secretly held by the Reverend Moon.

The subcommittee had heard testimony suggest-
ing that associates of Moon secretly brought millions
of dollars into the United States from South Korea
through diplomatic channels and failed to declare the
money. The allegation is interesting, for it could
mean that some of the billions of dollars that have
been sent in foreign and military aid to the Park government may have been funneled back into the country to buy influence with the American lawmakers.
Federal law requires that any person who brings more
than $5,000 in or out of the United States must report
the transaction to the Justice Department. Congressman Fraser's letter raises the question whether
Moon's associates hold the bank stock in their own
right or whether they are only nominal stockholders,
fronts for Moon's secret control of the bank. Columnist Jack Anderson was a member of the bank's
board of directors until he resigned when the controversy of Moon's connection with the bank became
obvious.

Moon himself does own nearly $80,000 worth of stock in the bank, a substantial investment for a man who supposedly owns nothing in his own name. It has also been reported that Moon helped the church make a mortgage payment to the Bronfman family on the Belvedere property with a personal check for $175,000.

In "The Eclipse of Sun Myung Moon," published in *New York* magazine, Chris Welles wrote, "In 1974 over a third of the MFT's (Mobile Fund-raising Teams) were organized as a specially selected group of 'Father's MFT's' that are said to channel money directly to Moon for his personal needs. . . . Moon is reported to have told a group of MFT leaders in 1973 that he had $13 million in his own bank account."

God or fraud? Only time will tell. Alan Tate Wood remembers a line from a Unification Church pamphlet published in Washington, D.C., in 1971. He told the congressional investigators about it. "Since a church is the safest and most recognized form of social organization, Mr. Moon founded the church in 1954 in order to have the greatest freedom of action."

COPING WITH
THE CRISIS

Your Child Is Involved . . .
Now What?

It would be comforting to think that tightly knit families with well-developed parent-child relationships could avoid what many parents view as the destructive effects of their sons' and daughters' involvement in religious cults. Unfortunately, it is not always so.

What does seem obvious is that for many families any kind of strong religious involvement on the part of their youngsters is cause for serious alarm. The further removed a new belief is from the religious home base, the more justified the parents feel in snatching the young person away from his new love. But it is just as true that a need to find God, group unity, and love can be stronger at times in everyone's life than the complex ties of even the closest family.

In these highly secular times, parents' stories of their children in religious cults are tales wracked by guilt and pain, indecision and doubt. Even those families who give approval to their children's spiritual lifestyle, and they are many, say they were at first doubtful about what they saw as a radical departure from what they would have chosen for their offspring. The way each family faces such a crisis de-

pends on how it coped with earlier family problems
and successes.

The makeup of each story is as different as the
weekly sermons heard around the world. And the
ways parents and their young arrive at their life-
altering decisions are as varied as religion itself. Almost everyone thinks his way is best. Here is how
one mother met the challenge. Not everyone could, or
would, do what Dee Dee Fischer did to get her son
Michael out of the Hare Krishnas. But then not
everyone is like Dee Dee Fischer, with her glamorous
style that blends somehow with her milkmaid skin
and figure.

Right now Dee Dee admits to being about 50
pounds overweight. Has she succumbed to the guilt
and self-denigration that even the slightly obese feel
in a society obsessed by the motto "You can't be
too rich or too thin"? Not on your life. From her
perch in a gorgeous penthouse apartment with a
view of Lake Michigan, Dee Dee confides that she
may one day lose her excess poundage, but in the
meantime, she's too busy to think about it and
she'll just wear caftans and other cover-ups. "You
can't do everything at once," she says, and admits
that she has too much to think about and work at to
spend her life depriving herself of something she
loves: food. As it is, Dee Dee and Charles Fischer
(a successful Chicago businessman and Michael's
stepfather) devote many hours of their busy lives to
counter-cult work.

Dee Dee Fischer's perception of life and mother-
hood has not come from any of today's popular formulas. She probably read Dr. Spock during a few mid-

night stomachache crises, but she is one of those
few individuals who has enough strength of character
and personality—along with vitality and charisma—
to make her own theories work. Dee Dee's strengths
have allowed her to formulate a unique and intelligent pattern for life. "My Way" could be Dee Dee's
theme song.

When the question of the Chicago area's Hare
Krishna temple's zoning variance was discussed by
the Evanston City Council Planning Committee, the
Fischers were there. Jerry Yanoff, a father with legal
custody of his twelve-year-old son who disappeared
into the Hare Krishna underground with his devotee
mother, spoke at the meeting, and Dee Dee and
Charles Fischer wanted to meet him and lend moral
support.

It is important to dwell on who and what Dee
Dee Fischer is because her special qualities are what
enabled her to get Michael, her only son, out of
what she viewed as the unhealthy clutches of the
Krishna religious cult. This mother of three is an
eccentric. But she is an individual who gets approval
from an intolerant society because of her unforget-
table style and because she makes her life work so
well. Dee Dee Fischer is nobody's victim.

Dee Dee spends hours on her telephone every
week, answering frantic parents' questions about
cult life, wondering whether they should sanction or
disapprove of their sons' and daughters' involvement or kidnap or rescue them. Frequently she simply offers her comfortably padded shoulders to cry
on. The Fischers get calls from all over the country.
Many hear of them from anti-cult parents' groups, or

from congressmen who tell worried individuals that
Mrs. Fischer seems to have a solid understanding of
the subject, or from any of the variety of near-
accidental ways that parents of cult members find
others who offer solace.

What most parents know when they call is that
Dee Dee did what they often want to do but don't
know how: She got her son Michael to leave the
Hare Krishnas on his own. After devoting months
of intense work trying to get him to "think for himself again," she succeeded in persuading him to walk
away from the International Society for Krishna Consciousness.

It has been three years now since Michael left
Krishna, and he completely approves of what his
mother did to get him out. Michael says the Hare
Krishna years are a period of his life he would prefer
neither to talk about nor to remember, though he
knows he'll never forget it. And so, this story is seen
through the eyes of his mother.

"Michael was the youngest Eagle Scout ever, in
Evanston, Illinois," says Dee Dee. She explains how
her competitive son always did well in school, had
lots of friends, played hard at sports, and, although
family finances didn't force him into it, worked as
hard as they'd let him at a variety of jobs. At seventeen, Michael got a Maritime Union worker's card and
used to hang out down on the docks, taking whatever
odd jobs came his way. He had always professed a
love for the sea (from his Midwestern lakeside view
of it), and his odd jobs led to a stewardship (a cov-
eted position) on several ocean-going cruises. By the
time Michael was twenty, he had not only earned

more than his share of honors in school and in life, but also seen the world.

Dee Dee now looks back and wonders if the death of her husband while Michael was still a teen didn't inflict on her son a compulsion to succeed. Since his father (the natural competitor) was no longer around to allay his son's fear of failure, Michael went on competing and working and trying to be everyone's idea of the perfect son. To his mother, without even trying, Michael was just that.

As a widow, Dee Dee was not financially strapped. The family stayed in their spacious Evanston home, in a community that takes pride in its typically middle-class mixture of intellectuals from Northwestern University's local campus, plus a cross section of fairly affluent families of all races and creeds. When they left the family home, it was to move to one of the most glamorous lake-front buildings in Chicago, where the rich and famous have their penthouses and multilevel apartments. Michael never wanted for material possessions. This family, even without a father, maintained a warmth that kept it, with the two daughters married and living away from home, and Michael in another city, still in close personal communication.

Sometime in his early twenties, after graduation from the University of Michigan, Michael began to experiment with drugs, in much the same way that many young men and women did in the late sixties. On an extended trip to London, Michael tried LSD. He began having mystical experiences and, he later told his mother, all the pieces in the puzzle of life began to fit together in a miraculous way. He had visions. But he also had an experience where all the problems didn't seem so easy to solve. In fact, they seemed insurmountable. Kids who experimented with psychedelics sometimes experienced great highs. Some thought they were supermen and leaped to their deaths from the tops of tall buildings. Michael's experience was the opposite. He went into extreme lows that took him into the depths of depression. He tried but could never communicate the full horror of this drug-induced nightmare to his mother. "My kids have always told me everything. There have been times when I wished they hadn't," says Dee Dee with a slight attempt at humor.

Sometime during this condensed and not unusual version of life in the late sixties, Michael ran into the Krishnas, who at that time were recruiting heavily among the young, affluent drug experimenters. Krishna literature of those years promised twenty-four-hour highs and genuine spiritual experience. "Stay high forever, no more coming down, practice Krishna Consciousness and end all bringdowns. Turn on through music, dance, philosophy, science, religion, and spiritual good." (Some parents of Krishna devotees still say the religious movement saved their youngsters' lives, but Dee Dee says that's nonsense. "All those kids who played with drugs are straight now. Some of them suffered, but the limits of Krishna are much worse," she says.)

And so Michael joined the International Society for Krishna Consciousness, obeyed the rules as he'd always done, shaved his head like a good Krishna devotee, and grew a *sika* (pony tail) that ultimately, according to Krishna, would be used to hoist him into heaven.

Dee Dee Fischer wanted her Michael to have his heaven on earth. You can imagine her consternation when Michael showed up in his peach-colored robes, clicking his prayer beads and ostentatiously chanting and meditating. Dee Dee wanted to be tolerant but says that more than anything else she wanted her son to live a full and happy life. She claims no one ever pushed Michael to conform to any specific ideal of success. She wanted him to make up his own mind as he always had. But she knew in her heart that Krishna was bad, bad, bad for her son.

The mother and son continued to call and write long letters to each other when Michael left to return to a Krishna temple in another city. Dee Dee bought all the Krishna reading materials the group so aggressively sells, read everything about the movement she could find, and began to lay the groundwork for getting Michael out.

She began by comparing the Hare Krishna movement founder Swami Prabhupada's translation of the Krishnas' bible, the Bhagavadgita, to other translations of the Hindu holy book. In the different translations of the ancient Vedic scriptures Dee Dee found differences she believes account for the life-limiting views that Prabhupada's Krishna devotees adopt. "The Bhagavadgita is a beautiful and very spiritual book," she still tells astonished parents of Krishna members who call to weep and wail. "You owe it to yourself and your child to look at it before you criticize it," she tells them gently. "They think it will bite them," she says as an aside.

Dee Dee listed what she saw as the discrepancies in the translations of the holy book. In one version a gentle view of life espouses some acceptance of life's disappointments. But Prabhupada's Krishna translation accepts none of life's compromises. Dee Dee carefully saved this and other information she could gather about Krishna, its leader, its aims, and its finances, all for the time when she could discuss them with Michael. Dee Dee envisioned some kind of life and death debate, where, if she won a logical argument with facts, Michael would be convinced to come home. Her idea was, in fact, not so far from the truth of what has become that mythologized encounter, the deprogramming.

Within a few months Michael wrote that he was settled in a new rural Krishna home, and so Dee Dee and one of her two daughters made a visit to New Vrindaban, the Krishna farm in West Virginia where Michael was living. Dee Dee and Michael's sister Linda walked several miles over nearly impassable dirt roads that led to the farm's enclave of ramshackle buildings. At this time Michael had been a Krishna devotee for several months. He had lost 40 pounds.

Michael told his mother of a mystical experience he had had, when he was standing alone in the woods and God appeared to him saying that his responsibility was to help the world, even if doing so cost him his life. Michael also told his mother that he had been handling snakes, and this so unnerved Dee Dee that she says she never even found out if they were the poisonous variety used to test faith in some fundamentalist Christian sects, or merely harmless garden snakes. Outwardly, Dee Dee kept her composure.

Michael had become so spiritually involved his mother found it difficult to carry on any conversation at all. They discussed mundane necessities such as food, clothing, and shelter, with Dee Dee trying subtly to emphasize man's need for each. Michael was subsisting on the strict vegetarian diet of the Krishnas, without even the fish or eggs that are usually included in similar diets, and Dee Dee thought he was starving himself. "I told him I thought he had an incredible need for perfection that had served him well in his life outside, but was now being perverted into fanaticism. 'You're still trying to be the youngest Eagle Scout in Evanston, only this time you're doing it for much higher stakes. I think you're trying to give your life here. Krishna is not giving you peace. It isn't working for you.' "

Although Michael's mother found her son's new-found spirituality somewhat dismaying, she says she attempted to talk to him on his own terms. If he wanted to discuss God, the way God influences human behavior, and God's role in life's meaning, then that was what they discussed. The way she explains it now, she would have preferred talking about something else, but if this was Michael's sole passionate interest, then that was what they would share. Dee Dee and Michael talked, at length, about God and His ways. She did not laugh at his beliefs, or do anything but gently question his new direction in life. Then it was time to leave.

A weaker person might have gone home in tears and taken to bed or to drink or to hysterics. Dee Dee says she left New Vrindaban knowing there was nothing she could do at the time but promising to work harder until her chance came again.

A few months later Michael moved into the

Krishna temple in Brooklyn. He now had a full-time job as part of the Krishna public relations team, making photographs and printing them for both the organization's magazine and a documentary film. Dee Dee was heartened, thinking that being part of what she calls "the yeast of life," in one of New York's most lively urban neighborhoods, would help Michael see what he was missing. That isn't exactly what happened, though in another sense the location had a decisive impact on his ultimate "salvation."

Her own state of mind, in an ironic way, contributed to the outcome of the story. With a bad cold and a high temperature, Dee Dee would not allow her visit to the Brooklyn temple to be cancelled, but she was feeling weak, a far-from-normal state of affairs for this platinum-blond whiz-kid grandmother.

It was in Brooklyn that Dee Dee got what she calls the biggest shock of her life. Her strapping six-foot son had shrunk to an emaciated 110 pounds with blue fingernails and a gaunt, nearly unrecognizable face, with every vein standing out on his shaven head. They spent the day together in the darkroom of the film studio Michael had constructed in the temple's sub-basement. The light was poor; Michael had jury-rigged wiring for his equipment; there was a strong odor of chemicals (like sniffing glue, she said). Dee Dee looked upon the job, with its regular chores and specific goals, as an advance for Michael. At least he wasn't meditating all day and playing with snakes and pondering the imponderables. But in view of his physical condition, she became desperate to get him back home.

The physical surroundings of Michael's work space

did not please this daughter of comfort, and Dee Dee was very depressed when she left the temple at mid-afternoon. Since she wasn't feeling well herself, she found a doctor who gave her cold tablets. When Dee Dee described her son's condition, the doctor confirmed her suspicion that Michael was probably suffering malnutrition.

Dee Dee went back to the nearest hotel she had been able to find and prepared for a long, bleak evening and night. Dee Dee is convinced that the hotel she stumbled into was known in the neighborhood for two-hour room rentals rather than the more commonplace overnight stays. Her feelings of disorientation led Dee Dee into one of the worst nights of her life. She thought she heard people screaming in the rooms down the hall and spent the night praying and crying, crying and praying for Michael, for herself, and probably for the world at large.

The next morning, Dee Dee woke up feeling physically sick and emotionally depressed. She began to walk aimlessly in the Brooklyn neighborhood. A light mist soaked and chilled her, but she kept walking and thinking, sometimes losing control and crying, knowing that others on the crowded urban sidewalks thought she was some kind of nut. "Which I probably was," Dee Dee now says, laughing.

Then something happened. Dee Dee, who is Jewish and deeply spiritual but only nominally religious, tells the story haltingly with more than a slight twinge of self-consciousness. She remembered it was the beginning of Passover, the annual commemoration of the time the Angel of Death spared the firstborn of the Jews. "The feeling came over me that my own

Michael would be saved, and God would help me to do it." She says a sense of peace overwhelmed her. She returned to her hotel room, changed into dry clothes, ate breakfast, and felt much better.

On her walk to the Krishna temple to visit her son, Dee Dee passed a fire station. "Something propelled me into that building, and I began to tell a fireman of the horrible living conditions in the Krishna temple." He listened politely, but Dee Dee thought he wasn't too interested.

She spent that day with Michael, trying to persuade him to enter a hospital. He wasn't entirely convinced, but seemed to waver in his determination to chant and pray away his poor health.

That night, Dee Dee slept soundly and awoke refreshed, prepared to return to the temple and persuade the temple president that they must hospitalize her son. To her astonishment, when Dee Dee arrived at the temple, the president didn't let her get in a single word. "Take him," said the president, "just get out of here." Amazed, Dee Dee listened to his account of a visit by the local fire inspectors, building inspectors, and zoning examiners. "What you've done will cost us thousands of hard-won Krishna dollars," he told her through clenched teeth. "Take your son, and please don't ever come back."

Dee Dee's spontaneous visit to the neighborhood fire station had accomplished more than she might have hoped. An inspection of the temple turned up fire hazards so severe the inspectors threatened to close it down if immediate safety provisions were not made. And Dee Dee got her son back—for a while.

She had her son, but also the problem of finding

space on a flight from New York to Chicago, since the season of Passover falls close to Easter. After waiting as stand-by passengers at Kennedy Airport they got the last two seats on an evening flight home. Since there had been no time to order a vegetarian meal for Michael, Dee Dee conferred privately with the stewardess, who plied Michael with all the untouched, leftover desserts from other passengers' trays. He ate them with undisguised glee.

Back in Chicago, Michael was immediately hospitalized. He was fed intravenously while his family hoped he would gain both weight and emotional equilibrium. His mother and sister spent hours of every day with him, mostly just chatting, but also trying to reassure him that he would get well and that everything would turn out all right, whatever all right was to each of them. They purposely did not question his religious beliefs, although they discussed them, and he continued to chant and meditate, causing concern and amusement along the quiet hospital corridor. "Let them laugh," Dee Dee said. "I felt we were fighting for his life and didn't give a damn what anyone thought. I refused to let anyone else's expectations dictate what I should do, and I didn't feel it was time to question his Hare Krishna beliefs and practices."

Then it was time for Michael to come home from the hospital. He was almost well. Dee Dee says she continued her moral support of Michael while she began to analyze his Krishna beliefs and encourage him to think about them. The two compared translations of the Bhagavadgita and discussed how the Krishna version was always the life-limiting one.

They talked about man's right to fulfillment, happiness, and challenge, both inside and outside of religion. What, they pondered, would be Michael's path to a satisfying life? What conditions would comprise happiness for him? She feels now that the family, working together with some visits from outsiders—a psychiatrist, a Roman Catholic priest friend, and a theologian—did the equivalent of what formal deprogrammers do, but at the same time allowed Michael gradually to return to reality, something Dee Dee felt was necessary. Everyone thought Michael was home for good.

Six weeks later, he reminded his mother of her promise to let him do whatever he wanted when he recovered his health. Michael had made his decision. He was going to return to Krishna.

"I thought it was the end of the world. I had tried my hardest to bring him around, and I had failed." With a lump in her throat, she stuck to the bargain, packed two grocery bags full of food and canned goods, gave Michael $50, and kissed him goodbye.

For two days Dee Dee did nothing. On the third day she resumed her work. She called the West Coast head of the United States Immigration Service to question Michael's use of his passport. She was concerned he would disappear into the vast population of India. Dee Dee called the FBI and the CIA, her state and national senators and the mayor. She talked to everyone in power who would listen, to convince them of the danger of religious cults, their recruiting techniques, and the Krishna conviction of being above our laws. She wrote a moving letter to Indira Gandhi, asking her why Swami Prabhupada was preying on American youth and asking if, in this other mother's opinion, he was sincere. She talked to the Indian consul, who would only counsel patience. Dee Dee says it was about this time that she learned a valuable lesson. "Bureaucracies are made up of individuals who will listen and work for you if they can."

Dee Dee then began to sense a growing disenchantment in Michael's attitude toward Krishna. She swears it was nothing he said or did. Dee Dee now says it was a mother's instinct, but she thought that Michael just might need some excuse to leave this group that had such a strong psychological hold on him. Dee Dee's feeling is echoed in the stories of other parents, deprogrammers, and psychologists, who say that with many young cult members there seems to be an almost desperate cry for help. Many former cultists confess feeling unable to leave groups on their own but recall wanting to be "rescued."

Michael's mother tried one more course of action. She blushes when she tells the story; the flush spreads as she almost whispers the secret. During a visit to Los Angeles, Dee Dee Fischer told her son that if he would not come home she would kill A. C. Bhaktivedanta, Swami Prabhupada. Michael came home. His stepfather, Charles Fischer, an engaging, irascible man who combines an interest in Eastern philosophy with an avidly right-wing form of intellectualism (an odd combination even in a world of eccentrics), now helped Dee Dee persuade Michael that a life of personal choice, available only outside the restrictive Krishna Consciousness group, was the world he deserved.

Michael has been away from Krishna for three years. He thinks of the experience as an extended nightmare and is sorry he lost those years he now considers a waste of valuable time and energy. Michael's passport, which Dee Dee managed to have revoked so he couldn't disappear into India's vast sea of humanity, was returned to him. The Fischers received a warm letter of concern from Indira Gandhi that is a family treasure.

After Michael had been home for a few months, he asked his mother the inevitable question. Would she really have killed Prabhupada?

"No," says Dee Dee mischievously. "I wouldn't have. I just would have smashed a few deities."

There are those who will say that for every rich, glamorous, and forceful parent like Dee Dee Fischer there are many more average, ordinary "just plain folks." Yet we found that the average American parent is as much a myth as the "average American family," with its 2.1 children and Archie Bunker ways. In every suburb and city, wherever we looked, we found no such stereotype. It is not that those we got to know were abnormal or wacky or crazy or any of the words that seem to mean the opposite of regular or normal. It's just that no family is really average.

Each has its own story and has developed its ways of interacting and making decisions and getting things done. We saw families where powerful fathers and weak mothers had raised strong sons and daughters. We saw assertive women and equally strong men whose offspring seemed to inherit none of their strength. There was intense feeling, even passion, in the coolest of families. Some strong parents were the least able to accept what had happened to their cult member children, or do anything about it. We saw gut-level fear and an equal amount of near-panic and indecision. We saw intellectual malaise and bewilderment, and we saw loving acceptance toward sons and daughters in their new religious lives.

We saw some parents guided by raw instinct and little knowledge who were able to take more direct and positive action than some of their more cautious, thoughtful counterparts. But not always. We saw equal numbers of reflective parents who moved just as fast as those who never stopped to think.

What we discovered shouldn't come as a surprise to anyone. It should be no shock to find that a nation that has developed pride in individuality to a fault is populated with individuals. In interviews with hundreds of families, we had no trouble seeing the differences.

We saw some as caricatures. Some were as funny as they were sad. One set of parents told us repeatedly how much their son and daughter loved one another. At first meeting it was obvious to us that their sensitive intellectual son was embarrassed by his gum-chewing, seductive sister. The two seemed to share more spite than love for one another, but the parents labor on in their delusion.

Some families broke down in our presence. One father verbally attacked his Moonie daughter, saying, "I've worked so hard to give you everything."

His daughter replied, "You did it because that's what you wanted to do. It was easier to pay our bills than pay attention to us."

In some middle class homes the children were treated as unwelcome guests. The furniture was either covered with plastic slipcovers or off limits, and cleanliness was a fetish. We saw, too, many comfortable, inviting homes, not all as posh or expensive as Dee Dee Fischer's eclectic penthouse with its contemporary furnishings, antiques, and huge pillows spread around the floor for lounging. But in the finest or the most conventional neighborhoods we saw homes where everyone, including outsiders, was made to feel welcome.

We also witnessed sadly misplaced energies. One mother cried bitterly while telling how she fought to control her emotions and hide her tears during the deprogramming of her daughter from the Unification Church. Now she weeps because she sees the deprogramming as a failure. Her daughter has returned to the Moonies, and the family has not seen her for more than a year. We feel her emotion was wasted and regret that she didn't spend it on her daughter, honestly confronting her with her pain and maternal love. This mother, outwardly the epitome of self-control, gave her daughter "good reasons" why she wanted her to leave the cult, "to teach or do something respectable." But never did she communicate to this child of hers how desperately she wished for her to have a whole life and how much she loves her. When this young woman scorned her mother, charging that the deprogrammer she had hired was not a social equal and "wasn't even educated," we sensed that the daughter had inherited some of her mother's highly visible snobbery.

"I wish I could fight like those Jewish mothers,"

said this Protestant physician's wife, "but I can't bring myself to do it."

The Reverend Kent Burtner, O.P., a thoughtful Catholic priest in Oregon, told us the story of a Lutheran family he counseled. The young Moonie daughter and her parents, an alcoholic father and a neurotic mother who had both given up on their own lives, came together with the priest for a deprogramming or series of talks. During one early discussion Father Burtner asked the young woman why she thought of the Reverend Moon and his wife as her true parents. Her response, a screamed indictment of her natural parents, so jolted everyone that the father promised to stop drinking (and has) and the young woman and her mother promised to be more open and accepting of one another. Father Burtner says that when the parents were able to see themselves through the eyes of their daughter it was the beginning of a healing process for the whole family.

We visited some families who were so wracked with guilt, fear, and bitterness that we wished we had brought along marriage counselors and psychiatrists. But these families were the exceptions. Most of the parents we saw were trying to do the right thing, struggling to keep their families intact. They were honestly attempting to assess if what their children had found was salvation, as they claim, or slavery, as the cult critics claim, or something in between. These parents were humble as they questioned their own abilities to raise moral, aware youngsters who were properly trained to make their own decisions. These families were the rule.

Unfortunately, there is no magic formula for making a family complete and whole. There was no single correct method for childrearing during those important formative years before a child became a follower of any of the hundreds of exploitative gurus who solicit followers around the world, and there are no absolute rules to guide them through these crises of postadolescence.

But one pattern emerges. Honest parents with strong value systems (who may not dwell on or think of either very consciously), who are willing to work hard to do what they believe is right, people who can honestly face their emotions and their instincts and each other, and are not afraid to confront their children, stand the greatest chance of having their families survive intact. It almost seems too simplistic, too moralistic, too judgmental to say. But it is what we have seen.

One of the easiest ways for parents to recognize signs of cult membership is also one of the most obvious. Telephone calls and letters home from a cult member will be very changed, for in many cases young cult members don't know how to explain what has happened to them and rely on group leaders or other members to help them compose letters and conversations. We've heard parents tell of telephone conversations when they were certain their child's conversation was being dictated by someone standing nearby. They heard whispered consultations and sensed the cautious choice of words. And they noted that sons and daughters were willing to give only partial answers to questions. Former cult members confirm these suspicions, telling of leaders who stood by for "moral support" while they phoned their parents and who also helped compose letters home that told about their new lives in the vaguest of terms.

But parents must also face the problem as it is seen by their youngsters. Since most religious cult members were raised in families where once-a-week religious services or semiannual religious involvement are the rule, the newly converted youngsters guess their parents will panic at the mention of a life centered around God or a special set of God-centered values. Sitting in a park after a recent rally, some young Unification Church members (who called themselves Moonies with a twist of ironic humor), told bitterly how their families hate and fear their smiles. But these Moonies said they have found peace and that God has helped them achieve an inner tranquillity that makes it easier for them to smile now than it ever was in their lives "outside." They said they were afraid at first to tell parents of their new lives because they knew they wouldn't understand and would condemn them simply because they were different.

While some young cultists claim to have found a direct line to God in the form of some self-proclaimed messiah who heads a group, others tell their parents they are part of a life system dedicated to "world peace" or "inner tranquillity" or other idealistic goals.

Some parents have their suspicions diverted, for though they are already aware of the Reverend Sun Myung Moon's Unification Church, they have never heard of the Creative Community Project, the Committee for Responsible Dialogue, the Collegiate Association for Research of Principles, the International

New Ideal City Ranch, or any of the other scores of aliases the Unification Church uses to confuse the public. And the Unification Church is not alone in deception. Many of the new religious cults, aware of their poor images, frequently use aliases and names that sound similar to mainline religious groups.

But whatever the religious group's title, Dr. John G. Clark, Jr., a suburban Boston psychiatrist who has been working with ex-cult members and their families for several years, says the manner of speaking and writing often changes. In a recent speech on cult life before a committee of the Vermont legislature he said, "Formerly bright, fluent, and creative individuals are rendered incapable of the use of irony or of metaphor, and they speak with a smaller, carefully constructed vocabulary filled with clichés and stereotyped ideas."

Dr. Clark goes on to say that the richness of language parents once heard their children use totally disappears in cult members, and in its place is a narrowing of thought processes that results in a terrifying and sudden change in the style of language.

Dr. Clark contends there are two distinct groups of people in the religious cults. The first group is made up of chronic schizophrenic borderline personalities whose problems get them involved. He believes that sick minds gravitate to the new religions, but he condemns his colleagues in the mental health field for frequently considering such instability the only cause of cult membership.

Dr. Clark's second group is made up of normal, developing young people who were going through the "usual crises of development on the way to becoming

adults and who had fallen into a trap laid by the cults
and had been taken in." The strength of these young
people—their adaptability—is now part of the problem, since they are so receptive to the "psychic, social
and psychological processes" used to recruit and keep
them in the cults.

We observed a variety of highly entertaining and
creative letters written by young people to their parents before they met the cults. In later correspondence
from the same young people, many of those who had
written the most amusing, ironic, and questioning letters, often with drawings, cartoons, and sketches,
wrote robotlike brief notes full of clichés.

Those in the first group, according to Dr. Clark,
the young people with serious emotional problems,
often write letters that change very little from the
style of their precult days. If they seemed confused
before, now they are dogmatic and rigid. But, of
course, it is impossible to divide people into two
groups. The line between sick and healthy, between
neurotic and psychotic is a fuzzy line that people
rarely agree on. Although the most emotionally unhealthy may reveal obvious scars of illness, others
simply do not. A careful examination of correspondence is not a foolproof way to know just what kids
are up to.

Communication is, of course, the only way humans
have of keeping in touch with each other. Some families have perfected the art, while others have never
learned to talk to one another with any kind of honesty. Communication difficulties may be further complicated by the normal problems of adolescence, but
they are often more muddled by distance. These days

it is not unusual for young people in their late teens
and early twenties to be away from home, and not
always in college or on a job in a specific location.

Group odysseys in vans or campers have become
commonplace among young people who want a better
look at the world. Many young men and a few young
women hitchhike around the country, looking for adventure as they travel. But if family ties are reason-
ably close (as we have found they are in most families of cult members), these wanderers usually check
in with parents by frequent collect phone calls. Some
parents insist that their children call home at least
once or twice a week. So when there are long periods
of silence and they don't know how to get in touch
with their young, parents often become frantic. They
start calling the parents of the fellow travelers and
usually, but not always, track errant sons and daughters down to some particular location.

Here again, parents tell stories that are merely variations on the same theme: "I finally found out he
was in a commune in San Francisco (or Boston or
Minneapolis or New York), but whenever I called
they told me he was out. No one could tell me exactly what he was doing, so I left messages to have
him call home as soon as possible."

All the former members of religious cults we know
have told us how they were cautioned to avoid problems with parents who might not understand their
new religiosity.

That telephone call often alerts parents to potential problems. Here is a typical call:

MOTHER: Tell me what this group you are living
with does.

DAUGHTER: Oh, we live together like a family and are trying to show the world how love can improve things, and we are very idealistic and we live in harmony. . . .

MOTHER: Yes, but what do you do?

DAUGHTER: Well, we study and are learning about world unity and why everyone is so unhappy and how to avoid conflict and we live together in harmony. . . .

MOTHER: Yes, well that sounds very . . . harmonious. But what do you do when you are out all day?

(Here the responses may vary. The young person may wonder whether to tell her mother she is out fund-raising because it might "freak Mom out," so maybe she'll tell her mother she's doing volunteer work, or some story that will calm her mother's obviously mounting suspicions.)

DAUGHTER: Oh, you know, I do some work for the house, like getting others to come and live here and telling people what we hope to accomplish. . . .

When it begins to sound like one of those cosmetic pyramid sales schemes where selling lipstick is secondary to selling franchises, most parents decide to press for more information. They may find, as hundreds of parents have, in the case of the Unification Church, that there are no volunteer programs. The young Moonies often claim, in their street-corner soliciting, that they work with the aged, the retarded, or drug addicts, when, in fact, they do not.

The only volunteer work Moonies do for society is done for public relations value, as it was when they dressed up in Unification jump suits and swept the streets of New York for a few days before their rally there in the spring of 1976. The real work of this group is street-corner sales of flowers or candy or candles, and bringing in new members through witnessing.

At this point there are several options, each aimed at gathering information about their child's new group.

Parents can visit, if the new home is nearby or if they can afford a trip to wherever the youngster is. There's no substitute for a careful analysis based on eye-to-eye contact with group members. During this stage, it is important to remember that this may not be a religious cult in any pejorative sense, but an honest attempt at communal living, a legitimate exercise in idealism where young people continue to grow and mature in a familial setting away from home.

A concerned individual can get in touch with one of the counter-cult parents' groups. Most of the men and women who volunteer their time to these groups have themselves had youngsters involved in one of the religious cults. They have files filled with information, heads filled with facts, and lots of sympathy for whatever parents or a brother, sister, or friend are feeling. Among the specific information they have is a list of the aliases used by cults to avoid accountability, legal difficulties, and loss of tax exemption. (Remember: legitimate, mainstream religions do not need or use aliases.)

But here again we urge caution. Some parents in the anticult groups are as much victims of "group-think" as they claim their sons and daughters are.

Some groups will urge instant deprogramming before parents have even determined if their child is indeed in a cult. In many cases, parents who do not want to deprogram their sons or daughters, even though they view the religious cult as a negative influence, say the parents in these counter-cult groups seem to prefer that they lose their children if they don't take the group's advice. This, of course, is not always true, but it is wise to sift and weigh all advice and information through one's own common sense and an uncluttered view of what is best for the young person and the family.

In addition to the new religions we concentrate on or mention in this book, there are hundreds more spread around the world. Some are less insidious than others. Some are, in fact, harmless, even positive, social forces.

Dr. Clark has put together his own brief checklist of qualities to look for in determining whether a group is, in fact, what we are calling, in the most destructive sense, a cult. He says:

1. All the groups have living leaders who are demonstrably wealthy.

2. Their systems of governance are totalitarian.

3. The beliefs of all these cults are absolutist and intolerant of other belief systems.

4. A cult's interest is very low or nonexistent in encouraging individual development toward some kind of satisfactory individual adult personality.

5. Almost all of the cults emphasize money-making in one form or another, but a few concentrate

very much on demeaning or self-denigrating activities or rituals.

Another common denominator in the cults, in addition to continued amassing of real estate holdings and funds which are controlled by the cult leader, is the presence of a leader who claims for himself special powers or allows himself to be thought of as a messiah who will bring peace and love to a world which needs both.

A parent may have determined that his child is inextricably involved with such a religious cult and may suspect that the involvement is not healthy, but is still not sure.

Many parents tell how during this stage of confusion they sought advice from a variety of experts. It is hardly surprising that, in our world of specialization, each authority sees the religious cult through the microscope of his own experience. Everyone has to have his say, and not all the advice given is either helpful or positive. Beware of accepting too narrow a view of the cult experience, for this view alone will not provide all the comfort, solace, or answers to the search for whatever action is in the best interest of a child and family.

The following is a list of opinions generally offered by these experts:

—*The moralistic cynics,* and there are a good number of them around in these disillusioned times, will say that this self-centered generation is getting no more than it deserves. It is, in fact, the individual's unrealistic ideals that have, say the cynics, created the small worlds of nonchoice where "Boy Scout" solutions and total lack of conflict surround spoiled middle class youngsters in cocoonlike warmth. "He's getting what's coming to him," goes this line of reasoning. Read Eric Hoffer's *The True Believer* for a variation on this theme.

—*Lawyers* will probably want to know if any laws have been broken by the group the young person has discovered, whether property has been confiscated by the cult leaders, or whether the young person is being held against his will. Their questions are pertinent.

—*Psychiatrists,* on the other hand, generally view religious cult membership either in terms of thought disorder or as part of the normal transition between adolescence and maturity. They may explain how group pressures compel young members to conform and adapt themselves so readily to religious beliefs they barely understand.

—*Social scientists* who study these groups see highly structured societies where human interchange is as ritualized as it is in the meetings of Freemasons, and where group action supersedes individual thought. Neither are they wrong.

—Many *clergymen* will agree that there's some truth in all of these opinions but see the main problem as one of returning a prodigal member of the flock to the front-row pew of their own church or temple. After all, they reason, "God is on our side," and not with some self-proclaimed savior.

—The *religious historian* or *theologian,* who sees the cults as mere examples of the cyclical and inevitable resurgence of gnostic, heretical splits from

mainstream religions, can be even more confusing.
This scholar will talk of gaining an historical perspective on the sudden arrival of a multitude of messiahs and look back to three decades in the nineteenth century when the Rosicrucians, Theosophists,
Shakers, and Mormons were the Johnny-come-lately
religions. And while a thirty-year period may look
like a brief time in the pages of a history book, it
looks more like a wasted lifetime to a distraught
parent with a child in one of today's religious cults.

While none of these traditional experts may have
a total picture of religious cults, their opinions are
valid. The family lawyer, for example, may be able
to help if parents decide to remove their sons or
daughters from the group by legal means. A clergyman may be able to help if the cult member professes
a strong spiritual need when he returns. The whole
family may benefit from the attentions of a psychiatrist or family counselor when the going gets tough,
or when the family is back together again and having
a difficult time.

The social scientists and theologians may write
books for each other that may someday be read with
a grateful sense of déjà vu, so nothing learned in an
investigation will be a total waste. But few of these
experts will have the same interest in the subject that
parents have: their own sons or daughters. What any
concerned individual needs is enough information so
that he or she may decide what to do.

There are many avenues open to parents of cult
members. Some families consecutively pursue several
different courses of action as they change their minds,

or gather more information and see things differently, or simply as the situation changes. Here are some of those choices:

—There is *the rescue* (kidnap and snatch, as it is sometimes called) and deprogramming, a debriefing session where the young cultist listens to information he has often not had the chance to hear. Most of this information is carefully gathered and organized by the deprogrammer and his assistants in opposition to cult involvement. Those who favor deprogrammings say that only in this way can young people be returned to personal choice and freedom of thought.

—*Legal removal* of a young person from a cult is often accomplished by a court order remanding a young person (whether legally a child or an adult) to the custody of his parents. This is usually carried out in conjunction with a formal deprogramming.

—*The bargain,* or contract, between parent and child. Here, a parent might say to the child, "If you plan to spend the rest of your life in this group, you owe us one week (or month or any reasonable period of time) to hear our side of the story and to discuss the other side of your story." Then an informal, though well-organized series of talks with authorities on cults and former members might take place.

—*Wait and work.* Some parents feel it unscrupulous to remove a child from the cult without his consent, but at the same time they are opposed to their child's commitment to the new religion and so they work at accumulating information about the religious cult. There is a danger here that positions will become polarized and communication will be impossible. But if parents attempt to listen and ask non-threatening questions, and adopt a neutral or low-key attitude, there may be the possibility of instituting a nonthreatening reevaluation (informal deprogramming) or deprogramming without losing contact with a son or daughter.

—*Wait and hope for the best.* Like the proverbial ostrich with his head stuck firmly in the sand, some parents wait and do nothing, hoping that a son or daughter will "come to his senses" and leave the group on his own. One mother tells of spending a year drinking and praying. With her subsequent feeling of loss of control over both her own and her son's life, it's not surprising that she now considers that year a waste of time. She has since had her son legally removed and deprogrammed from the Church of Armageddon, the Love Israel Family, in Seattle.

—*Conditional approval.* There are parents who, in fact, condone a son's or daughter's cult membership because it has ended a pattern of drug experimentation, brushes with the law, constant psychiatric care, institutionalization, or just general aimlessness. This is a parent who may say, "He's better off there than he was on drugs," or "He's never been so self-confident."

—*Complete approval.* There are many parents who think being a member of the Unification Church, or the Children of God, or any other religious cult is a constructive way of life. One set of parents, the Dwayne Blacks of northern California, attended a Creative Community Project meeting and said they were amazed at how different and clean the young

Unification Church members look within weeks of their "conversions." Mrs. Black told us that church members' attitudes are so much improved, their general demeanor so much more wholesome than before, that she and her husband fully approve of son Dwight's involvement and do not understand other parents' negative attitudes.

Getting Out

Adults may develop thick skins and cavalier attitudes toward the realities of their own lives. But when it comes to the lives of their children, most are as mawkishly sentimental and blindly optimistic as *Gone with the Wind's* Rhett Butler was with his Baby Bonnie. When the buoyant optimism of youth fades from the adult psyche, an individual's hopes are often channeled into the closest avenue of immortality: the lives of sons and daughters. As in a final effort at vicarious fulfillment, mothers and fathers want nothing but the best for their children. They again become hopeful, not for themselves but for their young.

And so, when they watch a child's chances for success diminish because of membership in a religious cult, it is not surprising that many parents panic. As they see the plans they've made for their child buried in incomprehensible Bhagavadgitas and Divine Principles, see the funds they've saved for a college education spent on courses that seem to lead nowhere, or see a child's life being spent in service to a dubious godhead, even strong parents can be moved to the brink of hopelessness.

The hope that educations and careers will provide the affluence parents have worked hard to achieve or, more important, the chance to live lives of free choice seems to fade for their cultist children.

Yet it may be true that surprise is our only teacher. Most parents are surprised, shocked, and bewildered when facing this situation. Still, some families are not only durable enough to survive a cult ordeal but manage to come through it with strengthened bonds of love and affection.

It may be a sign of deathless parental optimism, or perhaps it's only confusion, but at first many parents refuse to admit that a child's cult membership could be the most complex problem they have yet had to face in parenthood. Later, as basic questions go unanswered and as they analyze the content of evasive letters and telephone conversations, they may come to realize that a son's or daughter's commitment to a religious cult and its belief system is a more formidable adversary than they had expected.

Parents who've known a close and caring relationship with a child go through several emotional stages. We have seen expressions of these attitudes again and again, often in this order: shock, confusion, anger and guilt, and helplessness.

Shock: How can this be happening in my family? Can it last forever? Or is it temporary? If the family is not a religious one, the question might be "How can he find satisfaction in a religious life?" But underriding all the questions during the stage of shock is the one every parent seems to ask again and again, "How can this disaster have befallen us?"

Confusion: After the first stage of shock has worn off (for generations parents have proven that they can get used to almost anything, after all), the befuddlement sets in. "Why will she tell us nothing more about this group than the vague generalizations about love and changing the world? Is it really a religion? If so, how does it differ from mainstream faiths? Why is there so little information that I can understand, read, or study? How does this movement attract so many young disciples?"

Anger and guilt: If the parent of a cult member is able to get information and to see what the group is attempting to accomplish, anger may mix with guilt in the next stage of response. A heavy shadow of questionable financial and political goals hangs over many of the new religions, and parents often have access to information about the cults that their cult-member offspring never have a chance to see or hear. And so they became angry at the cult itself. Often the anger is edged with guilt. "Where did we go wrong?" parents may ask. "How could our nearly grown child fall for this kind of stuff?"

If parents get together with other families of cult members at this stage they may be able to assuage their own guilt by seeing they are not alone. Some parents want to lay all the blame on the cult. They may accept the theory that brainwashing has tricked their son or daughter into accepting a new lifestyle so that they can ease the pain of their own feelings of failure.

Techniques of social coercion and thought control do figure in the recruiting and indoctrination practices of many of the new religions, but in order to

assess the situation rationally, it is wise to keep in
mind what many religious figures tell us, "There is a
time in everyone's life when his values, his ideas,
and the foundation of his life are up for grabs."
Brainwashing, or not, some young people will join
any group that promises structure, love, and some
definite answers.

Rabbi Shlomo Schwartz works in campus ministry
as leader of Chabad House at U.C.L.A., one of a
group of revivalist Jewish ministries that preach and
practice fundamental Judaism. The rabbi is a blunt
realist who claims, "If we get them first, they're ours
for life. But if the Jews for Jesus or the Hare Krishnas or the Moonies get them, then they're theirs."

Rabbi Schwartz encourages parents to reassess the
values they have offered their children. He says that
while parents should not feel overwhelmingly guilty,
they do have a responsibility to examine the quality
of the life a young person left behind. Rabbi Schwartz
believes everyone has a need for strong religion-
based moral values, and few have been given them
in religious homes, he says.

While anger can be a powerful motivator, it can
also be a destructive force that could ultimately result in complete severance of ties between parents
and their sons and daughters. During the stage when
parents are most angry toward the new religious
group, some panic and plunge headlong into deprogramming plans that can very easily fail.

Helplessness: This is what happens to parents
who have not heard from a son or daughter for
months, even years, because their antagonism further damaged what was left of a fragile parent-

child bond, or because they rushed into a deprogramming that somehow failed. Helplessness breeds hopelessness. If parents fully understand the scope of the problem, if they are willing to work very hard and to face the situation with honesty and understanding, this stage may be avoidable.

The Reverend Kent Burtner, O.P., is assistant director of campus ministry at the University of Oregon in Eugene. Father Kent, as he prefers to be called, switched from counter-cult theorist to counter-cult activist when faced with a request to deprogram the daughter of a Lutheran family who sought his help.

After an article quoting him appeared in a Roman Catholic diocesan newspaper and was picked up by a national wire service, the priest was flooded with requests for information and help. "I tell parents to do four things," he says.

—"Try to learn where your kids' heads are so you can understand how they got involved. What are the problems in their lives, what are their needs and vulnerabilities?" Father Kent suggests that parents save all letters and keep the lines of communication open. "Try not to be negative, but tolerant and neutral," he cautions. "Don't set up a polarity that can't be breached. Keep all the literature cult members send home, gather information on the subject.

—"Keep a diary of your own thoughts and feelings." The priest explains that this puts parents in touch with their children and their own feelings, a process that will be very necessary, no matter what the parents decide to do about their son's or daughter's new life.

—"Get in touch with the parents of other cult members." Father Burtner reasons, "When you can see you are not alone, it alleviates some of the guilt.

—"Examine deprogramming as one option."

Deprogramming. The once unknown word has assumed mythical proportions. Some parents are convinced that it offers the only possible salvation for a cult member. Each deprogramming story is different, but the technique can be defined as a process in which a person is forced to question his beliefs by someone opposed to them, and to examine the process of conversion which led to the adoption of the religion and its practices. A deprogramming is a confrontation of opposing viewpoints. Those who favor the process say it "returns a person to his free mind and allows him to make decisions for himself." Once a parent has decided a son or daughter is better off away from his new life, deprogramming becomes one of the few clearly defined ways to set about accomplishing a permanent break with a cult.

"Deprogramming is the bottom line, the only foolproof way to help a young person see how he was duped into a religious cult," Neil Maxwell, stepfather of a longtime Unification Church member, tells us. Mr. Maxwell says the deprogramming he helped to organize and witnessed was a gentle process and that everyone involved grew through the experience. And, most important, he and his wife "saw her daughter return to life. We owed it to her to do it." The young woman approves also, saying she would

probably never have left the church if she hadn't
seen and heard the information presented to her by
deprogrammer Joe Alexander during their sessions
together.

There are others, however, who call deprogramming unjustified and indefensible. These parents find
those who resort to "reverse brainwashing"—as deprogramming has been called by its detractors—just
as evil as the similar techniques used by the cult to
recruit the young. "Holding a person against his will
and subjecting him to a highly emotional intellectual
battering is wrong, no matter who does it," they say.
The end never justifies the means, say these civil
libertarians.

But if the term deprogramming conjures any image in the mind of the general public it is a controversial one, due in no small measure to the style of
the forced, locked-door deprogrammings Ted Patrick
writes about in his book *Let Our Children Go.* "I
firmly believe the Lord helps those who help themselves, and a few little things like karate, mace, and
handcuffs come in handy from time to time," he
writes. Judging from the stories of many young people he has successfully deprogrammed, Patrick seldom uses any of these props. But their presence lurk-
ing nearby, if out of sight, does contribute to an
atmosphere of potential violence and illegality.

Even without violence, deprogramming has come
to mean an involuntary confrontation of opposing
viewpoints, carried out behind locked doors and
bolted windows. Patrick and the other deprogrammers claim that when they force a cult member to
listen to opposing views they can change a subject's

mind about a cult in a few days. Many deprogrammings take only a few hours, others one or two full days; some have lasted nearly two weeks.

Sylvia Buford is one of those who was successfully talked out of cult membership by Ted Patrick. Her deprogramming took place at a round table discussion in her parents' family room. Later Sylvia traveled and assisted Patrick in deprogrammings. She outlines some of the elements of the technique:

—Discredit the figure of authority: the cult leader.

—Present contradictions (ideology vs. reality): "How can he preach love when he exploits people?" is an example.

—The breaking point: When a subject begins to listen to the deprogrammer; when reality begins to take precedence over ideology.

—Self-expression: When the subject begins to open up and to voice some of his own gripes against the cult.

—Identification and transference: When the subject begins to identify with the deprogrammers, starts to think of himself as an opponent of the cult rather than a member of it.

In spite of Patrick's tendency to take on more deprogrammings than he can handle effectively, and his talent for self-congratulatory publicity, it seems obvious that he is sincere in his belief that what he is doing is right and good. And he is subject to tremendous pressure from parents across the nation to help them in their time of distress.

The question of the inherent danger in the use and misuse of deprogramming may someday be settled by the courts. In the meantime, the question "Do parents, no matter how well-intentioned, have the right to hold an adult against his will and badger him about his religious beliefs?" is an important one.

Daphne Greene, a formidable and sensitive counter-cult activist on the West Coast, says she will never force a deprogramming on her daughter Catherine, a member of the Unification Church. "If my parents had been atheists and had seen me beating my breast and sticking my tongue out for Communion [in the Roman Catholic Church], they too might have wanted to have me deprogrammed," she says. Mrs. Greene has, however, helped and encouraged many young people to leave the Moon church by spending countless hours talking to them and their parents. She says she will talk to anyone who willingly comes to listen.

Hundreds of young people have been convinced to leave religious cults during thoughtful discussions with concerned individuals such as Mrs. Greene, Rabbi Davis, and others. These reevaluations of the cultists' religious experience were not carried out under lock and key, but voluntarily. A parent who seeks to remove a son or daughter from the clutches of a cult must consider whether or not that young person would willingly hear the other side of the issue. Whatever alternative a parent decides to choose, it should be clearly defined and thought through before it begins. There are far more failed deprogrammings than anyone is willing to admit. We have seen them, along with the successes, and they can only worsen an already shaky family relationship.

Sandy Cole is "underground," perhaps in Europe with the Children of God, in spite of the $1,500 her parents have spent to have her deprogrammed. Sandy was supposed to be deprogrammed by Ted Patrick, who sent two young ex-cult members in his place when he got tied up on another deprogramming that lasted longer than he had anticipated. Patrick himself came to see Sandy two weeks after the initial deprogramming, because her parents were not pleased with the results of the young ex-cultists' work. Sandy was away from COG for six months after her deprogrammings, trying to restructure her life and "find a place" for herself.

The Coles wonder if the deprogramming was conducted poorly and destined to fail. Yet they defend Ted Patrick, saying, "He never knows how long a deprogramming will take and often runs days behind on his tight schedule." And they accept much of the blame for Sandy's return to COG on their own shoulders.

"Maybe we should have worked harder before the deprogramming and found some alternatives," they say. They did, in fact, help their daughter get involved in a religious volunteer program, but it didn't seem to hold her interest. "If we'd found a substitute for the Children of God, perhaps she would have stayed home." As it is, they haven't seen or heard from their daughter for many months.

"She just couldn't seem to take hold of her life," her father, a high school teacher and athletic coach, says. "We tried so hard to help her, but we couldn't find the right thing for her to grab onto."

Sandy Cole, a beautiful young woman who once

had high hopes for her life, is in the underground the COGs call the "catacombs," hidden from her family and the world. Her parents have frequent nightmares about the fate of the eldest of their six daughters.

The Reverend Kent Burtner, the Oregon chaplain who offers cult members' families a way to analyze their situation, has for years observed the rapid growth and expansion of the cult phenomenon and makes no effort to hide the strength of his convictions. "I am sick unto death that those kids are being used and exploited," he says. For nearly a decade, Father Kent has been watching the followers of the Reverend Moon work to increase his flock. "The ways the Moonies recruit followers are deceitful," he says. "And the ends to which the energies of Moon's disciples are aimed are just as indefensible as the ways their minds are captured."

Before his charge in Oregon, Father Kent was a graduate student at Berkeley's renowned Graduate Theological Union. In those days, the priest watched the changing political and religious scene and saw the Moon movement burst into bloom just as the flower children began to fade in the garden of the counter-culture.

Unification Church theology disturbs Father Kent. The message that Christ failed as a savior, along with the intricate plan whereby the Reverend Moon will unite and save the world, is offensive and upsetting to this Catholic priest. But a stronger reason for his counter-cult work is his fervent belief that the rights of individuals are being usurped by religious cults.

"Any belief system that so polarizes the forces of good and evil is mere negativism, is inhuman and intellectually dishonest," he says. "The idea of the Manichaean split between good and evil denies the value of the human person. Moonies are asked to hold their objections and to drop them behind them. Pretty soon, if they ever turned around, there would be a huge pile of questions sitting there unanswered." The priest points out also that not only are cult members discouraged from examining their questions, they are never even left alone for long enough to contemplate at all.

Father Kent on the West Coast and Rabbi Davis on the East Coast are two of a very small number of clergymen who speak out against religious cults and who could be called counter-cult activists. Both of these men of the cloth are cautious about getting involved in activities that could be interpreted as illegal. But each will speak to any young cult member who is willing to listen.

When Father Kent was called to deprogram the young daughter of a Lutheran family mentioned earlier in this chapter, he agreed to help the family and the young woman with a reevaluation of her life. She was not physically constrained or imprisoned in any way. Father Kent explains that he invoked her own intellectual integrity to make her listen to the sometimes "uncomfortable" facts about Sun Myung Moon and his Unification Church. The young woman is Karin Hegstrom, a college graduate from an Ohio farm family. Karin's parents and her closest friend from childhood were all involved in the reevaluation.

One Sunday morning just as he was about to celebrate Sunday Mass in the campus chapel, Father Kent received a frantic phone call from Karin's father. Mr. Hegstrom asked the priest's help in deprogramming his daughter. Several weeks earlier she had disappeared into the Unification Church and was now at the group's New Ideal City Ranch in Boonville, California, 200 miles north of San Francisco.

In order to reach her, Karin's father was considering swearing out a warrant for his daughter's arrest, since she had taken some of the family's possessions, including a car, into the church with her. Mr. Hegstrom was aware that this move might mean getting involved in a potentially irreversible legal action: His daughter could end up in jail. But arrest seemed to be the only way he could be sure she would leave the ranch. She had refused to come home and she had hung up on all her parents' phone calls.

First Father Kent cautioned the Hegstroms not to do anything they might regret and advised them to wait until they could all get together to make some plans. "Yes," he promised, "I will help as much as I can." The Hegstroms had to understand that the priest would not break any laws, but he would do everything in his power to help. In the meantime, he would serve Mass and be free in an hour.

After the service, they spoke again and discussed Karin's situation. She had broken off several conversations with her parents. She would not tell them much about her new life. In fact, she was very secretive. The Hegstroms were anxious and concerned about their daughter and on the basis of the phone calls, had driven across the country with Karin's close friend, Louise. They didn't know how they were going to "rescue" their daughter; they only knew they were going to try.

The plan was made. The Hegstroms would visit their daughter at Boonville and convince her to come with them to visit an aunt and uncle who live in a small town nearby. They had already tried to phone Karin but were unable to reach her. The parents felt they had been given a runaround, so Father Kent gave them the phone number of Martin (Noah) Ross, director of the Boonville ranch and an ardent follower of the Reverend Moon. Mr. Hegstrom told the young man that he and his wife would, under whatever circumstances necessary, see their daughter. The ranch director agreed that Karin would meet her parents at the ranch gate.

Karin came out of the padlocked gate, which is located miles from the ranch's lodgings and main buildings, and met with her father. After much talking, Mr. Hegstrom convinced Karin that the only way she could demonstrate her sincerity about the Unification Church was to come with them for an overnight visit and explain her feelings. "We need to talk. And, if you feel you must, we'll let you come back," he told her.

The two drove off to the home of Karin's aunt and uncle, where her mother and her friend, Louise, were waiting. There was an emotional reunion, especially between the friends, as Karin told Louise she wanted her to experience the joy of being a member of the Unification Church. "I want to convert you as my first spiritual child," she said.

Father Kent was also waiting, and Karin abruptly

questioned his presence at the reunion. "He's here for me, isn't he?"

That evening, Karin tried every ruse she could think of to avoid talking to the priest. First she and Louise went for a long walk. Then she said she wanted to spend some private time with her parents, then her aunt and uncle—all to avoid the confrontation she knew, by now, was inevitable. Although the young woman was trying to avoid having her belief tested in a discussion with the priest, she was not held against her will, doors and windows were not locked and bolted, but she made no attempt to leave. Karin Hegstrom had promised to spend the night with her family and she seemed determined to live up to her bargain.

Ultimately, Karin sat down with Father Kent, Louise, and her parents. They asked questions about her new life, cautiously and without hostility, and she attempted to answer them, saying only, "It is so wonderful. You will have to visit and see for yourselves. Your might not like it," she grudgingly advised Father Kent, "since you are a priest."

After several hours of questions, to which Karin responded only with bits and pieces of vague information, everyone was frustrated.

Then Father Kent asked a question that was calculated to arouse emotion. "Why have you accepted Moon and his wife as your true parents, and not your mother and father here?"

Later the family said they feared the entire neighborhood heard Karin's screamed response. "You always drank, and made us work on that farm. And you hit us all the time," she yelled at her father.

And to her mother she screamed, "You were so helpless. You wouldn't lift a finger to help."

Karin then turned on the priest. "The church was so hypocritical. And no one cared about anyone else or about living any kind of decent lives."

Pain that had for so long been denied and camouflaged in this family had finally surface. Karin stopped screaming and ran into the kitchen, tears streaming down her face. Her parents wept too. Karin's father followed her into the kitchen, and everyone present heard what he told his daughter. "Maybe we did make some mistakes. But it's not too late. Honest honey, we'll try to make it up to you. Please listen to what we have to say. I never knew how you felt."

They returned to the living room, and Karin asked Louise to come with her to talk. They excused themselves for a few minutes and when they returned they told of a bargain they had made. Karin would listen, but she would not respond. She would stay at the house, but only if no one questioned her. She would listen to anything they wanted to tell her, and that was all.

In exchange for Karin's attention, Louise promised to visit one of the Unification Church's Creative Community Project houses in San Francisco, where Karin had been recruited by the Moonies.

Father Kent says he "quavered inside" when he thought of how often a young person attempts to rescue a friend or sister or brother and ends up being converted to the church herself. "We might," he said, "end up having to rescue both young women." But it was too late to worry. The bargain had been made.

They spent a few more hours talking to Karin about Unification Church theology and practice; then everyone went to bed. Father Kent, who was bunking on the living room sofa, went over his copy of the Unification Church's 120-day training program, making notes of salient points to refer to the next day. Just as the sun rose over the horizon, the priest decided he'd crammed all his tired brain could absorb, and dropped off to sleep for a few hours.

That morning he sat with Karin and Louise around the kitchen table and continued the one-sided discussion. The priest had decided not to violate Karin's bargain but to encourage her to explain views she had never really clarified for herself. He set his copy of the 120-day program nearby, but took pains not to refer to it. Instead he talked about Unification Church theology, explaining how the belief system differs from Christianity. Finally, to clarify a point she wanted to make, Karin reached for the 120-day training manual.

"Ah-haaa," the priest said to himself. "This is the beginning."

Studying the manual, Karin began to feel that the verbal interpretations of church philosophy she had been given were not always based on fact. By the end of the second day of reevaluation Karin was feeling betrayed, confused, and angry. She jumped up, caught Louise by the arm, and pulled her outside. "I won't stay a minute longer," she told her friend. They walked together until Karin spotted a pay telephone. The priest was following them, at a distance, but he was close enough to hear what they were saying.

"You're running away from the one person who can help you out of this mess, who can help you understand what to do with your life," Louise was shouting. "And you won't even give him a chance to talk to you. You're turning your back on the one person who can help you. You may never have another chance."

Then, just as the two young women came to the phone booth, Karin threw her purse down and began to cry. "Okay," she sobbed, "I'll listen. But I am going back tomorrow."

Father Kent drew Karin aside and tried to comfort her by telling her how he once questioned his faith when he was a seminarian. "I felt like the loneliest soul in the world," he said, "and I know you do too. But please listen to us. I want you to believe that we want to help you. You are mixed up in something that is much bigger than you know."

She picked up her handbag, and they walked back to the house. After more discussion, the priest and Louise conferred privately. "All of Karin's doubts," Louise told him, "seem to hinge on who and what the Reverend Moon is, charlatan or savior?" Karin knew little about her adopted religious leader. She had not even learned of his existence until weeks after she joined his church.

"I know someone who knows a lot about the Reverend Moon," Father Kent told Louise.

And so they planned a visit to Daphne Greene, who lives nearby in Ross, California. Mrs. Greene, mother of two children who have been involved in the church, one a former Moonie and the other still a member, is also a former president of the board of trustees of Berkeley's Graduate Theological Union, a highly respected coalition of theology schools. This wife of a prominent Bay Area attorney is deeply religious and politically attuned. She has been watching the Unification Church with a wary eye since before her own children became involved.

"Bring the girls and come on over," she said. "I'll make sure Ford" (her son who left the church on his own) "is around; they can all spend some time together." The next day the threesome went to the Greenes' hilltop home, and after a meeting the three young people set out for a day at the beach.

That day, Ford Greene and later his mother told Karin facts about the Reverend Moon, his origins in Korea, his questionable political and financial goals, and how his brand of religion is not always compatible with Christianity.

By the end of the day, Karin had decided not to return to the Unification Church. "How could a girl like me get involved in something like that?" she wondered.

Father Kent knew that Karin and her parents still had some unfinished business to discuss, so when they returned to the relatives' home they all sat down with her mother and father and discussed the indictments Karin had screamed at her parents a few days earlier. Her parents wondered, "Could we have made Karin's growing up less difficult somehow? Has life been so tough for our kids?" They didn't have answers, but they decided they would make an attempt, however belated, to improve their lives. Karin's father promised to join Alcoholics Anonymous, and he has. Karin's mother began to understand why she was chronically depressed, how she

had lost control of her own life. The family promised
to seek regular counseling.

Karin and the priest discussed her personal problems. Karin had had what in the Unification Church
are called "chapter two," or sexual problems. Karin
is a big girl, not fat, but far from petite. She said
she felt unattractive and inadequate with men and
couldn't always trust her own feelings. They agreed
that it is not easy to learn to deal with members of
the opposite sex. But Father Kent encouraged Karin
to deal with doubts by facing rather than avoiding
them.

No one in the Hegstrom family solved their
problems that day. But it may have been the first
time the family recognized them and promised to
seek counseling. And they decided that they do
care for each other and that each member would try
to be kinder and more considerate. And Karin was
no longer a Moonie.

With planning rather than haste, a reevaluation
such as that done by Father Kent, or a deprogramming, can be arranged for optimum success. And, as
is apparent from the success of Karin Hegstrom's experience, it needn't take place outside of the law,
behind locked doors, or with force, to be effective.
Anticult parent groups, whose members are often parents of young people who have been successfully returned to lives of free choice through kidnappings
and forced deprogrammings, often believe the
forced deprogramming is the only route. They
rarely state, but are quick to imply, that if a troubled

parent wants his child out of a cult, this is the method he must choose.

A network of people working in the field of deprogramming has grown up around these anticult groups, and they may be recommended by troubled parents. However, few of the groups have established any criteria for judging the abilities of a deprogrammer, and a parent should be wary of those who may be recommended. Parental haste and desperation often lead to the selection of a deprogrammer whose knowledge of the cults is based on exaggeration and half-truths and whose counseling skills are scanty or nonexistent. This lack of skill is especially obvious in some young former cult members who travel around the country trying to get other young people to leave the cults. Vindication for their own deception by the cults may be their sole motivation. But these young people are often ill-prepared to interfere with the lives and dabble in the sanity of other young people.

We believe the best system for a reevaluation is to have one adult, with a knowledge of the cults and counseling techniques, in control of the process. This person can be a psychologist, a counselor, a clergyman, a favorite aunt or uncle, or a skilled and kindly deprogrammer. Anyone who takes on this task should be willing to learn all that he can about the cult and the individual before the process begins.

In most cases, parents should be prepared to pay for the deprogrammer's services. Deprogramming is a chore that requires training and skill, and so the services of a deprogrammer should not be expected to come free or cheaply. Neither Rabbi Davis nor

Father Kent will accept payment, but others who offer these services must support themselves and need to be recompensed.

Parents ought to spend time with a person who may direct a deprogramming for their child and insist on knowing what kind of knowledge or training he has for the task, what his approach to religion is, and they should learn in advance how much the process will cost. It is shocking to see how parents, in their desperation, have hired deprogrammers with less information than they would require of a housemaid or building contractor.

The debriefer or deprogrammer needs to be made aware of sore spots in the family relationships and should learn as much as possible about the background, personality, and life of the potential subject. Not all family problems are as easily unearthed as those of the Hegstroms, and neither are most families as willing to face difficulties with honesty and openness. In the hands of an insensitive, untrained amateur, deprogrammings can turn into disasters. Even well-meaning professionals, without counseling skills, can play havoc with families and their cult-member children.

Ideally, a reevaluation of a cult member's life and beliefs should be the result of a parent-child bargain. "If you intend to spend the rest of your life in that group, you owe us a week [or two weeks] of your time," is one approach. Rabbi Davis has himself conducted well over one hundred "rescues" that came about this way. The young people Rabbi Davis has talked out of religious cults were probably no happier about a confrontation with him than Karin Hegstrom was about hers with Father Kent. But each came and sat in the rabbi's unlocked study, across the desk from him, or sharing a sofa with him, and talked and listened. And each ultimately left a cult. He reports few "failures."

Parents who are unable to strike a bargain with a child to get him voluntarily to come home and "listen to the other side," and still don't want to resort to an illegal kidnapping, have yet another option. Some parents have gone to the courts to secure temporary conservatorships or guardianships of their offspring.

A temporary conservatorship is granted by a judge when it can be proven to his satisfaction that the cult membership of a young person has resulted in mental incompetency or impaired judgment in that person. Initial conservatorships are always temporary, and the subject and his parents must reappear together before the judge, usually after a deprogramming, in order for the court to determine if the conservatorship should continue. If the deprogramming is hasty and fails, so may the conservatorship.

The law is arbitrary, as it must be, in determining the legal age of consent and adulthood. In most states it is eighteen. Age, though, is not an issue in conservatorships. And many opponents of the new religious cults believe that the conservatorship (combining guardianship with deprogramming) is the only reliable way of guaranteeing that an individual consider all sides of the issue of his cult conversion.

Some parents say they have used the courts as a last resort, since there seemed to be no other way to free a son or daughter from emotional or physical attachment to a cult. Many of their children, after successful deprogrammings, praise the conservatorship, saying it gave them a chance to see how the cults had deceived them and gave them an opportunity to change their minds.

Getting a court-appointed conservatorship may be a time-consuming and costly procedure, and it is still only the beginning of a young person's struggle to regain control of his life. Michael Traucht and Wayne Howard, two young lawyers from Arizona, specialize in obtaining conservatorships, but the procedure is not complex, and, armed with sufficient information, the family legal counselor may be able to do the same thing.

Parents who believe their children are unwilling prisoners of the cults may not always consider the costs of legal extrication excessive when weighed against a young person's freedom. Many have mortgaged homes and future earnings in these efforts. But conservatorships are not always necessary.

Whether a family resorts to court-appointed conservatorship and deprogramming, deprogramming without the legal custody of the cult member, or attempts to strike a bargain by simply insisting that the cult member give equal time to other ideas, no course of action should be undertaken without some rational analysis of the situation. If a family begins the process of extricating their offspring from a cult, armed only with wrath and self-righteousness, they could be headed for more trouble than they anticipate.

Before they make a decision, parents should face some important life issues. Those who try to understand how this "conversion" came about must also try to find out what had been happening in their son's or daughter's life, and how the conditions of life prepared him for religious group life. What matters to this young cult member? What goals and aspirations did he have before joining the group? How does the family interpret success? How does the young person's definition of success differ from that of his parents? What are the cultist's options for a productive lifestyle? Does he realize that the cult may not be his only option?

Parents must honestly ask themselves, "How well do I know this young person?"

Deprogrammings behind locked doors are alarming, and even more alarming is the fact that these forced confrontations can fail. A reevaluation, resulting sometimes from a hard-won bargain, has never, to our knowledge, failed. These bargains take more arranging than the deprogramming, where parents relinquish the outcome and the responsibility to a deprogrammer for a flat fee. But the stakes of involuntary deprogramming are high. Failure is a possibility, and once such a deprogramming fails there may never be another chance.

Young Moonies, Hare Krishnas, full-time Divine Light premies, Children of God, and hundreds of members of lesser-known religious cults dedicate their lives to prayer or work within the group and never have a chance to talk, either privately or publicly, with disillusioned former members. In a reevaluation they get a chance to have their beliefs questioned by an adult who has taken the time to amass knowledge and expertise on the subject of their new faith.

After they leave religious cults, many young people say they had wanted to leave, as Dee Dee Fischer's son Michael did, explaining they had had vague feelings of dissatisfaction that they could not put into words. But many say that they could not have come up with a reason to part company with the new faith and new friends. It was not until their parents demanded that they come home or insisted that they listen to the other side that they were able to make a decision to leave what they later said was an unhappy experience.

Young adults, in or out of the cults, are living through those years when family ties must be severed if they are to mature. In order for them to make the often difficult transition from adolescence to adulthood, some emotional distance from their parents must be maintained. We have not learned of a single case where the parents of a cult member, by themselves, were able to talk a son or daughter out of a religious cult. Mothers and fathers should be on hand for a reevaluation or deprogramming and be ready to take part or monitor the process, but they are usually too close to their family situation to conduct a reevaluation effectively themselves.

Psychiatrists, psychologists, and therapists are often trained in counseling skills. But those skills alone offer no panacea for cult membership. Parents should be cautioned that many psychiatrists, due to the demands of their own practices, are unwilling to take the time to study cult materials and often, because of their training, view cult membership either as aberrant behavior or as part of the normal alienation of adolescence.

On the other hand, the professional ethics of any psychiatrist who will attest to the insanity of a cult member so the young person may be institutionalized to "protect" him from a cult must be questioned (unless there are specific symptoms to support such a diagnosis, other than parental hysteria or disapproval). We know of one psychiatrist who routinely hospitalized cult members until at least one hospital refused to allow him to use its facilities for that purpose.

Keeping in mind that so many forceful deprogrammings fail, it is interesting to note how Father Kent's gentle confrontation with Karin Hegstrom resulted in her abandonment of the Unification Church. Karin says she was shown the truth. Timing may have been an important factor in her case. She had been a member of the church for only a few weeks. But short-term involvement with a cult is no guarantee that a young person will give up cult membership.

Even long-time cult members acknowledge the early fanaticism and the wide-eyed "spacey" looks of newer converts.

Neither does lengthy involvement in a cult guarantee that members will not, as Alan and Giovanna Wood did, leave the church on their own after many years. Alan, Giovanna, and nearly thirty other Moonies walked away from a Unification Church center in Maryland, after realizing that the church was not filling their own spiritual needs. In Karin Hegstrom's case, the presence of her family and her friend, Louise, was definitely helpful. "Without them, it might not have worked," Father Kent says. "It's like pulling someone back home through a maze. They are so confused," the priest avows. "They have been subjected to constant lectures and reinforcement that are repeated over and over. You must find the right things to say, the ideas that evoke an emotional response, and use them the way cults do, by repeating them again and again."

Rabbi Davis, as well as most of those involved in anticult work, describes the process as "watching keenly for emotional responses and inserting a wedge of doubt." Most cult members do not ascribe to each of the cult beliefs with equal fervor. They seldom have had a chance to question or to analyze every part of the complicated theology and practices. Since most have not had a chance to examine doubt or to enjoy solitary contemplation, finding out just what parts of the new religion they do question is an important part of the reevaluation process.

Dr. Sargant writes in *Battle for the Mind: A Physiology of Conversion and Brainwashing,* "Those who wish to disperse . . . beliefs . . . and behavior patterns and afterwards implant saner beliefs and attitudes are more likely to achieve success if they can first induce some degree of nervous tension or stir up sufficient feelings of anger or anxiety to secure a person's undivided attention and possibly increase his suggestibility." Deprogrammers and those who have worked with cult members in reevaluations of their lives seem to know this instinctively.

Randy Wilcox came home from the Unification Church and he didn't want to go back. He just had trouble finding a "reason not to go." Randy's parents, his brother and sisters, clergymen, and Alan and Giovanna Wood all helped Randy to decide to put

the Moon experience behind him. Randy's parents
say they knew they could not have helped Randy
alone. Randy might not have even begun to question his beliefs if his parents had not been able to
gamble on his affection for them and demand, "If
you love us, you will come home." They promised
Randy they would not deprogram him, but they made
it clear to him that he had a responsibility to explain
his new lifestyle to them "in person." A family with
a relationship that was less close might not have been
able to make such a demand.

If parents keep the lines of communication open
with a cultist son or daughter, they may be able to
recognize signs of disillusionment or anxiety. Letters
home, from members of new religions, are often so
foolishly simple and cliché-ridden that they are not
valuable sources of information. However, telephone
conversations, if they are kept nonthreatening and
nonargumentative, can help parents know if disillusionment is setting in, if days of endless fund raising
are taking their toll. Group life, in a cult, where
love is dispensed in equal amounts to everyone, can
be frustrating, and many former members say they
stopped feeling special. Attempting to change the
world by selling peanuts or religious tracts they see
discarded must, at times, seem futile to all who
do it.

We became somewhat unwittingly involved, first
as observers and then as active participants, in the
deprogramming of a young Unification Church member, John Ashley. If it began as a forced deprogramming, it ended as a gentle reevaluation.

With the help of one of the loosely organized

groups of anticult parents which has surfaced in recent years, John's parents hired a young ex-cult
member, a former Moonie, to deprogram their son.
John would be home to be a member of his sister's
wedding party, and the deprogrammer, in so many
ways more a child than an adult, would "snatch"
and deprogram him. The Ashleys, John's mother and
his stepfather (John's natural father died after a long
bout with leukemia when John was a young teen-
ager), agreed to pay the young man $400 (though
the price was increased later), and they began to
lay plans for the deprogramming.

The deprogrammer bought handcuffs, rounded up
a crew of volunteer bodyguards from the family's
Lutheran Church, and held rehearsals of the snatch.
They even drove a dry run from the family home
to a motel room about 30 miles away, where the
deprogramming was to take place.

A room rental had been arranged in the nearly
empty country motel by the mother of an ex-Moonie
who also happens to be a township supervisor in
the municipality where the motel is located. She had
spoken to the township police and received a guarantee that the police would take a "hands off" policy
toward the deprogramming. Finally, everything was
ready.

After the wedding reception, with John still in his
stiff rented evening clothes, the deprogrammer handcuffed him, taped his mouth shut, threw him into the
back seat of a car, and sped off to the motel.

Once in the motel room, he handcuffed him to a
chair, and the former Moonie proceeded to make
dramatic statements right out of Ted Patrick's book.

"We're prepared to stay here for as long as it takes you to promise you'll never return to that fake church." He ripped up a picture of the Reverend Moon, told John that Moon was a "rip-off artist," and called the Korean evangelist every name he could think of. He thought of many, none of them flattering. Between histrionics, the deprogrammer read quotes from the Bible, showing John how many had been distorted and used out of context for Unification Church purposes. When he was able to engage John in conversation and challenge a theological point, which was seldom, the young deprogrammer would grapple with his suitcase, filled to overflowing with anticult materials. "I know I have the answer to that question in here somewhere," he would say while he groped through his untidy files, looking desperately for the appropriate material. As a deprogramming, it was comic opera at its worst.

The young former Moonie seemed particularly fascinated with the sexual allegations about the Reverend Moon and told with obvious relish a story about Eve's alleged intercourse with a serpent in the Garden of Eden, a story that is taken by some to be part of Unification theology. "Beware of false prophets," he shouted with great drama.

With great relish the young man told John about ritual blood-cleansing ceremonies the Reverend Moon is said to have practiced in Korea. The allegation, which has been neither proven nor adequately discredited, claims the Reverend Moon engaged in sexual intercourse with his young women followers to "cleanse their blood of the taint of Eve's original sin with Lucifer." The Reverend Moon's opponents contend that sex orgies which surrounded the ritual resulted in his imprisonment in Korea. "Do you want Moon to have sex with your wife before you even get a chance to have sex with her yourself?" the deprogrammer asked John again and again.

Before he joined the church he had been a moderately religious person, John told the deprogrammer. But he said he joined the Moonies for the purpose in life and friendship that the group offered, not for the religious aspects of the movement. Still the deprogrammer kept quoting the Bible and trying to discredit the Unification Church on the basis of theology.

Just before dawn of the first full day, the deprogrammer handcuffed John's arm to a chair next to a bed in the motel room and let him go to sleep. To the observers the deprogramming of John Ashley seemed destined to fail. Then, early the next morning, the deprogrammer played a tape made by a former Moonie, Bill Hansen. On the tape, Bill explains clearly and articulately how he, when he was a Moonie lecturer and recruiter, was encouraged to deceive prospective converts and to withhold information from them. Bill's tape struck familiar chords for John. He began to wonder if he, too, had been deceived and began to confide to the observers that he was getting a little tired of being a Moonie.

John said he was disenchanted with the life he led as a Unification Church member. He didn't like the way he and the other young Moonies had to live —fund raising for long arduous hours on street corners, sleeping in sleeping bags for months on end,

using the same towels that everybody else used, and
getting up day after day at 5 A.M. to begin the difficult and boring existence all over again.

John told the observers that he especially despised
the lying he felt he had to do in order to meet
quotas set for him as a fund raiser. It really bothered
him, he said, to tell people he was raising funds for
a children's home that didn't exist. But he was afraid
if he told the truth, that he was soliciting for the
Unification Church, he would come back at the end
of a day empty-handed. Still, he felt loved and
wanted by the Moonies. He enjoyed having friends
who loved him. And, after all, the saints who went to
their deaths in dens of lions weren't happy about
their fate, but they knew they were doing the right
thing, he said.

So we sat down with John and asked him to make
two lists, one with all the good qualities of life in
the Unification Church, and another with all the
negative aspects of that life. We discussed each point
with him and told him he seemed like an honest and
intelligent young man. Didn't he have a responsibility to control his own destiny? First his parents ran
his life. Who was running it now? we asked. What
were his goals before he joined the group?

At first, John just wanted to talk, and we tried to
ask open-ended questions that led the way for him
to examine his situation. Finally, several hours later
(the deprogrammer had taken a break and was
gone), John admitted that the bad seemed to out-
weigh the good on his list. Did he want to go back?
No, but he still couldn't be sure that his own dissatisfaction was reason enough to leave.

"What will I do with my life?" he wondered. John had completed his education and he had a career, though it was one he wasn't sure he liked to fall back on. He also said that he liked girls. John admitted that he missed having sexual or romantic attachments in his church life. There was one young woman he cared for; she was a former Moonie. He thought maybe he could get a job and save enough to pay her a visit at her home in the Southwest. What did we think of that? he wanted to know.

John decided he was not going back to the Moonies. He agreed to go home with his parents for a while until he got things together. The young deprogrammer and another former cult member went along for what they called John's "rehab." John's mother told us later that they took over her home. "They ran up long-distance phone bills, tried to make my son feel guilty because he joined the church, and tried to pit members of my family against each other with tricks and secrecy."

The family finally told the young men to leave, but not before a psychologist warned them that John was either going to have a nervous breakdown or go back to the Moonies if they didn't get him away from the young men. And the cost of the deprogramming came close to $2,000 with hotel bills, food, and telephone bills charged by the young deprogrammer.

John has been working, trying to save enough money to visit the young woman he met in the Unification Church. The two young people write frequently, exchanging long, confiding letters. They are looking forward to meeting again, anxious to see if they do, in fact, have a romantic interest in each other.

Deprogramming has been condemned by those who call it "reverse brainwashing," but it has also been highly praised. Many former members of religious cults say they would never have been able to leave the groups if they had not been deprogrammed. Sylvia Buford, the bright Texas debutante who is now on her way to law school, calls it "a return to the normal thinking process." Janet Taylor, a former Unification Church member, has said deprogramming is helpful and necessary if one is to think clearly again. "I was in a whole different reality in the church. I couldn't reason."

Many advocates of deprogramming think the process is helpful, even if one decides to leave the church on his own. "It takes a lot longer to get it together again without deprogramming," says Dr. George Swope, the father of a former cult member and head of a counter-cult group. "Some young people who left cults without deprogramming suffered months of inertia and nightmares trying to do it themselves."

Jenny Michalsen, who was involved with the Unification Church, says she wanted to leave but might never have been able to cut off her new ties of friendship in the Moonies but for deprogramming. "I wonder if I would ever have left if I had not seen the negative information. Sometimes I think I would have. But you never have the time or the opportunity to face your doubts in the church, and so maybe I would have stayed." Angelo LaFava and Gene Leone returned to their theological educations at the Unification Church seminary after failed deprogrammings. After attending classes with them, it is easy to see how they were seduced back to lives of religious academics (even though unaccredited) and the warm security of the small band of Moonie students at Barrytown. They are committed to the goals of the Reverend Moon, as they know them, and want to be missionaries in his behalf. But most of those deprogrammed from the cults don't leave such satisfying lives behind. The masses of cult members spend long, tiring days recruiting and raising funds for their faith, or working within the structure of a group for just enough money to allow them to live as full-time members.

Randy Wilcox was not deprogrammed in the classic sense of the word, but he did take part in a round of activities that, along with his parents' love and respect, helped him put his life back together again outside the cult. Randy has found religion within the framework of orthodox Christianity. He has decided to dedicate his life to God's work and has joined a Mennonite voluntary service program. This is not a life his liberal Unitarian parents would have chosen for Randy, but they respect their son's decision. "When Randy talks about his love of God, I feel like a fellow who is listening to a friend who has just fallen in love. I don't deny he feels the way he says, I only wish I would meet someone (God) who could make me feel that way," his father says.

Elizabeth Albertson, mother of successfully deprogrammed Terry and Nini Coleman, says that because she appears to have a firm grip on her own life, people often ask her what to do about their lives. "It's very tempting to give advice. But I restrain myself. And that's what parents must do to help a kid find his own way in life. A deprogramming or a reevaluation is after all only a return to free choice. Parents must understand that there's no guarantee that a child will do what they want and they must be able to accept the outcome."

Deprogramming . . .
No Guarantees

The small band of Moonies are relaxed and laughing as they listen to Angelo LaFava finish his story of a deprogramming that failed. The irony of the situation is as rich in conflict as the young man's story. The dozen Moonies are sitting in the study of a seminary that once served the princes and peerage of the Roman Catholic church, a religion that the Reverend Sun Myung Moon, messiah to these young theology scholars, claims has failed.

The seminary had been closed and was quietly sold to the Unification Church. It happened several years ago as part of the national trend away from religion that resulted in fewer believers, fewer students in Catholic educational institutions, fewer choices by young Catholic men to become part of the clergy, and finally, the sale of massive properties like this one.

Not even the newly installed sky-blue shag carpet and motel-modern furniture that looks as though it came from a warehouse outlet can remove the opulent and impressive aura of the Order of Christian Brothers, who for so long inhabited this study and seminary. Remnants of Roman Catholic influence are everywhere, with crosses and statues, grottoes, and prayers carved in stone at every turn around the splendid grounds. This monastery in the Hudson Valley at Barrytown, New York, once housed the mighty church of Rome, with its trappings of age and acceptability. Then, because it was nearly empty, it was sold. Now it serves as a learning center for the growing gnostic religion of a self-proclaimed Korean messiah and houses some of his zealous band of followers.

Each of these Unification Church seminarians claims to feel nearly as persecuted as the early Christians, and they point to the monastery as a symbol of the power of money. The Catholics worked their way to world respectability and acceptance, "and so will we," they say.

Angelo tells how he realized after several days of being held against his will, when his religious beliefs were intensely questioned by a deprogrammer and several ex-Moonies, that "if I just acted like the good all-American boy again, they would all leave me alone. I never renounced my faith, and I still can't believe how easy it was to fool everyone."

Angelo is in his mid-twenties, handsome and blond. He is the son and namesake of a self-made man, and he has told everyone in the study on this damp fall evening of an escape that sounds like some perverse rendition of an Andy Hardy tale. A practiced long-distance runner, Angelo paced himself while jogging with his "keeper," a stocky young man who, he knew, would not be able to keep up with him.

The plodding runner is a former member of Moon's Unification Church who had been charged by the deprogrammer and Angelo's parents with keeping an eye on him, in case he attempted to escape. The ex-Moonie is overweight and out of shape, and as the two jogged alongside each other Angelo knew that when it came to the final sprint he could outrun the other young man and make it to the car of a Moonie brother stationed at a prearranged rendezvous point.

"We were just running along, and I knew we were coming closer to the restaurant at the bottom of the hill. Just as we approached the spot where I knew I had to take off and get away from him, God provided a curve in the road. I said to my running partner, 'I've just got to sprint. It's been so long since I've had a good run.' Then I ran like crazy, and oh, how I wanted to look back to see if he was trying to keep up with me, even though I knew he couldn't."

Angelo gets up from his easy chair in the study to show everyone how, during the final laps, he tried to "look cool," gazing around as though he were taking in the scenery, while his legs were pumping as hard as they could for the last half mile. As Angelo rounded the bend and came into sight of the restaurant, he recalls praying, "Oh, please, God, let him be there." And sure enough, the car was in its appointed place with the driver leaning against a tree reading a newspaper, just like in the movies.

His keeper, Angelo saw from the safety of the waiting car, was just rounding the bend, sagging, plodding, barely able to move his legs.

The story is told with ease and great dramatic

flair as Angelo demonstrates how he won the race and how "they" lost it. By the time he is finished with his great escape story, there isn't a dry eye in the crowd, everyone is laughing so hard.

Then Angelo takes his seat again and is serious. "I had to get back to Washington. There was so much work to do for the church rally. As soon as I got there, the same day I left, I called my family in California and told them again and again not to cry for me. Even while they were crying, I said, 'Don't grieve for me, save your tears for something worth crying about.' "

Angelo LaFava has been a member of the Unification Church for several years and says he thought, before his attempted deprogramming, that his family had come to understand the deep conviction of his faith. He still says that they would never have "kidnapped" him and tried to break his will if a deprogrammer and several anticult parents had not pressured his parents into believing he was "brainwashed," and being held against his will.

Now Angelo is back in the church, working for a master's degree in religious education at the still-unaccredited Unification Church seminary in upstate New York. He will be cautious about visiting his home in California, the lovely place built by his labor-leader father for Angelo's Italian-American family, atop the hill he raced down to escape.

"All my family really wants me to do is not be so calm, play a little ball, and act like the all-American boy. The all-American boy," he says over and over, "that would satisfy them." His life of godliness, Angelo muses, does not.

Most of the half-dozen church members in the formidable Gothic study have not heard Angelo's story. Neither have they heard Gene Leone's, though several know the highlights of these two dramatic tales. They are, however, full of sympathy for the two young men who describe how their parents want them out of this church at any cost.

The Moonies in that room, like most of the followers of Sun Myung Moon, say that their parents approve of their life choice, once they understand how challenging and fulfilling a life in the Unification Church can be. They claim they are not afraid of deprogramming, because they say that their own parents would never resort to such drastic measures or feel the need to rescue them.

But, they tell with great bitterness of members who were not only "kidnapped" (church members make little distinction between legal or other means of removal by parents or deprogrammers), but in some cases falsely accused of being psychotic or dangerous and placed in mental hospitals until they could be trusted not to return to the church. In some cases, it took church members only a few days to convince psychiatrists they were perfectly sane, but at other times it took much longer. Some returned to the church after these ordeals. Many did not. Several, according to the Moonies, were "made crazy" by being institutionalized. They are neither at home nor with the church. They are still in mental hospitals.

These young people say, very simply and with absolute sincerity, that each is doing exactly what he or she wants in life. It is difficult not to envy them their idealism, even while you mistrust it. Unifica-

tion Church members are dedicated to world unity,
nothing less. Each says he hopes fervently that
Christians the world over will see how they must
unite under the Reverend Moon.

Each of the Unification Church seminarians is a
college graduate. A baccalaureate degree is one of
the entrance requirements at this seminary that still
lacks, and desperately seeks, accreditation and acceptance as a graduate school of theology. Fellow-
ships, grants, and student visas for foreign students
are all unattainable until such accreditation is forthcoming. They explain they are being denied accreditation only because they are controversial. All new
religions go through periods when they are not accepted, members explain.

Movingly, they tell us of their love for God, for
the Reverend Moon and for each other. They describe how this love allows them to live together
and shape lives that are challenging and fulfilling.
They address each other as brother and sister, this
band of faithful Moonies huddled together in one
small corner of one of the many buildings in the
vast empty seminary.

They call us "sister," too, and it is uncomfortable,
the way the title Ms. is for those unaccustomed to it.
In a convent and some parts of the feminist movement, "sister" is acceptable, for Catholics and devout feminists at least, but here it makes outsiders
uneasy, the way Protestants and Jews must feel the
first time they address a priest as "Father."

Here, on the Moonies' home turf, biases we don't
even know exist surface over the most trivial issues.
We two outsiders later said jokingly to each other that

we wish the Moonies would wear their hair a bit longer, look just a little more hip. As it is they spark old prejudices from our college years in the sixties. They are set apart by dress much as the engineering students were back then, with their plaid flannel shirts and nondescript work pants with a slide rule inevitably sticking out of a back pocket. Square. We know, as we laugh, it is as much from embarrassment at our own prejudices as from amusement.

Hair has always been a symbol of conformity and rebellion. Back when almost everyone wore his hair short, we remember the home permanents we hated, but were given to "keep the hair out of your eyes." Then came long hair and an era when principals and others in authority sent students with hair below their collars home for haircuts. Hair got longer, and soon principals' sideburns crept down toward their neckties and Americans laughed together about hair and what a silly symbol it had become. Today the curly locks of "hardhats" peek out from beneath their protective shells and we feel justified laughing at Moonies with their cropped heads.

While overwashed and outworn denims and shirts have become a national uniform, both the young men and women in the Unification Church are uniformly tidy (though a definite odor of the unwashed hovers around many of them), in clothing that looks as if it came from a ten-year-old mail order catalog.

It is necessary to remind oneself that these are radicals, causing at least as much concern as the left-wing political activists did a decade ago. And each Moonie tells his story with the conviction once reserved for campus politics, war resistance efforts, and other "antiestablishment" goals.

Gene Leone, more than most young men in the Unification Church, has the wholesome sun-tanned good looks of an Olympic athlete. He is powerfully built. His handsomeness is not the pretty-face kind that movie stars must have, but the rugged sort typical of campus football heroes. Gene, with his curly blond hair and easygoing personality, has what many women his own age might call "sex appeal."

Gene's story pits brother against brother in an inner-family war—brother against brother, such a well-worn cliché, from the annals of civil and religious war history. But when we hear this engaging young man tell of his own great escape and his feelings of betrayal by a brother, we see the pain in his eyes. This is no Moonie with a plastic smile and synthetic enthusiasms. This story of two young men, who will cry for each other and are separated by a river of belief, is a sad one, even in a time of sad stories.

It began with Gene at home visiting his family. He had left the Unification Church for a few brief days to return to his Ohio home to spend time with his mother and father and his brother Mario. Gene's two sisters and other brother were away from home. Mario had been to a Unification Church introductory lecture and had left in great haste and with intense disapproval. "He didn't even stay for the whole thing," Gene tells us.

During the visit, Gene and Mario didn't discuss

the church. They did, instead, all the time-filling
things young people do together, all the activities the
Moonies laughingly say it makes their parents feel so
much better to see them do, but that they privately
consider meaningless: bowling, basketball, touch
football, games of chess and scrabble.

In the midst of this reunion Gene's father told the
boys he had an appointment with a business associate and invited his sons along for the ride. Gene
declined, but Mario said, "Oh, come on, let's go
along, it will make Dad feel good," and so Gene
agreed to accompany them. The three took a short
ride, then stopped at a motel.

"I thought to myself, This is sort of weird, meeting a business associate at a motel," Gene tells us.
"But I got out and walked in with them." While Mr.
Leone and his "friend" conferred alone for a few
minutes, Gene and his brother waited and began
talking to a young woman Gene assumed was the
man's daughter.

"Which one of you boys was going to be the doctor?" asked the older man, when he and Gene's
father had completed their business.

Gene said he was the one but added that he now
plans to become a missionary.

The man replied, "What a shame, throwing away
a chance like that."

Gene didn't defend his new career choice but said
he was happy to have found something so fulfilling.

The young woman then professed curiosity about
his church, and Gene began to give her what he calls
"Divine Principle lecture number one." She got very
angry at many of the ideas, including the one about

world unity, which she said is impossible. Gene suggested that she visit a Unification Church Center sometime and hear for herself of this wonderful new philosophy.

"How do you know I haven't?" she asked.

Gene didn't jump at her bait but continued to tell her how he found peace. Everyone in the room disagreed with Gene, and he said to his father, "Come on, let's go, there's nothing to be gained by staying to talk."

His father convinced him that everyone did, in fact, want to listen to him, and pleaded with his son to "sit down and talk to my friends."

After another ten minutes, the young woman, who was calling the older man "uncle," asked Gene again, "How do you know that I don't know anything about the Unification Church?"

Suddenly Gene remembered. "You were on a television show—the one about the Unification Church?" Gene confesses how he felt "sort of excited to meet her," recalling the television image of an attractive young woman.

"And then," Gene recalls for his Barrytown audience, "it finally dawned on me. These were no 'friends' of my father's."

"Why am I here?" he asked.

"If we have to stay in this room for four months, you'll never go back to that church," replied the man Gene then knew was a deprogrammer.

Gene says his first emotion was shock. "You can't do this to me, Dad. It's not even legal. I want to leave." Gene still can't believe that his father and brother would have conspired to have him held against his will. "But almost right away I told myself, 'I'll get through it all right.' "

Heads nod in agreement among the audience in the seminary study as Gene relates his experience. There is an obvious warmth in this room and a sense of quiet self-confidence. No one interrupts anyone's story or intrudes an opinion on what another person is saying. The atmosphere troubles us, perhaps because we are used to discussions where there is challenge and disagreement, where the artful game of polemics is often played. It is disquieting, this unity of purpose and constant agreement.

Gene's story continues. "I felt so sorry for my dad. He understood how bad I felt, and how angry I was at being held. I wanted to tell him I understood why he was doing this, even though I was very angry. But I wouldn't do that." Then another thought intrudes on Gene's consciousness: "I had always wondered why church members changed their minds. Now I was going to find out."

The first day of Gene's deprogramming was devoted to questioning his beliefs and to analyzing the Divine Principle, where the Reverend Moon's philosophy is explained. The deprogrammer and the former Moonie spent time talking, sometimes calmly and rationally and sometimes emotionally, about Gene's reasons for being in the church and what he hoped to gain from his commitment.

"I sat in the same chair for eight hours while they battered me with words," he says. "But I never felt I was losing my faith or even that they were forcing me to seriously question it."

Gene tells us that the second day of deprogramming was his own private production of "This Is Your Life." Everyone in the church study laughs as though they've heard this line before. "They got some old hometown friends together and paraded them through the motel room. It was really weird, seeing them all like that, wondering how they got involved, and what they thought about it all." This day was more emotional than the first. He says he was finally permitted to flop on the bed and to sleep for six hours after eighteen hours of steady questioning and talking the second day.

They said things that seriously disturbed this young man. "They called the girls prostitutes for the Reverend Moon," he recalls incredulously. "They kept telling me I didn't have my own mind and said all the men in the church were pimps.

"I told them to get any psychologist and to let him judge my state of mind. They refused.

"And they kept doing things that really annoyed me, like following me into the bathroom. Finally I said, 'Don't follow me into the john. If someone has to come with me every time, it has to be my brother. He's the only one.'" Now he explains it was a matter of dignity.

Gene again and again told the deprogrammers that he was being held against his will. "You have no right to do this," he told them.

"So leave," the ex-Moonie told Gene, pointing to the door. But the deprogrammer blocked the doorway. When Gene told him to move out of his way, the man said, "I can't let you go, Gene."

Gene says, "Something snapped. I had had enough. 'Get out of my way. Get out of my way,' I told him. Then I hit him and knocked him against the wall. Suddenly there were people all over the place. Two guys got me down and were holding my arms with their knees.

"The deprogrammer came over to me and put his hand back as though he was going to hit me but then seemed to think better of it. I was shouting, 'Let go, let me out of here, you can't do this to me.'

"Everyone was yelling and screaming. The girl was yelling, 'You're not a Christian; you're not even a good Moonie.'

"Then I reached up with a free foot and kicked the deprogrammer in the ear. He ran and got a crucifix and held it over me real close—like this was some sort of exorcism. I couldn't believe it. Then the girl got a bucket of water and threw it on me.

"My father came in the door and was appalled by the scene. 'What are you doing to my boy?' he asked. But then he backed off when the deprogrammer said, 'You get out of here, we'll handle it.' "

Gene tells his story with feeling, but mostly with growing detachment, as though it happened to someone else. Perhaps he is telling it with special care, laundering it for slips of the tongue or remarks that might make him seem less sure of his faith in the eyes of his fellow church members. During the part involving his brother, Gene shows intense emotion, but it is quickly checked. The memory of full-blown anger during the fight is recalled in flat tones, devoid of excitement, with a sense of resignation. Still there is confidence and control in the telling of this personal tale. Perhaps it is this curious lack of animation that gives parents cause to call their cult member sons and daughters "robots." And yet, if one is admiring, it makes Gene appear very mature, very gentle, even very sweet.

Gene continues his story for his, by now, spellbound audience. "The third day, I thought to myself, I'm going to start lying to these people. They had told me the day before that if I didn't agree to stay out of the church I'd be taken to a mental hospital. That scared me, but I rationalized, 'it can't be any worse than where I am.' In fact, I thought to myself: I might be able to convince the doctors that I am sane since they wouldn't have any vested interest in keeping me away from God."

On the third day, right after he woke up (and after about six hours of sleep), Gene told his deprogrammer, "I had a dream last night. Jesus was crying."

The older man replied, "It's because you're in the wrong church."

"I was real quiet and then I said, 'Maybe you're right,' as though I'd finally seen the light. It was so easy to convince them I'd changed my mind. So simple." He shakes his head. "Incredible, that they'd think I'd lose my faith so easily."

After what is, in the lingo of deprogramming, called the "breakthrough," Gene was moved from the motel room to the deprogrammer's home for what is called "rehabilitation."

"I just wanted to be alone so I could figure out how to get away, but they would never let me alone." Gene remembers the deprogrammer's wife as a very kind and motherly woman. "I used to call her a witch, because she could almost read my mind.

If I found a quiet spot to sit and think, she'd come by and say, 'You shouldn't be thinking about that. You're floating again.'" He recalls her with some amazement and grudging admiration, "She was really something.

"I knew I'd have trouble getting away from there, because they have all the phones bugged [others in "rehabilitation" had told Gene this], and the police make rounds and keep an eye on things for them." After a few days Gene finally decided to get up in the middle of the night, run to the nearest highway, and hitchhike back to the church. His plan didn't work out.

Gene, tiptoeing, shoes in hand, to the front door, awakened the deprogrammer's wife. "And so I pretended to be going to the bathroom," Gene says. "I stayed in the bathroom for what seemed like ages, running the water and flushing the toilet."

The next morning, the deprogrammer came to Gene's bedside and questioned, "What's wrong, Gene?"

Gene says, "He was so gentle and so nice. I just couldn't argue with him and so I didn't say anything."

Gene's escape attempt had not gone unnoticed. That night he was put through more deprogramming. "I'd told them I was a born-again Christian, and so they said I must accept Jesus Christ as my savior. They thought that would be some kind of momentous thing for a Moonie to do—a real denial of my faith—but they don't understand Divine Principle.

"I said, 'I accept Jesus Christ as my savior.' But they could not let go."

Gene says they insisted, " 'You tried to escape this morning, and Jesus Christ does not want you back in that church. If you accept him as your savior, you must reaffirm your commitment to him.' My brother was so choked up by all of this he had to leave the room. I just felt so sorry for them."

Gene then tells, without emotion, about an event that took place several days later. He says this was one of the most painful parts of his whole ordeal. "I asked my mother about my clothes and books. She put her arms around me and told me not to worry, she'd burned all my clothes, all my church books, and all the letters from my friends. All of my tangible links with the Unification Church past were gone. I almost cried. How could she do this to me? I wondered."

But Gene has learned to control his emotions. He says he didn't, even then, show any feelings. "I felt more determined than ever to get back to my friends in the church."

Weeks after the deprogramming of Gene Leone began, he and the deprogrammer and several other young people were settled into a friend's vacation home.

"I kept thinking, How can I get away? How can I get out of here?" Gene tells of being heartened when another church member who'd been with the group in Ohio and at the vacation house was able to escape and return to the church. "She told them she was calling her college to see if she could reenroll, but she had really called the church."

In that phone conversation the girl made plans with her church friends for an escape. She made it.

"I was jumping for joy," Gene recalls. "After the young woman made her escape a police officer came to the house to investigate, and all of them told him how unstable she was. I could see the policeman becoming negative."

The deprogrammer and his aides called Gene outside so he could tell the police officer how awful the church was, and how emotionally unstable the young woman was. "I wouldn't do it. So I just said, 'Well, it seems that she thought what she was doing was the right thing and that's why she ran away.'

"No one seemed surprised that I wouldn't make an anti-Moon statement; they just assumed that I agreed with them."

In the meantime, a church member phoned the house and asked the deprogrammer if Gene was being held against his will. "He put me on the line, and the church brother on the telephone asked, 'Do you want to get out?' "

Gene answered, "Yes!"

After that conversation the Moonies were ready for a call from Gene to come at any time.

Gene began to lay final plans for his breakthrough. He asked the deprogrammer to take him for a visit to an aunt and uncle who live in a small town nearby. "We went bowling and had dinner with my relatives and my brother. We had a really good time," he remembers.

Just after midnight, Gene told the small crowd in his aunt and uncle's living room that he wanted to take a shower. "I had the car keys, because they had let me drive the car for the first time. So I took them into the bathroom and hid them under the

wastebasket, turned on the shower, and squeezed
through a tiny bathroom window. I bolted and ran
like crazy down the road. I got to a bar that had just
closed, banged on the door, and asked the bartender if I could use his phone. They [the deprogrammer and others] never let us have a penny
because even a dime is enough to make a collect call
to the church."

The bartender was suspicious of Gene and didn't
want to let him in. But he went to his cash drawer, got
a dime, and directed Gene to a nearby pay telephone. Gene called the church, arranged for them to
pick him up in a nearby supermarket parking lot,
and then, thinking his family would have found the
car keys and would be looking for him, decided to
take back ways to the nearby market.

"I prayed, 'Heavenly Father, it's just me and you.
Please help me.'"

Gene's troubles, like his escape, had just begun.
"I ran to the parking lot, looking for a place to hide.
The garbage bins were overflowing with bags full of
rotten food, and so I couldn't hide there," he says. "I
jumped over a fence and was looking in a junkyard,
looking for anything big enough to hide me. Then I
noticed a huge semitruck, parked under a tree. I
climbed on the roof of the van and spread the tree
branches around me."

Then, Gene tells us, he just lay back and watched
a drama unfold before his eyes. "It was like watching World War II. I could imagine I was hiding
from the German Gestapo. There were police cars
all over the place with their searchlights going everywhere. I'll tell you," he says shaking his head, "I

was scared all over. My knees were knocking; my whole body was shaking."

In the midst of all the excitement, Gene's safety was even further threatened. A truck cab backed up to the van where he was hiding and hooked on to it. "All of a sudden we started to move, with me still on top. I couldn't believe this was happening to me. It was like something you have bad dreams about when you're a kid."

Gene rode for a few hundred feet, and before the truck had a chance to gather speed he grabbed onto overhanging branches of a tree and dropped, like Tarzan, to the ground. Back to the supermarket lot he scrambled, but this time he hid under a large cardboard packing carton that allowed him, when there were no passing cars, to move around under his protective coverage. "One car came through the lot, but it didn't stop and I couldn't get their attention. They drove off."

The story moved from the bizarre to the ridiculous as Gene, safe under his box, peered out from his shell like a turtle and watched his cousin, a member of the local police force, with another officer confer with the Unification Church member who had come to pick him up. Gene kept quiet, and eventually both cars left.

"After they drove off, I said another prayer. 'Well, it's just you and me, Heavenly Father, you've got to help.' And I said to myself, 'I'm going to make it back to New York, no matter what.'"

The question for Gene was no longer if he would make his escape, but how he could make it out of an area surrounded by police cars, in a town where his cousin had alerted everyone within radio distance to be on the lookout for him. Gene says he wondered how he would be able to lie low enough to keep out of the way of the law and at the same time move in the direction of the Unification Church headquarters in New York—"to freedom," as he defines it.

"I decided there was only one way. I'd have to steal a bike and ride the back roads to Newark, and then take a train or bus to New York." Gene feared that all the thruway entrance ramps, bus depots, and train stations would be watched, and he later found out this had been true. (While the bicycle idea may have been the result of logic and some desperation, there is that story in Unification Church legend that the Reverend Moon once escaped from pursuers by riding a bicycle 600 miles while carrying a crippled man on his back.)

"I didn't want to steal a bike, but I figured I could get it back to the address after I was back in the church."

The first bike Gene came upon was a shiny new ten-speed girl's bike. It would have been perfect. But Gene says he knew it would break someone's heart to find that bike missing, and so he kept looking.

The next bike was far from perfect, but Gene felt it wouldn't be missed much. "It was old and rusty, painted green and purple, with a banana seat and no pedals. It was almost hidden under a bush, and one tire was nearly flat." Gene salved his conscience with the thought that it might have been discarded.

"I got on that bike and started pedaling south, avoiding all the major highways. As I pedaled, I prayed, asking for guidance." He recalls that his legs

were just about to give out when he reached Newark
at dawn and decided to "fund-raise" to raise money
for a ticket into New York. He panhandled a few
coins; then a man gave him a dollar and told him to
get something to eat and go back to his church. A
dollar seemed like a huge amount of money to the
weary young man. Gene says he thanked his bene-
factor profusely and asked if he could mail the
money back to him. The stranger assured him it was
not necessary and wished Gene good luck.

Gene avoided the police in the Newark terminal,
boarded a train, and within minutes was in Manhattan and then back at the Unification Church
Headquarters, where he was greeted by scores of
delighted church members.

The first thing Gene did was pray and thank God
for his safe return.

Then he called his father and let him know that
everything was okay. Gene says, "I told him, 'I'm
still very angry about what you have done to me.'
And my father came very close to apologizing."

Gene tells us that his family relationship was
badly damaged by this attempted deprogramming
and that the entire family suffers for it.

A few months after the failed deprogramming of
Gene Leone, his father was the victim of a tragic
automobile accident. As his father lay near death in
a hospital, Gene explained to his family he was
afraid to come home, afraid that even in their grief
his family might try again to hold and deprogram
him.

He told his brother, "Mario, the reason I'm worried to come and visit Dad is that I don't trust you."

Gene describes his family religious ties as inactive Catholic and says his own religious involvement has brought his family closer to God and back into organized religion. He does not know whether the pain of his own involvement or the accident to his father is the cause of the family's new religiosity.

In the beginning of high school Gene had become a born-again Christian and was a member of the Campus Crusade and Youth for Christ. Here Gene appears to be an exception; most Unification Church members appear to have joined with no deep religious conviction. "My religious experience gave me a deeper understanding of God and God's heart. It prepared me for membership in the Unification Church, where I can devote my life to God's work," Gene says.

Before Gene met the Moonies, he had planned to become a missionary doctor. "Even then my parents would have preferred that I just be a 'doctor-doctor' and leave God out of it."

Gene Leone is a likable young man. He seems, except for a certain missing enthusiasm, to possess the qualities any parent would hope to see developed in a son or daughter. He is pleasant and gentle, he is strong and direct. He is bright, blessed with intelligence, untroubled by genius. Not necessarily shallow or simplistic, Gene's wit is not honed to a fine inquisitive edge.

He has asked his questions. He seems content that he's found all the answers. He claims that not only his life but his salvation and future are in good hands in the Unification Church. He is dedicated to a life of self-denial in his quest to help others find the God he knows.

Gene wished us well in our work. He did not try to convert us. He asked sincere and thoughtful questions about our families and looked at pictures of our children with interest and sensitivity.

There may be, as critics of his faith claim, an arrogance in his humility. There may even be a fanatic in his soul. But if there is, it does not show. (We know there could also have been a decision made before our visit not to proselytize or attempt to convert us.) After our visit, we are convinced that some of the Unification Church members have found peace. Whether it is temporary or permanent, we cannot guess.

Angelo LaFava and Gene Leone, in spite of their affiliation with the Unification Church, are still counted in the ranks of 50 million Americans who are considered, by archdioceses who still keep a count, to be Roman Catholic. The number of active Catholics has been shrinking in the past few decades, as seen in the decline of students in Catholic educational institutions from 6.1 million when enrollment was at an all-time high, to 4 million in 1975.

Some think a disproportionately high number of Unification Church members come from the Roman Catholic church, part of what Bishop Louis E. Gelineau of Providence, Rhode Island, describes in a pastoral letter as "the church that is coming apart." According to Bishop Gelineau, attendance at Sunday Mass varies between 10 percent and 25 percent of the total number of Catholic church members. "The times," he has said in masterful understatement, "are such as to test our faith."

But then, too, the numbers of Catholic souls accounted for in the records of this mammoth religious institution don't always reflect its true membership. Two young women who left the church, married outside of it, and are not raising their children in it, say they think they are still on the roll books. "After all, nobody even said goodbye," one told us. "I'm sure they don't even know I left."

In direct contrast, the new religions know, sometimes to the point of harassment, where each and every member is and the state of his faith.

But it is not only the Róman Catholics who see a troubling number of their young involved in religious cults. Rabbi Maurice Davis and some of the parents active in counter-cult groups contend that the percentage of Jewish youngsters in the cults is far higher than their percentage in society.

However, a study done by the Unification Church of its own membership claims that the young people who join the church represent varied religious backgrounds in almost exactly the same proportion they are represented in the rest of society.

Stan Bernstein, that Ph.D. candidate in Michigan, says the membership of the Hare Krishnas, his special field of study, reflects nearly the same pattern of Protestantism, Catholicism, and Judaism as the society it inhabits.

In their pain and desperation, many parents have turned to deprogrammers to help them rescue their cult-member sons and daughters. The first in this field, and author of *Let Our Children Go,* a book that describes his activities and gives his reasons for deprogramming, is Theodore Roosevelt Patrick, Jr.

Ted Patrick is certainly the best-known of the deprogrammers.

Today he is not alone. Now there are several adult deprogrammers and a host of former cult members who "deprogram" others out of sincere conviction that no one should be a member of a group that allows so little freedom of thought and personal choice. They espouse their new causes with the same fervor they once reserved for the Unification Church, the Children of God, Hare Krishna, the Divine Light Mission, or whatever new religion they swore allegiance to.

Most of the men and women who seek to help return cult members to the waiting arms of parents and families are, we feel, honest human beings with the best intentions. And, contrary to the allegations of their most severe critics, we believe most are not opportunists seeking to make a fast dollar from the misery of their fellow men. There is no shame in selling services, after all, and most of the adult men and women involved in deprogramming have given up other professions or jobs to devote their lives to their cause.

Still, many of them are ill-prepared and untrained in handling the psychological aspects of the intricate task they so readily undertake. Many, too, are lacking in the practical organizational skills that are necessary for projects that involve the sanity and self-images of those they seek to rescue.

It seems that for every deprogramming success story we found a nearly equal number of deprogramming failures, where the young persons involved have returned to their churches. The deprogram-

mings of Angelo LaFava and Gene Leone are not
the only ones that have failed. Many families, who
have paid deprogrammers fees of $1,000 and more,
have had to insist that an adult deprogrammer
come to their aid when the deprogramming, handled
by young former cult-members, produced no apparent results.

Hundreds of young people have been rescued
from religious cults and are living happy, productive lives. In many cases, "post-cult" lives are still
not what parents had in mind for their sons and
daughters. But when a "rescue" attempt has failed,
it often ends in despair that is more final than the
pain the deprogrammings were designed to rectify
in the first place.

Rabbi Davis tells, poignantly, how he attempted to
"rescue" a young woman from the Unification
Church. He had known Janet for several years; she
had been a member of his congregation in White
Plains. Rabbi Davis blames his failure to rescue
Janet on his own ignorance of the Reverend Moon's
religion. He now says that it was this failure that
pushed him to seek information and to try, with a
vengeance, to throw light on what he sees as the mis-
representations and malevolence of the church.

Patrick, highly acclaimed as he is by many par-
ents and former cult members, has had his share of
failures and is frank about them in his book. Kathe
Crampton, Ed Shapiro, Dan Voll, and Sandy Cole
were all subjected to his deprogramming techniques.
Today, Kathe Crampton is still known as Corinth
Israel in the Church of Armageddon, the Love Israel
Family in Seattle. Ed Shapiro left his college to re-

turn to the self-deprecating lifestyle of Krishna Consciousness. Dan Voll returned to the fundamentalist-style faith of his guru Hannah Lowe. Sandy Cole has been, for several years, underground and out of touch with her parents, serving the Children of God and their leader, David (Moses) Berg.

These failed deprogrammings did little to weaken the religious convictions of the young people they were designed to "rescue." They may, in fact, have further alienated them from their already distant parents. With the greater dedication and resurgence of faith that inevitably follows a failed deprogramming, it is yet to be seen if the subjects will ever be able to reintegrate into society.

Some parents claim the deprogramming might not have failed if the young persons had something to return to in their lives, something the religious cults clearly were not providing. This may, in fact, be the missing ingredient in many "rescue" attempts that fail.

Candy Harrison, a young member of the Unification Church, has been "rescued" twice by her parents and has gone through two rigorous deprogrammings. Twice she has returned to the Moonies. Candy's case has been highlighted by lawsuits and counter suits with both the church and Candy's parents charging that she was kidnapped against her will.

During a visit to the Unification Church headquarters in Washington, D.C., the day after the Reverend Moon's Washington Monument rally, Candy was ready to meet two reporters. Suddenly she disappeared. She had been spirited down a rear fire escape and out of town because her sister, accompanied by a friend, and with two police officers waiting nearby, had come to visit her at the headquarters. Candy must have feared that her parents and a court order remanding her into their custody were not far behind.

Many cult members flee from deprogrammers, or from their own families, after an actual deprogramming has taken place, during a period deprogrammers call rehabilitation. They return to their churches because they are "floating," a word coined by deprogrammers to mean a time when cultists cannot decide which lifestyle they want to choose. The churches, with their highly structured lifestyles, and specific demands on young members, offer the "easier" answer to questions about how to continue living.

Although floating is not defined in any dictionary, counter-cultists say it is the time when a young person vacillates between lives—when he is most likely to daydream about his shattered religious dreams and long for the security of the life within the religious cult.

Some cultists never question their choice of lifestyles and escape during the actual deprogramming. Donald and Charlie Robertson were two such "escapees," and the legal system, in their case, worked in their favor.

These two brothers, each Divine Light premies for more than five years, had come home to visit their parents and to take a short seashore vacation with their family. Both the young men are in their twenties and have, they say, carved out satisfying lives as part of the Divine Light Mission. When they arrived at their parents' cottage on Cape Cod they discovered, to their amazement, that all of the windows had been nailed shut and the locks on the doors had been changed. When they entered the living room after a quick tour of their vacation home, they found a deprogrammer, a bodyguard, and three former cult members.

Charlie and Donald decided to "go along for the ride," to "play it cool," and to wait out the deprogramming. Then Donald discovered a bathroom window that had not been nailed shut. He opened it and ran to the local police station, where he asked for the assistance of the patrolman on duty. Together they went back and freed his brother.

"I didn't want to get my parents in any trouble. I just wanted to get my brother and get out of there," he says. "We have the right to live our own lives."

Donald Robertson, intelligent and well-educated, has the hollow cheekbones and gaunt pallor that Dee Dee Fischer says she saw in her own Hare Krishna member son, also a vegetarian. Donald's mother says he has looked this way only since he started eating the strictly vegetarian meals of the Divine Light premies. "His physical condition was what prompted us to get him out," she says. Donald says he's always been thin.

The police officer, who insisted Donald and his brother be allowed to do what they prefer, as free men, charged the young men's parents and the deprogramming team with "false imprisonment," though Donald says he only wanted the police to free his brother and "forget about it." At a subsequent hearing both the parents and the deprogrammers were exonerated.

During a visit with Charlie at the Divine Light

Mission headquarters in Denver where he works, he chatted pleasantly in his office. But then he refused a ride back to his ashram for fear that we were deprogrammers hired by his parents.

The two young men say they love their parents. Charlie has recently been transferred to a Boston job, closer to his family's home. He says he wants to see them, wants to get them to accommodate themselves to his lifestyle—a lifestyle his parents see as foreign and incomplete for their sons.

One of the more ironic stories of a deprogramming is told by the mother of a former political group member who employed Ted Patrick to "free" her daughter. That's one version. The other story, nearly unrecognizable, is told by the daughter herself, an attractive and intelligent woman in her early twenties. Each of these stories, according to the teller's reality, is true. Somewhere between the two is what we'll call "objective reality."

The mother tells how the daughter was deprogrammed, after an emotional breakthrough where she "saw the light." Then, however, the daughter began to "float," as the family drove to Indiana to visit aunts, uncles, and cousins. During the drive to Indiana the young woman attempted to escape. She slipped notes to desk men in motels, tried to phone the group to come rescue her, and tried to get back to the political commune every chance she got.

"When she wasn't 'floating,' she was fine. She was our normal daughter again, not the zombie spouting political philosophies," says her mother. Then, when they got to Indiana, she was fine. "We finally knew we had our daughter back," says Susan Kaplin's mother.

Here's the daughter's story. "I was never deprogrammed. I was pretending to be so they'd leave me alone. After hours of being deprogrammed and shouted and laughed at, I couldn't take it anymore. But I was NOT deprogrammed. I was still a member of my group, in my heart, in my spirit, and in fact, when Ted Patrick left and we started our drive to Indiana," she says.

It wasn't, according to Susan, until the family arrived in Indiana and she had the chance to sit down and talk to a cousin, a lawyer several years her senior, that she seriously questioned her beliefs even enough to begin to doubt.

"My cousin said to me, 'I don't know you and you don't know me. I don't really care about you that much; you're my cousin, but I haven't ever really known you. I haven't seen you in years. But if you want to talk to me about it, I'll talk. And,' he promised, 'I'll listen.' "

Susan says now that the deprogramming her parents paid a small fortune for never worked. "Actually my deprogramming began miles from home, miles from any deprogrammer, miles away from Ted Patrick.

"My cousin was the first one I told my politics to. I told him there were slave labor camps in the Rocky Mountains [Susan was a member of a left-wing socialist political group], and that they were all run by Nelson Rockefeller, who was also, according to the group, going to take over the country.

"He said, 'That's really off the wall.' Then he told

how he flies his own plane through the mountains. 'There are no such camps. There couldn't be. All kinds of small planes fly through the mountains all the time, and they could not possibly be there without being seen.'" He asked Susan questions about the logistics of such camps. Where would they get food and supplies? How could they be kept such a complete secret in a country with a diligent press that loves to poke around? Susan had no answers. She began to feel foolish.

"He was the first person who treated me like an adult. With the rest of them, it was like they'd forgotten about me, as though the individual didn't really count for anything. The system of deprogramming was what they wanted to talk about. 'He was deprogrammed. She was deprogrammed. It's all brainwashing.' I finally talked to my cousin because he was normal, and treated me like an adult, someone who wouldn't cry at the drop of a hat, at the least mention of my ideas. He was rational.

"My cousin said he knew for a fact there were no slave labor camps in the Rocky Mountains. And I believed him. He never made fun of me [as the deprogrammer had] but really talked. Within a few hours I wondered how I had ever been able to believe all that stuff. Ted Patrick," she emphasizes, "never deprogrammed me, or even made me question my beliefs."

Why then, we ask, do her parents believe so fervently that Patrick alone was responsible for the change in her political beliefs and life. Has she talked to them frankly, told them what she is now telling us?

"Oh, yes, I've told them all this. They just don't

want to believe it," says Susan. And so the parents
and the daughter never discuss it.

Susan's mother is head of one of the counter-cult
groups in the Midwest who contends that Rabbi
Davis could not, as he claims, have deprogrammed
or debriefed nearly 100 former cult members while
they sat peaceably across from him in his temple
study. "I just don't believe it can be done that way,"
she says.

Readjusting

Sylvia Buford, who wrote this thoughtful personal essay in her diary after she left the Unification Church, will not return to the Moonies. Sylvia is now helping other former cult members during their own difficult readjustment periods, and she's good at it because she knows how difficult it can be to leave the church and pick up the pieces of a life left behind. Still, when a member of Sylvia's family read these words, she feared the young woman was on the brink of returning to the Unification Church. Parents and friends of former cult members say the fear never leaves them, the trust never quite returns.

Today a deprogrammed Moonie returned to Unification. I hear that his family is so stricken with grief that it is as though a death had occurred in the family. I felt some disappointment—but mostly sadness. He had tried so hard the past year to hold on. It was just too lonely for him I guess. He found nothing in this world and he had found something in Unification. There were warm bodies and songs and a higher purpose, no matter whether it was right or wrong.

Sometimes, on a cold day like today, I miss the warm sunshine of mornings at the Unification

Church Center in the Colorado mountains and the soothing tones of the Korean songs we sang there. A part of my heart is still there I suppose, and someday maybe I'll be able to figure it all out.

I don't like the word "brainwash." What happened to me was something more frightening, more insidious than I can ever explain. I suppose the word is Utopia. The Unification Church was the closest I ever came to Utopia. In spite of what angry parents say, the Unification Church doesn't need to kidnap. Its attraction is all-encompassing. They say, "Come with us! We can have an ideal world."

Perhaps it is heresy in religious doctrine, and unrealistic in philosophy, and dishonest in practice to the outside world. But all one remembers of the experience is the promise, the lure of the honey. So what is wrong with it—what is wrong with it?

It makes of those in its influence an exclusive novelty, a marginal commodity, a thing left out which takes no part in life. The boundaries of Unification are so limited that those within it can give joy to no one.

They become like a violin stored in a closet. The beautiful instrument renders no music, it neither adds nor takes away—it only lies dormant, becoming warped with age. But those in Unification don't mind waiting in the closet for the dream to become a reality, for the promise to be fulfilled, for the honey that can never be tasted. The tragedy comes when they can see that their dream will not be fulfilled and all that is left of the promise is a set of loose strings and a bent bow in need of repair.

Sylvia is waiting to hear if she's been accepted in law school. She says, "There's no way I'll ever go back. There's too much happiness in my life now to want to return to a life of nonchoice." Today she strongly disapproves of the Unification Church.

But her questions persist, and may be answered only as the idealism of her youth ripens into the realism of maturity. Now, Sylvia still craves the dream of sharing a common and universal goal of a world made better through sacrifice. Mourning for the lost dream can develop into a form of intellectual malaise with former cult members who are unable to replace lives of total dedication with something else that seems as meaningful. With love and support from her family, and with the understanding and help of a professional counselor, Sylvia says she knows there are no easy answers in life. But she still wants to be a part of a Utopian vision. She is still searching. Her quest gives her a common bond with most religious cultists. Cults are filled with idealists who have nowhere to go.

Dreams are slow to die. The hard facts of reality are not always powerful enough to kill a dream. This is why deprogramming, or walking away from a religious cult, is just the climax of a cult experience. A readjustment to life must follow if the encounter is to be put to rest and catalogued with memories of things past.

Many young people return to their cults after deprogrammings even after they have promised their friends, families, and themselves not to. Others float from one group to another, changing their religious beliefs, their college majors, and their goals by whim instead of reason.

When parents decide to rob a young person of a cult-promised dream because that dream appears false to them, they must be prepared to help their son or daughter find a workable substitute for it. The task is rarely easy. But it will certainly be less difficult if the parents can, with patience, encourage the young person to evaluate what is really important in his scheme of life and to analyze why he made the lifetime commitment to a cult.

Former cult members must understand how they got into the cult. Did they make a conscious decision to join? Were they avoiding life problems that seemed too difficult to confront? Did they allow themselves to be led into the cult because they weren't able to make decisions of any kind?

The self-esteem of young people who have just left a religious cult is often at an all-time low. They realize they have allowed themselves to be grossly deceived, and they have difficulty trusting their own instincts.

A young psychologist in California, who is familiar with former cult members since both her fiancé and his sister were once Moonies, understands this problem well. She explains, "There is a great fear of commitment when a person leaves a cult. Ex-cultists have tremendous needs to confide and be accepted, but at the same time they are so afraid to get involved."

In her book *Your Child's Self-Esteem: The Key to His Life,* Dorothy Corkhille Briggs states, "For high self-esteem [an individual needs to]:

—establish final independence from family and age-mates to become a confident other [individual];
—relate successfully to the opposite sex;

—prepare for an occupation for self-support;
—establish a workable and meaningful philosophy of life."

Unfortunately many of the young people who join these groups are suffering from lack of self-esteem and they use the cult experience as an alternative means of gaining it. They find it easier to look and feel confident by relying on the cult than to work for self-esteem within themselves. Cult membership does for them all the things Dorothy Briggs says they need to do individually:

—They become independent of family and peers by becoming dependent on the cult.
—They relate to the opposite sex by following the strict sexual mores of the cult.
—They engage in menial labor with easily recognizable goals in exchange for support.
—They adopt the philosophy of the cult rather than developing one of their own.

When they leave their groups it is natural that they feel a lack of self-esteem even more acutely than they did before they joined. They still face the long uphill push toward maturity. Since the cult experience may have debilitated them psychologically, some find the climb overwhelming.

If parents were aware of adjustment problems in a young person's life before his cult experience, they can be sure that the problems have not disappeared. A cult encounter can compound personality problems. It rarely alleviates them. Even if a young person seemed well-adjusted before his cult encounter, a parent should watch for cult-induced group-dependency problems.

When Fred Herbert left the Unification Church he endured months of crippling lethargy in the small Wisconsin town where he was born and grew up. "I could hardly move after I left the Moonies," he says. Fred wonders how he lasted as long as he did as a Moonie. "But," he rationalizes, "then it seemed like the best choice I could make for my life."

Before Fred Herbert joined the Unification Church he was a top student at the University of Minnesota, idealistic and intelligent. But, like so many other young people who enter religious cults, Fred lacked specific goals and direction. He says he changed his major "so many times I can hardly remember," before he settled on psychology—a field that still holds his interest.

Fred claims he left his idealism behind when he left the Unification Church, but he still clings to a dream of the Moonie promise. "I know there are no easy answers," he says. Still he wonders why he hasn't been able to find a substitute for the way he felt when he thought he was part of a movement that was going to change the course of world history.

Even though he has spent many of the months since he left the church helping a deprogrammer, Fred admits he still hasn't faced some problems he should have confronted before he joined the Moonies. At twenty-six he has not used any of his expensive college education or worked at any job that resembles a career. He has yet to set life goals for himself. According to the woman who deprogrammed him, Fred has considered returning to a religious cult several times.

In the darker moments since he's left the church, Fred says he wonders if, after all, the Moonie dream might work, wonders why he and others in the church shouldn't continue to try to change the world. Fred still has these conflicts even though he basically believes the Moon mission is destined to fail. Fred's father says the young man suffered frequent cult-related nightmares during the first few months after he left the Unification Church.

It's been more than a year since Fred was a Moonie, and now he is attempting to make some semipermanent plans for his life. He is particularly interested in mind control and other coercive techniques used by the new religions and plans to work with a psychologist who treats former cult members. He knows that becoming a mature individual is a long-term process, and he isn't alone in this realization.

Most former cult members tell of tremendous difficulties they experienced upon reentering life after a cult encounter.

Sally Spencer spent nearly a year in bed after she left the Unification Church. She pulled herself out of bed long enough to type one sentence at a time on her English honors course thesis. Sally says she finally completed the course and received a bachelor's degree. But for many months after she left the group —on her own—Sally says she thought she was "going crazy" or "losing my mind." If her college adviser had been less understanding of what she was going through or if her parents had been overprotective and had not allowed Sally to fight the demons her own way, she might never have made it. After graduation Sally was accepted at a top graduate school and is aiming for a career. As she nears graduation from law school she is eager to establish herself as a lawyer with a life and roots of her own.

"Very few members get out of the Unification Church by themselves. I consider myself lucky," Sally says. "Almost everyone who was a member of the church when I joined [seven years ago, when the movement was called the Unified Family] is still a member today.

"It is nearly impossible to leave. The members make it very difficult and work tirelessly to pressure you to stay. My own mind screamed that I maintain a commitment to this new life. I couldn't think clearly because I believed that all 'un-Moon' thoughts were Satanic," she wrote in a testimonial for other ex-cult members to read.

Still this young woman gathered the strength to walk away from a cult that had a firm grip on her life because she says she knew instinctively the life was too limited and that things were not as they should have been in the top leadership. When she left she was convinced she wanted more out of life than the group offered. But she never foresaw a tortured year of nightmares and the overwhelming worry that Satan could now possess her.

There are problems other than identity-related ones. The young California psychologist observes that while they are cult members young people forget the "dance of the sexes"—the ritual wherein young men and women tentatively explore the nature of intersex relationships. "The real world is far removed from the cocoon a cult builds," she explains, "and leaving the safety of guaranteed friendships with no threat of sexual involvement is very tough for many young people."

Many former cultists have residual problems with sex because of restrictions or prohibitions that have been taught in the cult. Except for a few groups that endorse free and perverse sexual behavior, the cults put strictures on sexual instincts that are ultraconservative. Like the Victorian bride who was taught all her life that sex was dirty and nasty but was expected to find it pleasurable within hours after she was married, those who have been cult members cannot easily put aside these inculcated values.

Sylvia Buford says she was afraid of any kind of relationship with a young man when she left the Moonies. "I was afraid he might expect something of me," she says. Since she's been away from the cult for a year and a half, Sylvia says she can have a "good relationship" with someone she really cares for and professes few problems with her own sexuality.

Some cultists discover they can no longer suppress their instinctual desires and decide to leave the cult.

Former Hare Krishna devotee John McCabe rose to a top-level position during his five years in the movement before he left the group on his own. At twenty-four, John is a college student again.

He confesses that while he doesn't tell anyone about his years in Krishna, he considers the experience a valuable one and has no regrets. He finds the attitudes of others toward Krishna critical and based on limited information and he says he doesn't want to explain again and again what Krishna represented to him.

John decided to leave the cult, after so many years, for a number of reasons. One reason, a minor one, he says, was his own reluctant celibacy. "I began to want very strongly to be free, on my own, and living exactly as I felt was right. The vow of celibacy was getting hard to maintain, because I was almost ready to turn twenty-three and my masculinity was in bloom. I was not feeling like a kid any more. I was feeling like a full-blown male adult with all the natural desires and necessities of one. In other words, the full-grown female was starting to really attract me."

John had taken the vows of total celibacy as a Krishna swami, and according to those vows his thoughts of women were to be suppressed. He eventually decided that holding back natural desire was "ridiculous and artificial," since the rest of Krishna life didn't offer enough in exchange.

John has had a few intimate relationships with women since he left the Krishnas and says they came about very "naturally." He emphasizes that his sexual conflict was not the only reason he left Krishna. If there was a single reason, it was because he felt he was prevented from making free choices of his own. John was finally convinced on his own that he could better serve the world and himself outside the movement. "How could I pray and just ignore the whole mess that lies in front of my eyes?"

he asks. "When one-third of the world is starving, when the waters, the air, and the land are full of garbage and pollution, peace is not experienced. How could I sit and meditate and try to save my soul and other souls?" he asks.

Now, John says, he has accepted the responsibility for what happens to him in life. But an important part of his story is his still-fervent belief that he could not have been deprogrammed. John McCabe believes his five Krishna years were a constructive part of his total development as a person. "Everyone in Krishna thinks about leaving, I know for sure," he says. He tells stories about many Krishna friends who left the group when they became disillusioned with its goals. "They didn't want to devote any more of their lives to it. One married couple with a child has settled successfully in Florida. They had very few problems with readjustment."

John says he has seen former Krishnas experiencing great emotional difficulties, but they are the ones who left the movement against their will and who continue to yearn for the dream of changing the world. Other former Krishnas just don't know what they want, in or out of the cult. He believes his own readjustment was fairly easy and painless because he spent months contemplating what to do until he had decided exactly why he was leaving and where he wanted to go.

Not all parents are willing to gamble for five years, as John's did, to see if their son or daughter outgrows a cult's structured life and peer-supported goals. Yet, in terms of long-range life adjustment, John McCabe may be better off than the young person who leaves his problems outside the door of a religious cult and is faced with picking them up again when he is forced to leave the cult because his parents cannot bear to watch him waste precious years as a religious zealot.

Among counter-cult activists, there is a theory that those who are officially deprogrammed have an easier time readjusting to life after they leave a cult than those who simply walk away. Actually, it seems nearly *all* former cultists have difficulty reentering a society they have been taught by their cult to despise. It is predictable that cultists will have a struggle when they leave behind lives of structure, love, and attention, all neatly packaged together with goals and purpose.

Many cult members say they were in bad emotional states before they found a cult. They often say they were drug addicts or so depressed they would have become suicide statistics if cult recruiters had not come along and "saved" them. The drug stories they tell are, on investigation, often overblown. Some young people who have had only passing experiences with marijuana say they were addicted to hard drugs. Others who tell of life crises and depression often do not exaggerate but tend to blame society for their problems rather than understand that personal conflict is often a normal part of the maturation process. Many former cultists say they had little motivation and no goals. They were feeling lost, helpless, and unfulfilled when they joined their groups. Some say they had experienced the end of a love affair and were feeling confused, hurt, and guilty about sex. Those within cults nearly always blame the evil, Satanic world for any such crises and claim God has "saved them" from their sinful lives.

There is a perverse sort of pride within religious cults, an extension of the prodigal son theory, that says the worse off a person was when he joined, the more pride he can take in being "saved." And so it is not surprising that many of the most elaborate stories of drug use often turn out to be the use of marijuana, hashish, or some experimentation with hallucinogenics, and the promiscuity is actually nothing more than an intimate relationship with a high school or college sweetheart.

One young man, still a Moonie, blames his parents for not stopping his "illicit sex" with a teen-age girlfriend. His parents say they never knew about it. If they had, they say, they would have considered it somewhat normal though it would have worried them and they would have discussed it. Now he talks constantly about sex as the "root of all evil." He discusses marriage but appears to believe it will be loveless, and wants to marry only out of duty toward his group and to father perfect, sinless children.

Another young man who had left the Krishnas blames his father for introducing him to a life of drugs and illicit sex. The young Krishna's father drove him back to his former college campus, where the young man settled into a new room and within a few days was invited to an informal party. At the party he smoked grass, seemed to flip out, and walked barefoot through twenty miles of snow to return to his Krishna temple. He has become something of a legend within Krishna as a hero who withstood tremendous temptation and who left behind the sinful ways of the world that even his father approved.

According to the authors of *People Reading,* Dr. Ernst G. Beier and Evans G. Valens, three major steps are involved in changing another person's behavior: "Disengagement, delivering a surprising response, and providing space for change."

The doctor-writer team explains how disengagement and analysis of the problem must precede any decision to alter behavior that seems antisocial. In the case of a cult member, this detachment is the thought and consideration a parent gives to the situation before any kind of decision is made. The "surprise" of which they write, in a cult member's case, could be a deprogramming reevaluation or simply recognition of reasons to leave. The "space for change" comes when the initiator of the change steps back after the "surprise" and allows the subject to come to conclusions that will allow him to alter his own behavior. This is the period of rehabilitation.

In the period of analysis that precedes a decision to deprogram, parents should not only be certain that they believe the forced removal from the cult is the right thing to do, but they must also be prepared in advance to help the cult member through the difficult period of rehabilitation. It would be naive to think that love alone can take care of the situation.

It is important to try to understand as much as possible about the individual—his background, education, and the conditions of his life before he entered the cult. It is also necessary to learn as much as possible about the cult in question. While some groups deceive potential converts during the recruiting process, others do not. The willingness and eagerness of young people to become part of these groups should not be ignored.

James S. Gordon, a psychiatrist and consultant to the National Institute of Mental Health, spent a year and a half observing and participating in the life of several of the religious cults of the 1970s. Dr. Gordon attended a weekend workshop in the Unification Church and a variety of other cult ceremonies and events, always as an observer who kept his professional identity hidden. The young bearded Harvard Medical School graduate argues that religious cults are neither as socially pernicious as cult critics say nor as positive as their members avow. Rather, the cults are, Dr. Gordon says, a natural result of a time of social and cultural crisis.

"In the religious cults which seemed, almost miraculously, to arise to meet . . . needs [Dr. Gordon defines them as the need for a transcendent experience, fraternity and sorority in a family setting, leadership and authority, community, and a sense of mission], young people found a confirmation of their longings and a group structure which could help them overcome their isolation. In the web of exotic and highly rationalized theologies, they discovered and have tenaciously held onto an unerring map, one that would take them beyond the limitations and uncertainties of secular and political goals." Dr. Gordon believes the idiosyncrasies and burdens of cult life are a cement which binds members together and distinguishes them from the "outside world."

Perhaps if they were not so personally involved

they could agree with Dr. Gordon's assessment, but most former cult members cannot be philosophical about their experience. They need a scapegoat—in this case the cult—as a focal point for their anger. Often it is useless to explain to these young people that they have intrinsic vulnerabilities which made them susceptible to the cults. They feel they must reinforce the separation with anger and blame.

The cult promised them salvation if they stayed. They left, and they are tormented by fears of eternal damnation and lives of hell on earth. When they evaluate the pros and cons of the cult, their fears often mount, unless they are helped to face them in an objective fashion. It is simply easier to reject the cult as totally bad.

Unfortunately, many "rehabilitation" programs conducted by deprogrammers are only forms of security, which serve simply to keep the subject busy and reinforce his new antagonism toward the cult. Many deprogrammers are themselves former cult members who reinforce their own need for vindication by deprogramming others.

Rarely can parents alone help a young person through the difficult adjustment he must make when leaving a cult.

Where, then, can parents turn? Cult rehabilitation programs are being developed by some community service organizations with the help of anticult parent groups and former cult members. It is conceivable that YMCA/YWCA and YMHA/YWHA groups with community mental health programs could sponsor group therapy sessions in communities where ex-cultists need help.

Also at the urging of the anticult organizations,

more and more psychiatrists and psychologists are becoming aware of the cult phenomenon and the problems that follow cult membership. Some young people have been helped back to reality by therapists who understand the problem. But even with professional help, the ex-cultists have a need to share their experiences with others who "have been there too." They need to know other ex-cult members and to understand that they are not unusual or sick or "dumb" because they succumbed to a cult's attractions.

Several live-in rehabilitation centers have sprung up around the country. Some have well-thought-out programs. But the best live-in program is little use to a family who can't afford one. These families will have to turn to friends and services within their own communities.

The director of a rehabilitation facility in the Southwest says she rarely recommends individual psychological counseling for the young people who come to the center she runs. While this woman doesn't deny the need for occasional counseling, she thinks ex-cult members mainly need love and attention and a reintroduction to good clean fun. This woman, the wife of a well-known deprogrammer, says many young people get involved with cults in the first place because "they were educated right out of their common sense." It is almost too obvious to say parents should use caution when selecting a deprogrammer, someone to help in a reevaluation, or a rehabilitation program for their ex-cultist son or daughter.

If there is one single course of action that appears

to be valuable for every ex-cultist whose family can afford it, it is the kind of rehabilitation program set up by Dr. George Swope, an ordained Baptist minister who is a professor and counselor at Westchester Community College in Westchester County, New York. He brings his experience as the father of an ex-cult member (Swope's daughter was a Moonie) and his years as a pastor together with what he has learned about young adults as a teacher, in the center he has established in rural New England. The center at his converted New Hampshire summer home, with attached barn-garage and carriage house, offers a program of psychology and religious studies for ex-cult members.

Dr. Swope decided to set up the rehabilitation program after he took over the leadership of Citizens Engaged in Reuniting Families (CERF), a counter-cult organization founded by Rabbi Maurice Davis. "I began to see that at least 25 percent of all deprogrammings were failing," Dr. Swope says, "and that the kids were heading back to the cults." He places the blame for failures squarely on the shoulders of some deprogrammers, describing them as "inexperienced." They rely, he says, on their own powerful personalities to sway young cultists' convictions. He believes they fail when they do not help young people try to find substitute beliefs and goals for those they left behind in the cult.

The cost of a four-week stay at the Swope center is $1,000. Here Dr. Swope tries to help young people see how their association initially came about and to see what needs they had that were filled within the group. Former cultists are taught not to feel guilty or ashamed because they were vulnerable to a cult encounter and are advised on how to cope with the problems of reentry into life outside the influence of the group.

Dr. Swope designed the program after consultation with advisers from the fields of psychiatry, education, medicine, law, and business. The system is divided into three parts:

Structured rap sessions are combined with a study of psychology and mind control techniques.

A study of the principles of biblical interpretation emphasizes the Bible as the basis for Judeo–Christian culture and how cult leaders distort the Bible's message.

The ex-cultists study the family, dealing with expectations of an individual, and the separation from parents, which is a normal part of the maturation process.

The educator says he isn't interested in imposing any religious belief on anyone but feels that "they need a positive view of religion, whether they accept it or not. We try to compare the mood of cult leaders such as Moon and Prabhupada with that of religious leaders like Christ and Gandhi."

In their study and discussions about family life, Dr. Swope explains to his young students why a clash between them and their parents—whether gentle or harsh—is an inevitable part of becoming an adult. They discuss the cult concept of the family and compare it to the expectations society holds for itself. A religious cult usually views all those outside its perimeters as misguided, at best—demonic, at worst.

Swope says, "There can be no such thing as a perfect society when it's made up of imperfect people."

Study and classes do not fill all an ex-cult member's time at the center. In free hours staff members and other former cult members are available for informal conversation. Dr. Swope encourages the young people to take part in outings, bowling, swimming, games, and other activities. The center is located near three colleges where the young people can also attend films, discussions, and other events.

After the basic four-week session, an ex-cultist can stay on longer at the center, and the cost drops to less than $250 per week. "By this time," Dr. Swope reasons, "the young person needs less supervision and fewer counseling sessions, so we don't charge as much.

"No one is detained at the center against his will," he says. Dr. Swope is never personally involved in deprogramming, but he will advise parents about legal conservatorships and the selection of a deprogrammer.

He believes most former cult members are not ready to go back to college or the job market immediately after breaking with a cult. "They have just left a high-pressure situation and are reluctant and unable to handle pressure." Dr. Swope calls the time it takes a young ex-cult member to get ready for work or study again, "decompression time."

Jean Merritt, who has worked successfully with scores of ex-cult members, is associated with Dr. Swope in the center. The young people Jean Merritt has counseled are often her strongest supporters and tell how she helped them unravel the mysteries of their cult experiences and encouraged them to shed the excess emotional baggage they carried away from the cult.

Since the center has been in operation, only one parent has resisted Dr. Swope's advice that his son see a psychiatrist or a psychologist during his rehabilitation. Dr. Swope says he thinks that father was afraid some family problems might be unearthed in the therapy and was not, himself, prepared to face them. Dr. Swope makes his belief clear. "If a young person needs psychological help, he should get it."

After a successful rehabilitation, former cult members usually are able to function in society. But many of them need additional time before they can get on a direct route to a career. It is time they may have needed to take even before they joined the cult.

Randy Wilcox spent nearly a year studying religion before he decided what to do with his life. The track Randy is on now still may not be the one to take him through his entire life. At the end of two years, Randy says he will either leave his Mennonite Volunteer program or seek guidance about where to continue his mission. Whatever Randy ultimately decides to do with his life, the odds are it will be a choice far removed from the one his Unitarian parents thought he would make when he graduated from college in 1975 with a degree in business administration.

Other young people may find purpose in voluntary programs such as the Peace Corps or Vista. Parish priests, ministers, and rabbis are often aware of religious service programs for young people within their own faiths. Father Kent tells of the Channel program in Seattle, where young people devote two years to study and community-service work.

While many families of ex-cult members dismiss these religious and secular service programs as a small step away from a group-dominated cult experience, there are obvious differences between them and the cults. A young person is always free to leave a voluntary program when his enlistment time is up, and none of the programs are founded or guided by a living leader whose ethics may be in question.

No Easy Answers

Our odyssey through the religious cult labyrinth confirmed what we suspected at the beginning of our journey. A few young people can flirt with cult life and then simply walk away from it. Yet the guileless can become so entangled in the web of a cult that they cannot extricate themselves without help. Those who want restrictive, structured lives of non-choice will either find or create them, and these individuals may remain with the new religious cults in spite of attempts to remove them.

A few of the religious cults, like the wayward Children of God, seem to be dispersing and becoming less effective in attracting new converts. Others, more perverse and unorthodox, have never been able to attract significant numbers to their folds. These remain scattered on the fringes of an omnipresent counterculture.

The Hare Krishnas, so reliant on the direction of their aged spiritual master, may not survive his inevitable death. The Divine Light Mission shows signs of change and may become more acceptable as an alternative form of spiritual expression rather than a total lifestyle.

The Church of Scientology may continue to arouse the ire of disaffected members, while others will claim their total commitment to Scientology has improved their lives.

Sun Myung Moon's monumental Unification Church seems to be growing richer and stronger, despite the criticism and force that have been mounted to stop it. Yet this group, too, seems capable of changing its ways to become part of the ever-expanding religious establishment.

On the other hand, some branches of the "Jesus movement" appear in danger of becoming cultlike as their leaders become corrupted by power and begin to claim divine sanction. This is how a cult begins. A leader emerges with a philosophy of a way of life that will, he claims, guarantee salvation and satisfaction. He gathers followers and remains the central figure in the group. Then, the pattern shows, the self-styled religious leader begins to tell of divine revelations or claims to have always had special powers. The history of each religious awakening is filled with stories about self-avowed prophets and god-figures and their propensities for power.

What then will become of young people who, in spite of their parents' attempts to deprogram and reintegrate them into secular society, insist on remaining cult members? If the Unification Church, the Children of God, Hare Krishnas, and other cults stay on the cultural scene, will these young people always be part of them? Many will not.

We have observed that those who pursue an ideology with great intensity are seldom able to sustain the pursuit for long. These fervent ones often reject one cause for another in what becomes an endless quest. Today's most fanatical Moonie is often tomorrow's most dedicated counter-cult activist.

Perverse and restrictive religious cults are but one symptom of illness in a society where all is not well. Even if religious cults disappear or become so controlled by law that they are forced into compliance with accepted values and mores, or if the groups voluntarily modify their practices to become acceptable to the broad spectrum of society, the cultural malaise which nurtured them may go unattended, and new, equally threatening movements may rise from their ashes. The cult phenomenon is an indication that many young Americans sense some missing elements in their culture.

In order to expose the roots of the sickness, an examination of society and its institutions—the government, the churches, the schools, and the family— is in order.

Government, the most pervasive institution, holds the most potential for controlling religious cult excesses. But an overly ambitious legal effort to control the cults is also dangerous. It would be a poor exchange to limit the religious freedom of the entire populace in order to inhibit the growth of religious cults.

Ted Patrick told a California legislative inquiry headed by Lieutenant Governor Mervyn Dymally, who was then a state senator, "Freedom of religion, this part of the Constitution is outdated. [It] is nothing but a license to kill, lie, and steal and do everything under the sun as long as you've got a non-profit corporation and say you're a church. This part of the Constitution should be changed. . . ."

Patrick's proposal is a radical one. Even orthodox Christian churches and spokesmen for other mainline faiths who decry cult practices urge caution, warning their members that the sort of action Patrick suggests could very well impinge on their own individual religious liberties.

Nevertheless, it is through our legal system that religious practices detrimental to individuals or society can be controlled. Constitutional lawyer Alan Goldhammer also testified before the Dymally Committee and explained the Bill of Rights. He pointed out, "While every person is guaranteed freedom of conscience in freedom of belief, the freedom to act is not guaranteed. When belief is translated into action, a person may be required to conform to regulations. . . ."

In his testimony, Goldhammer cited the case of the *People* vs. *Collins,* in which a conviction for possession of marijuana was upheld even though the defendant claimed he used the drug to intensify his religious belief and to increase his ability to engage in religious experience. Goldhammer explained that while the government could not legislate against the defendant's conviction that drug use would intensify his religious experience, it could prohibit him from carrying out that belief in a practice that is illegal.

Goldhammer advised the committee, "If conduct is occurring here which is wrongful, the first question is whether existing laws regulating criminal and civil conduct are applicable. And if such is the case, then the problem is one of existing law. If existing laws do not reach the problem and it is still felt that conduct is wrongful, assuming that a true religious belief is found and not a facade designed to conceal illegal activities, then legislation to prevent practices must be devised which will not interfere with the belief and which will demonstrate a compelling interest based on the protection of the health and safety of the public."

Laws restricting religious recruiting and proselytizing in school yards could be passed and vigilantly guarded. To protect the rights of prospective converts, it could become illegal to recruit young people to groups which operate solely as fronts for religious cults, when the group's true identity is not revealed to potential converts.

But overly ambitious state and municipal laws can backfire. Local control of solicitation and fundraising efforts, for example, could become so bureaucratically cumbersome that legitimate groups could no longer afford the time to register, explain themselves, and sell their wares. Zoning laws that are designed to keep "pernicious" groups out of "good" neighborhoods can also be applied to other groups and can set dangerous precedents. We may recall the plight of the Mormons, how their barns and fields were systematically burned until they were pushed westward into the territory of Utah. Jewish rabbis remind us of the troubles they have had buying or renting space for synagogues and temples outside of big cities.

Still, zoning laws can be applied without prejudice as they were in Evanston, Illinois, when the City Council ordered local Hare Krishna leaders to comply with city statutes that require property up-keep, adequate off-street parking, and noise control. The Krishnas were given plenty of time to meet the requirements, and yet they did not comply. Because of their unwillingness to obey existing laws, the Krishnas have been denied a zoning change required for them to remain in the community, and they are being forced to leave.

In another instance, a community has banded to-gether, before the fact, to keep the Moonies out. The action is being taken, not because Unification Church members have done anything illegal in that community, but because the citizenry fears they might do so in the future. A spokesman for that township zoning commission has said he will use the full force of the law to keep the Moonies out. Privately he admits his hope that the Unification Church will see that it is not wanted in his community and will look elsewhere for property.

Grass-roots ordinances, even with their potential for unjust restrictions, can hardly invoke the awe-some control of religious belief that could come about through constitutional amendment. The finer points of community control and exclusionary zon-ing are, of course, open for court decisions. Never-theless, care must be taken not to apply laws to religious cults more stringently than they are applied to other religious groups. In the Evanston case, sev-eral witnesses hostile to the Krishnas told zoning offi-cials of the group's alleged harboring of runaway juveniles, and of other problems. The officials lis-tened politely but said they could consider only the zoning questions. They suggested that the entire City

Council hear this testimony, since the zoning group did not intend to judge the group on their behavior in other areas.

Religious cults that violate federal laws such as the Internal Revenue Service code, the Foreign Agents Registration Act, or immigration and naturalization laws may be prosecuted to the full extent of the law and made to conform. If existing law is utilized to its full extent, some cults may find that the United States is not the gracious hostess they once thought.

In the area of education, religions that sponsor schools for their members or their members' children must operate those schools in accordance with state and local regulations that govern all educational systems.

In addition to attempting to control religious cults, the government sponsors programs that can serve as alternatives to the cult experience for idealistic, motivated young people. Parents and educators once discouraged this kind of temporary commitment, fearing that if young people took time off from their studies or took breaks before beginning careers, they might be sidetracked indefinitely.

But parents are discovering, as Katherine Sheehan, dean of Scarsdale High School in New York says she did, that "a year off frequently broadens a student's perspective and makes him less likely to take his education for granted."

University guidance counselors have watched generations of young men who couldn't settle down to study drop out of college and after a stint in the military service return to their studies as serious, conscientious scholars who had gained the self-discipline and motivation they had sorely lacked before their military experience.

"Several recent studies have argued convincingly that a year off between high school and college can be a stimulating experience and very beneficial to emotional and career development," according to Dr. Michael Balzerman, associate professor at the University of Minnesota's Center for Youth Development and Research.

One cannot observe the discipline, enthusiasm, and vigor of the disciples of Sun Myung Moon and other contemporary cult leaders without suspecting that this energy may be a great national resource and without wondering if it can be channeled into constructive, more positive directions than cult life.

Volunteers in Service to America (VISTA), the Peace Corps, Volunteers in Parks, and Volunteers in the National Forests have not made a serious attempt to recruit young people in recent years. Today, none of these programs seems to ignite the imagination of idealistic young people to the flames of intensity the cults can spark. At their inception in the 1960s, the Peace Corps and VISTA attracted thousands of young visionaries. But these programs began to lose ground when their ballooning dreams deflated into pragmatism and the age of disillusionment dawned in the late sixties and early seventies. Today they stand virtually forgotten, outside the mainstream of American life, while religious cults and their leaders benefit from untold hours of idealistic young energy.

In VISTA today, young people over eighteen can

work for a year in one of many social and environmental projects. The program provides food, lodging, and other benefits and is a sound alternative where young people can try their wings of adulthood instead of attempting to burst into full flight, unprepared and untried.

Volunteers in Parks, a volunteer group of young people within the National Park Service, receive no salary for their work—nature-walk guiding, working with conservation teams, photography, or cave exploration—but they do receive uniforms and are insured. They are not provided with room and board but must live at home or near enough to a national park so they can commute to work.

Young people who want to indulge their love of the outdoors and at the same time contribute to the betterment of the environment may consider enlisting in the Volunteers in the National Forests. In this program young people may work at a number of tasks that range from map making to trail maintenance.

Volunteering in the Peace Corps requires skill and training and is a more likely alternative for a young person who has completed his education and wants a chance to get some experience and help others at the same time. The Peace Corps needs skilled craftsmen, mechanics, farmers, nurses, and teachers.

The religious establishment, the social institution religious cults most vigorously seek to supplant, also offers some service programs for young adults who wish to volunteer their time in the cause of a better life for all, in the context of service to God.

Former Unification Church member Randy Wilcox has found expression for his idealism and love of God in the Mennonite Voluntary Service Program. Father Kent Burtner tells of a program the Roman Catholic church operates in Seattle, Washington. Mainline religions may look to such programs as alternative services. To young people they may provide a way of entering the world tentatively and cautiously, within a system where they can provide service that uses their knowledge, skill, and energy while they receive guidance and direction.

Interest in lifetime religious vocations has waned in recent years, and these temporary programs, if they were made known to more young adults, could provide the churches with the manpower to work in religious education and social service programs.

The United Church of Christ and the United Presbyterian Church of the U.S.A. offer 26,000 one-year volunteer assignments each year. These volunteer jobs, which provide room, board, and small stipends, are in homes for emotionally disturbed children, homes for the aged, inner-city programs, coffee houses, and community-organizing projects.

Many churches say they are looking within their own organizations to see what has gone wrong, asking why so many of their young members are deserting the churches of their childhood for unorthodox new belief systems.

Many clergymen say they fear that these new religions may be totally undesirable. Four such representatives of Roman Catholicism, Judaism, and Protestantism denounced the Unification Church, calling the Moon cult a threat to the world. "The Unification

Church has all the earmarks of the Nazi movement,"
they said. Church members immediately replied that
while the clergymen were undoubtedly men of good
conscience, they were not speaking for their respec-
tive faiths, but only for themselves, when they denounced the Moonies. Susan Reinbold, a public
relations representative of the Moon group, says,
"The research these men base their conclusions on
is shortsighted and unfair since it was gathered
only from former church members and others opposed to the church. They never consulted or entered into any dialogue with the Unification Church
or its members," she said.

The four clergymen were not the first to say that
Moon's Divine Principle is dangerous and anti-
Semitic, for the Principle asserts that man is responsible for the "failure of Christ's mission," and alleges
that those men who were responsible for his death
were Jews. Because of this, and according to the
doctrine of indemnity the Moonies espouse, the Jews
have suffered persecution, including the Nazi holo-
caust, to atone for that failure. Contemporary Jews
were appalled when a Roman Catholic Pope held
them responsible for the crucifixion of Christ, so they
can be no less insulted when a Korean messiah tries
to do the same.

Members of the Jewish community, with Rabbi
Maurice Davis, are concerned by the numbers of
young Jews who seem to be finding "salvation" in
the Principle of the Reverend Moon. They find the
current Jewish exodus to Moon and other religious
cults especially disconcerting because large numbers
of Jews have never converted to other faiths. And yet
somewhere around 10 percent of the Unification

Church members in the United States are young
Jewish men and women, according to Rabbi Davis
and other informed observers. "Not an alarming
figure, until one realizes that Jews only make up 3
percent of the national population," says Davis.

But the Jews are not alone in the problem of attracting and keeping their young. The old Roman
Catholic axiom, "Give us a child before he's seven
and he's ours for life," may no longer be valid, if it
ever was.

All orthodoxy sponsors vigorous programs for
childhood religious education—catechism, Sunday
school, Hebrew school. But after early adolescence,
following confirmation and bar mitzvah, most religions appear to take continued devotion and membership for granted.

Those who survive adolescence in their faith are,
according to the Reverend Derald Stump, Episcopal
chaplain at Pennsylvania State University since 1965,
"young people who have two advantages: they are
from committed, not nominally religious families,
and are members of strong, active congregations
where teaching and worship are emphasized and
reinforced by fellowship in a youth program." Some
sects offer such fellowship programs, but most neglect the serious study and worship they emphasized
before the adolescent religious rites of passage took
place.

The Reverend Stump agrees that interest in religion is enjoying a rebirth on college campuses. But
even so he says the number of students who participate in orthodox religious rituals is small when compared to the whole of a student body.

"We have an active campus congregation and

well-attended worship services and Bible study classes throughout the week," he says. But then he adds that only 100 of the 1000 Episcopalians who are registered at the large land-grant university participate in the campus ministry. He doesn't find the 10 percent turnout for church discouraging but points out that the national average for campus participation in the Episcopal church is only 5 percent.

Father Stump says the Lutheran church's campus ministry at Penn State has about a 10 percent following and that the Roman Catholic church, which has the largest religious contingent on the campus, has a Sunday Mass attendance of 4000 persons, about 50 percent of the registered Catholics. But the Methodists at Penn State aren't doing as well. "They recently canceled on-campus religious services because of lack of interest," he says.

Father Stump's ministry is designed to reach all Episcopalians registered at the university. He devotes little or no effort to recruiting and converting new members to his church. The same may be said about each of the other mainline religions' campus ministries. On the other hand, the highly publicized Campus Crusade for Christ is active on Father Stump's campus and hundreds of others around the nation. They do use recruiting methods similar to those used by religious cults. Father Stump calls the dogmatism and direction the group practices "simple-minded," but admits, "They're reaching some people we're missing."

But if Father Stump's young Episcopalians, in a sect that for years has jovially called itself "God's frozen people," can't adopt the Bible-thumping evangelical techniques of the Campus Crusade, they are taking a lesson from the Mormons. The young parishioners are planning a two-by-two visitation to each of the Episcopalian students who don't currently attend church services.

And this campus priest, whose church may seem conservative and aloof to less-restrained Christians, seems to understand that his ministry involves more than the spiritual well-being of his young parishioners. He counsels on emotional and social problems as well and understands, as only one who works with young adults can, how vulnerable they are and how fellowship in a community of "like souls" can mean so much to a lonely college student. "The Campus Crusade has been effective," he says, "Because it offers a warm place and definite answers for freshmen who are away from home for the first time and are feeling lonely and unloved."

If the mainstream religious establishment can provide a supportive framework for young people during their difficult transition years, perhaps they won't look elsewhere for guidance and spiritual nourishment, says Father Stump. His and others' activist approaches are good ones, but it seems vain for the churches to indulge in too much self-castigation, for the problem is not theirs alone.

The problem also arises in the schools, and any examination of society's ills, their sources and treatment, must include a look at our educational system.

While children cannot be taught values and good judgment in school, they can learn rational ways to examine alternatives, to weigh options, and to evaluate the consequences of their actions. In a changing world, the ability to sift information and to find answers to relevant questions may be the most important skill we can give our children.

Critics of the American educational system say that decision-making and critical analysis are not fostered in an educational environment that stresses preparation for a specific trade or profession.

American higher education grew out of the tradition of the great English universities and emphasized the classics, history, philosophy, and a study of the arts. But in most institutions, this broad-based program has been supplanted by practical, goal-oriented studies. Pragmatism dominates the nation's schools, where learning what to think sometimes seems more important than learning how to reason. When the New Jersey voters decided to allow casino gambling in Atlantic City, a nearby college quickly began to plan a degree program in casino management, and courses for dealers and croupiers.

Those who say the American educational system is seen as a service industry that rewards specific job skills rather than aesthetics explain that this came about as a result of the hands-off attitude early immigrants had toward the schools.

But today's parents have begun to question the role of education. And many young Americans, especially those who were told that a good, practical education is the key to everything that matters, have begun to doubt the value of that advice.

It is in society's primary institution—the family —that most social problems begin and end and where cultural myths and realities must ultimately be confronted.

Since its inception the family has served as the basic foundation of society. It is not, and never has it been, a static, unchanging institution. But certain realities that were true in the beginning remain true today; the predominance of the nuclear family unit, for instance.

In her book, *Here to Stay: American Families in the Twentieth Century,* Wellesley scholar Mary Jo Bane points out that the nuclear family (parents and children) is and has always been the predominant form of family life. The author says the elaborately embroidered myth of the extended family, where generations shared the same home in stress-free bliss, is just that: a myth.

We asked at the outset of our journey through the religious cults if society can allow the undermining of the family. Perhaps the response to the cult threat should properly originate within the family rather than with a larger segment of society. In a free society, it is more fitting that individuals, family members all, influence the larger, more pervasive institutions to help control the cults, than for those larger institutions to influence or attempt to control the family. One example of the way individuals can respond to social problems is seen in the counter-cult groups formed by parents and former cult members.

Yet is the family a healthy enough institution to counter the cult threat? The extended family has been highly overrated, and its passing greatly mourned, particularly by the mobile American middle class, whose generations are often separated by thousands of miles.

In addition, if parenthood is still a normal part of adult life, it is increasingly apparent that it is not, today, a universally popular state. When nationally syndicated columnist Ann Landers, with her unerring feel for the pulse of America, asked readers, "Would you become parents if you had it to do all over again?" she received more than 10,000 responses. The shocked columnist reported that more than 70 percent replied that if they had known then what they know now, they would not have had children.

In an article about the results of her survey in *Good Housekeeping* magazine, Ms. Landers divided her negative responses into four categories: young parents who were deeply concerned about global hunger, overpopulation, and the possibility we might incinerate ourselves with nuclear weapons; parents who stated frankly that their children had ruined their marriages; older parents who feel that their grown children neglect them; and parents of teenagers in trouble.

Dr. Martin Orne agrees that these are difficult times. "It's a whole cultural issue. We have created a society of instant everything, where happiness is a primary goal instead of a by-product as it should be."

He explains that a money-oriented society where happiness is worshiped as a goal is very destructive. Speaking to a group of upper-middle-class suburban women, the psychiatrist explained why it is difficult for an affluent family to raise well-adjusted children. "Having all the advantages is not a good thing for a child. When everything is provided, he may not be able to have any purpose of his own. And he may deprecate what he can do for himself."

One young man told a story that confronts the issue of parents who try to make things "too easy" for their children. The young Midwesterner had worked all summer at a menial job and had saved $500 to buy a car. He visited used car lots for weeks until he found a Volkswagen that was both serviceable and within his limited budget.

The young man invited his father to come along with him on the evening he planned to pick up the car. In the meantime, the young man's father, who admired his son's perseverance and thrift, decided to reward it. When the two got to the car lot, instead of picking up the dented and chipped Volkswagen, the young man's father presented him with a gift—a shiny new Mustang.

While few parents are so insensitive, the story illustrates Dr. Orne's point. If the family provides everything for a young person, it tends to delay his need to do for himself. Why take a low-paying, tough job if your parents can easily afford a hefty allowance that is bigger than the minimum wage?

And so affluence has its own set of problems. Orne warns parents not to be too judgmental when their children do things for themselves. "Don't deprecate the commitment a young person makes. Any commitment is better than none. If a person is committed to his work, his religion, his family—to anything—it decreases his need to jump on someone else's bandwagon."

But selecting any commitment, any option at all, is difficult when there are so many choices available to middle-class youngsters. Possibilities of what they can do with their lives appear limitless. These young people may find it difficult to narrow down the choices, or to make any decisions at all when confronted with so many possibilities.

Parents, of course, have an inherent responsibility to prepare their offspring to take care of themselves. It takes courage to let go, and many parents find letting go especially difficult when it is postponed too long. As children approach maturity and begin to strain at the family ties, a break is inevitable and must be allowed. But the question of just how long parental responsibility should continue into their offspring's adult life is a serious question. There are many answers.

In terms of cult involvement, it is difficult to imagine how a parent can, with a clear conscience, stand by mutely and watch a son or daughter join a cult that clearly exploits its members or uses drugs and sex as part of the worship and ritual.

But on the other end of the cult spectrum there are groups, however heretical their beliefs, that do allow the maturation process, with all its stops and starts, to continue. Families differ in the ways they handle cult-related crises and in the degrees of their outrage.

But there comes a time when the parents of a cult member, however enraged or embarrassed, must decide just how far they will go to retrieve a child from a cult. Some simply run out of alternatives when deprogrammings fail and their sons and daughters stop listening, or disappear. Just as parents increase the chances of a teen-age marriage by resisting it too much, unceasing opposition often acts to strengthen the cult member's conviction. Every religious movement needs its saints and martyrs. Within the cults, the most fervent believers, who "kept the faith" in spite of deprogrammings or total parental opposition, are revered by their peers.

And yet we have seen many cult members leave a group when the decision was their own, not their parents'. Those families who are secure in a belief that they have taught their children to be competent adults are able to wait for their sons and daughters to come away from a cult on their own.

One set of parents, whose three youngsters, a son and two daughters, followed each other into the Unification Church, vowed to sit back and encourage, but not demand, their children to leave the Moon group. Richard and Cathy Anderson do not believe in deprogramming, and they do not have a sense of finality about their son's and daughters' commitment to the church.

Cathy Anderson says she promised herself she would not be a domineering mother. In her forceful and definite speaking style, she tells how her mother and grandmother were strong, manipulative women. "They wanted me to do exactly what they thought was right for me. We didn't always agree." Mrs. Anderson says she never did exactly what was expected of her, and it is clear that although she has removed herself geographically from her family's grasp, she is still resentful of their ways.

"My husband and I tried to raise our own kids to be flexible, self-sufficient young people with lots of interests. I think we succeeded, so I know they'll come out of this intact." Mrs. Anderson laughs when she tells how their kids visit home and "preach at us. I tell them if they really want to change the world, they ought to continue their memberships in the Sierra Club and the Cousteau Society, movements we've always been a part of."

When Mrs. Anderson explained her feelings, one of her daughters had already left the Unification Church on her own. Kirsten Anderson said she began to see that the Moonie life was far too simplistic and restrictive to be realistic.

Since that time, the other Anderson daughter has also dropped out of the Moon church after a membership of several years. Now the family all want the remaining member, their son and brother, to leave, but they will only discuss issues with him. They do not demand that he leave the Moonies.

Neither of the two young women think their church membership was "the worst thing that ever happened" to them, nor do they feel the years they gave the Unification Church were wasted.

Their mother says each has matured in the process of discovering for herself (with the support of family and friends) that the Unification Church could not provide the life she wanted. The young women accept the responsibility for their decisions. Their parents are being supportive of them as they struggle to decide what they want to do with the rest of their lives. Chances are that it won't be any easier for them now than it was before their cult experience. But the Andersons are convinced it won't be any more difficult.

Mrs. Anderson sees the local group of counter-cult

parents in her community as nothing more than "hysterical, manipulative parents who cannot give up control of their kids' lives.

"So what if they spend a few years as a Moonie or whatever?" she asks. "No one can turn off the growth process, and they'll come out of it if they've got the stuff. Parents are so afraid they'll be judged by what their kids are doing. That's why they freak out. They're afraid that having a son or daughter in a religious cult means they've failed," she adds.

Not all parents can be as confident as the Andersons. Watching a son or daughter spend years in the service of a dubious religious cult leader is not easy. And the opinions of hundreds of former cult members who thank their parents for deprogramming them must also be considered. These young people say they would never have been able to leave on their own.

Thoughtful reevaluations and debriefings can and do help many young people to see the other side of an issue they could not comprehend while deeply immersed in a system that pits them against the "wicked world."

There are voids in contemporary society. Some of today's messiahs and gurus are culpable of exploiting the weakness they see. But it is also obvious that many of them are convinced that they do possess special powers and that they alone can lead mankind to salvation.

We have seen through our research how thoughtful parents who are willing sincerely to question their values, broaden their perspectives, and consider what they have to offer their young stand the best chance of helping their sons and daughters opt for satisfying lives of normalcy.

There will be some victims. Many families have worked hard, have tried to do what they believed was right, and still have failed to remove cultists from their groups. The fact must be faced that many have failed miserably. And many of the successful deprogrammings must be viewed as qualified victories for those young former cultists who still grope frantically for something to give meaning to their lives.

It is the responsibility of each family to respond in its own way to the threat of the religious cult that separates parents from sons and daughters. Members of families can call on the major institutions in society for help. The counter-cult parents groups are doing just that, and many of them are doing it well.

We asked if society had the responsibility to regulate groups that inspire contempt for our laws and values. The answer is implicit in the question for anyone who understands the basis of the legal system of the United States. Still, government must temper its temptation to act to control cults. The Vermont legislature took a look at the Unification Church, and a joint resolution was put before the state's general assembly calling for an investigation of the organization.

When it reached the House, after passing the Senate with a substantial majority, Representative Hugh Moffett of Brandon, Vermont, made these remarks:

"We are being asked to send messengers from among us to determine whether this Sun Moon is an agent of the Lord or an agent of the devil. Thus the immediate question before us is not whether Sun Moon is a stinker, but whether government shall interfere with religion, if it be that, or in any event with the quest for the souls of men and women."

The legislator expressed sorrow that the question had been put, but said that since it was a matter of concern to parents and young people alike, he agreed that the legislature must pay attention to it and address the problem.

"Some years ago," he said, "I knew two teen-age girls who made a decision for Christ and Billy Graham, and went around in a daze for ten years. They spent four years at fundamentalist colleges of dubious educational quality. They signed letters, 'Yours in Christ.' They seemed to have a permanent glaze in front of their eyes, a glaze impenetrable to reason.

"Now there are worse trips young people can take. I feel, however, that Billy Graham did those girls poor service. Shall we send then our messengers . . . to evaluate Billy Graham?"

Mr. Moffett continued his remarks with stories of the fighting between two Christian groups in Ireland and pointed out that he did not feel justified in "casting the first stone" at the Reverend Moon. He ended his presentation in this way:

"I would like to mention just one other case of a government interfering with religion. . . . This Jesus from up-country, apparently handsome and persuasive, was converting people. He was taking converts from old, established, proper religions. And he was dividing homes. The government stepped in with the proceedings now known around the world.

"Mr. Speaker, history shows many cases of governmental interference in religion. I suggest that in most cases it has been futile, unfortunate, or disastrous. Let us not add another attempt. Let us not try to play God."

The resolution was defeated 78 to 64.

We asked if a religious system can take all of a young person's time during the years of his life when he could be laying the foundation for a useful and productive life as a functioning member of society. The answer is yes, of course it can. It has been done for a thousand years and more in orthodoxy and it has been called a religious vocation. Each mainstream religion cares for its own. Rarely have any of those who chose in early life to devote their existence to God and his work become burdens on society. Many have served society as educators, counselors, and medical and social workers.

Viewing the religious vocation in other, more contemporary terms, few of the families touched by religious cultism would, they will admit, prefer any kind of religious vocation for their children, legitimate or not.

And in some of the newer religions the issue becomes even more complex as it is so difficult to see what a lifetime commitment will mean. In some cases a person never learns what he is committing his life to until long after his decision is made. Often he is manipulated into a nearly irrevocable life choice.

We have learned from history that religious awakenings are passing phenomena and believe that the cult experience of the 1970s is no exception. As today's religious cults either pass into oblivion or modify to become part of the mainstream, few new members will join and the acute problem will subside.

Yet what of the thousands who are already unwitting subjects of these self-proclaimed, exploitative gods and prophets? Are Americans so callous and insensitive that they can sit by and watch young men and women spend vital years of their lives selling peanuts on street corners or religious tracts in airports? Can society ignore the frustration of their parents? How would you react if it were your own child? And if it were you?

Bibliography and Reading List

Bane, Mary Jo. *Here to Stay: American Families in the Twentieth Century*. New York: Basic Books, 1976.

Beir, Ernst G., and Valens, Evans G. *People Reading*. New York: Warner Books, 1975.

Bettelheim, Bruno. *The Children of the Dream*. New York: Avon Books, 1971.

Bhaktivedanta, A. C. *The Bhagavad Gita As It Is*. Los Angeles: Bhaktivedanta Press, 1968, 1972.

Briggs, Dorothy Corkhille. *Your Child's Self-Esteem: The Key to His Life*. New York: Doubleday, 1970.

Cameron, Charles, ed. *Who is Guru Maharaj Ji?* New York: Bantam, 1973.

Cohen, Daniel. *The New Believers*. New York: Ballantine, 1975.

Dāsī, Krishna Devī, and Dāsī, Śama Devī. *The Hare Krishna Cookbook*. Radnor, Pa.: Chilton, 1973.

Garrison, Omar V. *The Hidden Story of Scientology*. Secaucus, N.J.: Citadel Press, 1974.

Glock, Charles Y., and Bellah, Robert N. *The New Religious Consciousness*. Berkeley: University of California Press, 1976.

Greenfield, Robert. *Spiritual Supermarket*. New York: Saturday Review Press, 1975.

Hewitt, Jean. *New York Times Natural Foods Cookbook*. New York: Quadrangle, 1971.

Hoffer, Eric. *The True Believer*. New York: Harper & Row, 1951.

Hostetler, John A. *Hutterite Society*. Baltimore: Johns Hopkins Press, 1974.

Klagsbrun, Francine. *Too Young to Die: Youth and Suicide*. Boston: Houghton Mifflin, 1976.

Klein, Carole. *The Myth of the Happy Child*. New York: Harper & Row, 1975.

Kelley, Dean. *Why Conservative Churches Are Growing*. New York: Harper & Row, 1972.

Kim, Young Oon. *Divine Principle and Its Application*. Washington, D.C.: The Holy Spirit Association for Unification of World Christianity, 1968.

Lappe, Frances M. *Diet for a Small Planet*. Rev. ed. New York: Ballantine, 1975.

Levine, Faye. *The Strange World of the Hare Krishnas*. New York: Fawcett, 1974.

Lifton, Robert J. *Thought Reform and the Psychology of Totalism*. New York: W. W. Norton, 1961.

Marty, Martin E. *Nation of Behavers*. Chicago: University of Chicago Press, 1976.

Mason, Alpheus T. *Brandeis: A Free Man's Life*. New York: Viking Press, 1956.

Mayer, Jean. *A Diet for Living*. New York: McKay, 1975.

Meerloo, Joost A. *Rape of the Mind*. New York: Grosset & Dunlap, 1961.

Patrick, Ted, and Dulack, Tom. *Let Our Children Go*. New York: E. P. Dutton, 1976.

Rosenfield, Edward. *Book of Highs*. New York: Quadrangle, 1973.

Rothchild, John, and Wolf, Susan Berns. *The Children of the Counterculture*. New York: Doubleday, 1976.

Sargant, William. *Battle for the Mind: The Physiology of Conversion and Brainwashing*. New York: Harper & Row, 1951, 1959.

Sheehy, Gail. *Passages*. New York: E. P. Dutton, 1976.

Skinner, B. F. *Beyond Freedom and Dignity*. New York: Knopf, 1971.

Toffler, Alvin. *Future Shock*. New York: Random House, 1970.

Counter-Cult Groups

Committee Engaged in Freeing Minds, Box 5084, Arlington, Texas 76011

Citizens Engaged in Reuniting Families, Box 348, Harrison, New York 10052

Citizens' Freedom Foundation, Box 256, Chula Vista, California 92012

Free Minds, Inc., Box 4216, Minneapolis, Minnesota 55414

Individual Freedom Foundation, Box 48, Ardmore, Pennsylvania 19003

Index